NOTRE DAME REVIEW

NOTRE DAME REVIEW

NUMBER 23

The *Notre Dame Review* is published semi-annually. Subscriptions: $15 (individuals) or $20 (institutions) per year or $250 (sustainers). Single Copy price: $8. Distributed by Ubiquity Distributors, Brooklyn, NY; Media Solutions, Huntsville, Alabama; and Ingram Periodicals, LaVergne, Tennessee. We welcome manuscripts, which are accepted from September through March. Please include a SASE for reply. Please send all subscription and editorial correspondence to: *Notre Dame Review*, 840 Flanner Hall, University of Notre Dame, Notre Dame, IN 46556. *The Notre Dame Review* is indexed in *The American Humanities Index* and the *Index of American Periodical Verse.*

ISSN: 1082-1864
Long Stories/Lean Poems ISBN 978-1-892492-22-7
Cover Art: Catherine Gass, from the "Faulty Diction" series, 30"x 40" digital pigment print, 2003.

Contents

YOU ARE MY HEART

Jay Neugeboren

It took three of us to move the sewer cover once we'd pried it up. Then the question was: who was going to go below and get the ball. Everyone looked at me, and I shrugged as if it to say: No big deal. Back then I was the kind of guy my friends would brag about to others because I'd take just about any dare—jumping onto the tracks in a subway station and waiting until the last second, a train bearing down on me, before vaulting back onto the platform, or, taking a running start, leaping from one rooftop to another—the gaps ran from five to ten feet—of four, five, and six story apartment buildings.

This was 1953, in Brooklyn, and it was Olen Barksdale, my best friend that year, who volunteered to hold me upside down by the ankles. We were playing stickball in the P. S. 246 schoolyard on a cool Saturday afternoon in late October, and the sewer—a drain, really, that we used to mark third base—was one I'd been down before.

Olen and I were on the Erasmus basketball team together—he was a senior and I was a junior—and he'd been Honorable Mention All-City the year before when we'd made it to the quarterfinals of the city championships at Madison Square Garden. Most days after practice we'd take turns walking each other home, and a few nights a week, when our homework was done, we'd meet and take walks along Flatbush Avenue, usually winding up in a cafeteria, Bickford's or Garfield's, where we'd talk about everything—not just basketball, but personal stuff: about our families, and girls we liked, and why I did the crazy things I did, and, most of all, about how much we wanted to get away from our homes, and what we'd do with our lives someday after college, when we were on our own in the world.

My dream, ever since I'd read Ayn Rand's *The Fountainhead*, was to become an architect. I was good at drawing and loved making model airplanes—I had a big collection of World War One and Two fighter planes—SPADS, Fokers, and Sopwith Camels; Messerschmitts, Flying Tigers, Spitfires, and Stukas—and not just the kind you carved from balsa wood, but the kind with rubber bands inside the fuselage, tail to propellor, that you wound up so that the planes would actually fly. You made the planes from what we called 'formers'—thin round or box-like pieces of balsa in which you cut slots with razor blades so you could install toothpick-like stringers and struts that gave shape to the planes, and over which you pinned tissue-thin Jap paper you glued down and painted with dope. I also spent a lot of time drawing imaginary houses, complete with floor plans, and during the previous year I'd begun making models out of some of them.

Olen's dream was to become the first person in his family to go to college, after which he intended to play pro basketball while also attending medical school. That way, when he retired from the pros he'd already be a doctor and could afford a house like those most of the doctors we went to had, where your family lived on the top floors and you had your office on the ground floor, and where, most of the time, your wife was your nurse or assistant.

1953 was also the year I became the only white person singing in the choir at Olen's church, The Barton African Methodist Episcopal Church, and this happened not because of what he did when I was suspended upside down in the sewer—though that had something to do with it—or because of any dare, but because of how much I came to love the music, and—more—because I fell in love with Olen's sister Karen.

Despite all my bravado, Olen knew I was pretty scared when I did a lot of the things I was famous for. He was a very quiet guy—I think I was the only guy at school, black *or* white, he'd ever exchanged more than a few sentences with—so that when I crawled over the edge of the sewer, belly first, and one of the guys yelled out "Geronimo!" and I pushed off, I was surprised to hear Olen call down to me that the sweat was making him lose his grip, and that rats in the sewers had a real thing for Jewish noses. Did I know about this Jewish kid, naked and blind-folded and with a huge erection, who ran full blast into a brick wall? "Yeah," someone answered, giving the old line. "I heard he broke his nose."

The sewer was about nine feet deep, and Olen swung me back and forth like a pendulum so that my head was about three feet from the bottom and my hands were free to grab at things. The ball, a pink Spaldeen, was resting on a dark clump of rotting leaves, and as soon as I had it—the odors made my stomach pulse—I yelled at Olen to haul me up. Olen was all muscle, about six-foot-three and two hundred pounds, with wide shoulders and huge hands, and I was only five-seven and a hundred and thirty-five pounds soaking wet—and when he'd pulled me almost all the way out and I was bracing myself on the sides of the sewer to hoist myself up the rest of the way, he suddenly grabbed my left ankle with both hands and shoved me off again, letting me plunge back down to within a few feet of the bottom. I flailed away, my heart booming so loud I was sure the guys could hear it, but without letting go of the ball and without giving Olen the satisfaction of crying out.

On the way home, I gave him the silent treatment, and he knew that when I did, nothing could make me be the one to talk first, so finally he gave in and put his arm around me, telling me he didn't know what had gotten into him but that when he went to church the next morning he was going to ask the Lord for forgiveness. At first I thought he was kidding, and I almost said something about him asking God for a new brain while he was at it, but when I saw he was really feeling bad I didn't say anything back, and a moment later he asked if Jews were allowed to go to church and would I want to go there with him in the morning.

Sure, I said, and added that we weren't like the Catholic guys, who had to get permission if they wanted to come to synagogue for our Bar Mitzvahs. He told me he wasn't asking just because of what he'd done to me, but because it was going to be a special service where his sister Karen, who was my age, had a solo with the choir.

The next morning I got up before my parents did, put on a white shirt and a tie and, my good black dress shoes in my hands, tiptoed out of our apartment. Our street was quiet on Sunday mornings, with nobody going off to work or school, nobody yelling things down from the apartment house windows, and only an occasional car going by. I sat on my stoop for a while after I put my shoes on, drinking in how peaceful things were—a rare moment for me because this was a time when my parents were always checking up on me, my mother especially—wanting me to account for every minute of my life: where was I going, and who was I going with, and had I done my homework or brushed my teeth, and even wanting to know if I'd been having regular bowel movements. When the door to my room was closed—I was an only child—my mother would barge in without knocking, after which—both my parents worked, my father as a piece goods finisher in a dress factory (this was seasonal work, so he often spent long periods sitting around the apartment doing nothing, which drove my mother crazy), and my mother as a secretary for an insurance agent—she'd demand to know why I insisted on keeping my door closed and what I'd been doing during all the hours I was home alone.

Subtlety was never my parents' specialty, and though they never actually said anything *against* Olen, they'd say that they couldn't understand why, with all the choices of people I had to be friends with, I chose to spend so much time with a *shvartze.*

I had a pretty nasty temper in those days, and I'd yell at my parents that they were narrow-minded bigots who wanted to run my life for me. Were they going to choose my wife for me too some day? When my father was around and I said things like that, he'd whack me across the cheek, open-handed, yelling at me that I was an ingrate and a no-good, and the two of us would go at each other for a while. The angrier my father and I got, though, the calmer my mother became.

"Well, I always say the best way to judge a person's character is by the company he keeps," she would declare, adding that she certainly had nothing against Negroes, and that Olen seeemed like a perfectly nice young man, although how could she tell since he never said anything besides hello, goodby, and thank you, and—who knows?—maybe the way my parents objected to him was part of the reason I was so determined to stick to our friendship.

Olen was a terrific ballplayer, but he wasn't the best player on our team that year. Our best player was a red-headed Irish kid named Johnny Lee. Johnny's father was a cop and his mother was a schoolteacher, and Johnny was not only first team All-City but, according to *The Sporting News,* a pre-season pick to make first team high school All-American. He was also an Honors student with dozens of colleges recruiting him, and the word was that he was going to go to an Ivy League school, probably Yale or Princeton.

He was almost as quiet as Olen—they were about the same size and build, with Johnny being leaner and an inch or so taller—and according to *The Brooklyn Eagle*, having the two of them work in tandem made us odds-on favorites to win the city championship. Although Johnny didn't have Olen's raw strength or open court one-on-one moves, he was a better rebounder, with a real nose for the ball, and he was a much better shooter. But then, there was probably no player in the city who was a better pure shooter than Johnny. In practice once, he hit eighteen straight jump shots from the right corner, and then followed with thirteen straight from the left corner before he missed. And he'd never leave the gym until he'd made twenty-five consecutive foul shots.

Most of the time Johnny would play in the middle, and Olen would roam along the baseline from one corner to the other, though they'd switch sometimes and Olen would move into the pivot. Even though Johnny often had to play against guys taller than he was, he had quick moves and such a soft touch, including a phenomenal fade-away jump shot, that eventually, in college, where he played at all five positions, sportswriters began calling him "The White O," after Oscar Robertson, who was probably the best player in the country during those years, and who, like Johnny, could play any position on the floor.

This was a time before college and pro basketball teams were dominated by black players—the first black player in the NBA, Chuck Cooper, didn't come into the league until the fall of 1949, more than two years after Jackie Robinson had joined the Brooklyn Dodgers—and it was a time before there were a lot of seven footers playing, so it wasn't unusual for guys Johnny's or Oscar's or Olen's size to play center. A few years before there had even been a player from the West Coast named Johnny O'Brien who was my height, or maybe an inch or two taller, who played in the pivot and had been an All-American.

It was also a time before sit-ins and freedom rides, before voter registration drives and bombed-out black churches received national headlines—before everything we know as the civil rights movement had come into being: before the Montgomery bus boycott and the Mississippi Freedom Democratic Party, before the Selma to Montgomery March and the March on Washington, before civil rights workers were murdered and governors stood in the doorways of schools to keep black children from going to classes with white children, before riots destroyed black sections of cities like Los Angeles, Detroit, and Newark—before organizations like CORE, SNCC, SCLC, and the Black Panthers came into being, and before most of us had heard of people like Martin Luther King Jr., Fannie Lou Hamer, Rosa Parks, Medgar Evers, Stokely Carmichael, and Malcolm X.

And even though it was also a time when what was called *de facto* segregation existed in New York City the way it did in most of the country, North *and* South, you wouldn't have known it from our neighborhood.

About a third of the students in my elementary school, kindergarten through eighth grade, were black, which was about the same percentage as Jews (Irish and Italians made up most of the other third), and virtually all the black kids, including Olen, lived in a three square block section—about a ten minute walk from my house—where their families owned their own homes.

Olen was the oldest of seven children, and he and Karen had come north from Georgia when he was in the fourth grade and Karen and I were in third grade. They came with their mother, grandmother, and brothers and sisters, but not with their father, and they moved into a two-story wood-frame house next to one owned by Olen's aunt and uncle—his mother's sister and her husband, who had five children, including the Tompkins twins, Rose and Marie, who were two years behind me. They also arrived with their Uncle Joshua, who pressed clothes in a dry cleaning store on Rogers Avenue, and it didn't occur to me until years later, after I'd moved away from Brooklyn and had a family of my own, that Joshua had not been a real uncle.

Starting in the fifth grade, Olen had a newspaper route in the mornings—he got up at five to deliver the papers—and from seventh grade on he worked after school, weekends, and summers delivering soda and seltzer, and he used to say that it was lifting the wooden cases and carrying them on his shoulders that had enabled him to build himself up so much.

Olen's mother, who worked as a cook in the lunchroom at P. S. 246—this was the elementary school Olen and his brothers and sisters went to with me—remembered that I'd had a reputation for being one of the smartest kids in the school, and about once a week she'd take me aside and make me promise to get Olen to study harder. Basketball was useful because it would get him into a college, but the main thing was for him to get his education. Before Olen was even fifteen months old, she told me, he could pick out any card you asked for from a deck of cards, and where they came from in Georgia people used to gather around in their house to Olen do this. Nobody had ever seen a brighter boy baby, she said.

Olen's mother was usually in the kitchen cooking when I was there, and since a lot of what she made was fried in bacon grease and my family was kosher, the smells would drive me crazy, and when they did, Karen would delight in tempting me.

"Oh come on and have just a little taste," she'd tease, and she'd offer me a strip of bacon or a sausage patty or some fritters. "What do you think—that your God will strike you dead if you do?"

I'd resist at first, but then Olen, Karen, and some of the others would get on me, and while they fried up thick pieces of bread in the grease, or passed a strip of bacon under my nose, they'd roll their eyes and smack their lips with pleasure.

Mrs. Barksdale would tell her children to leave me be, but she'd laugh when she did. "Not eat bacon? Well, I can certainly see why you people are known for your suffering!" was one of her favorite lines, and it was usually the one that made me give in, and when I did—closing my eyes while Karen or Olen or one of their younger brothers or sisters put the food into my mouth—declaring that I was being force-fed against my will—they'd all hoot and holler in triumph.

When I got to Olen's house that Sunday morning in October, Karen was at the stove, and her hair, which was shoulder length and straight, was tied back in a lavender ribbon. The family was getting breakfast ready and Karen was working alongside her mother, both of them wearing aprons over their white dresses while they fried up sausage, bacon, cornbread, and flapjacks. "Let us pray," Uncle Joshua said after we were all seated, and everybody clasped their hands and looked down while Uncle Joshua gave thanks to Jesus for His lovingkindness, for the food we were about to eat, for *all* our provisions, for our health and salvation, for the gift of song He had given to Karen, and for the young man of—his exact words—"the Mosaic persuasion" that He had given to us in loving friendship.

"That's you," Karen whispered quickly while everybody was saying "Amen," and she said it without looking up, her hands still clasped in front of her.

Mrs. Barksdale and her mother left before we finished breakfast, and when we got to church they were standing on the steps with several other women, welcoming us and handing out programs. The church was made of whitewashed cinder blocks, with a big painted sign over the entrance, in red, white, and blue—"The Barton African Methodist Episcopal Church"—and above the sign, a plaster statue of Jesus on the cross, the statue bolted into what appeared to be a large porcelain bathtub that had been turned upright. The women were dressed in bright white dresses, wore turquoise-colored berets, sharply angled in front, that looked like the kind British commandoes used during World War Two, and had purple sashes across their chests, with patches that identified them as "Spirit-Led Women."

Inside the church other women, also dressed in white—eight or nine of them—were sitting in the back two rows, wearing blue capes and white nurse's caps. A group of older men, in black suits, ribbons on their lapels saying "Usher Corps," showed us to our seats, and none of the men or women treated me as if it was anything unusual for a white boy to be there.

I recognized a bunch of kids I knew from Erasmus and had grown up with—of the five to six thousand students at Erasmus, only about a hundred were black, and just about all of them had gone to our elementary school—and, like Olen and his brothers and sisters, they were dressed in their Sunday best: the guys in shirts and ties—a few of them in suits—and the girls in fancy dresses. When one of them would look my way and smile, I'd smile back, but maybe because everyone knew how close Olen and I were, none of them acted surprised to see me there.

Olen didn't say much while we waited for the service to begin, and I didn't want to gape, so I kept my eyes on the program. "Shout to the Lord all the Earth! Let us sing Power and Majesty, Praise to the King!" the cover declared. "Nothing compares to the Promise I have in You."

What surprised me about the church was how *formal* everything was. Until I was Bar Mitzvahed, I had gone to synagogue with my father every Saturday morning, and I still went with him a few times a month, and in our synagogue there were no programs or ushers or women in uniforms. People came and went whenever they wanted, stood up or sat down to chant the service in their own way and at their own pace no matter what else was going on, and people talked so much—some of the old men even snoring—that the rabbi would come to the front of the podium a few times during every service to demand quiet and to remind us that we were in the House of God.

The Order of Service at Olen and Karen's church was printed out, and the program also contained a Church Calendar for the week, a list of Daily Bible Readings, and a list of people who were Sick and Shut-In, with their addresses. When the service began—it was a "Special Harvest Service"—all the seats were filled, Ushers and Spirit-Led Women stood at the end of each row of seats, and the room went dead silent.

Whenever Olen stood, I stood, and whenever he lowered his head in prayer, I did the same. Once people were paying attention to the Pastor, the Reverend Benjamin H. Kinnard, I relaxed, and when the congregation recited prayers—mostly Psalms from the Old Testament—I joined in, and when they stood and sang The Morning Hymn—"Jesus Hears Every Prayer"—I sang along with them.

As soon as we back sat down, an elderly woman in front of me turned around and smiled—"My, but you have a lovely voice, young man," she said—and Olen leaned into me, his eyes wide in astonishment—started to say something, then just shook his head sideways, and shrugged.

After that, the more Olen stared at me, the louder I sang. I didn't know the words to all the hymns, but I could latch onto the tunes fast and fake the words, and I found myself singing with gusto, so that when Visitors' Recognition came, and my name was called out, lots of people turned my way and applauded.

About halfway through the service, right after Tithes and Offerings (I followed Olen's lead and put fifty cents in the basket), Pastor Kinnard said that even as the harvest would be coming in, and not far down the road winter would be coming on, and even though dark times might be coming to any of us, still, with Jesus's love, and love in our hearts for Jesus, we could walk in the light, and when he said these words, Karen stepped forward from the choir. People in the congregation began talking out loud ("Walk in the light, oh yes, walk in the light," and things like that), and Pastor Kinnard said that Jesus had blessed us this Sunday with a young woman whose voice could make the angels weep, Mistress Karen Barksdale, who would now sing "Walk in the Light" for us.

"You watch this," Olen whispered just before Karen began to sing, and when she did—as soon as the first words left her mouth and rose into the air—it was all over for me. Her eyes were closed the way they were at breakfast when she was praying, and her voice was startling—clear, pure, strong—but it wasn't so much that I wondered how such a large voice could come from a girl her size—Karen was shorter than I was, and wirey—but that I wondered how she had ever known—how she had *first* known—that the voice she had was there inside her, and that it was hers.

The choir swayed from side to side, keeping the background beat by repeating the words "Walk-in-the-light," while, to one side of the choir, an elderly man played an upright piano, a boy of about ten or eleven played drums, and two of the "Spirit-Led Women" shook tambourines. People stood and waved hands back and forth, and when the music heated up some, and when Karen's voice soared above everybody's, singing out almost as if she were crying, but effortlessly—"*I want to be in love with Him!*"—I melted. I stood up then and sang along with everybody else, and when, warbling on the low notes, Karen's voice suddenly exploded into high ones and then shimmied back down, and when she sang out with all her might "*He's shining! He's shining!*" and the choir responded and they went back and forth with the words—"*He's shining! He's shining!*"—in what I would later learn was call-and-response, the place went wild—people stamping their feet and clapping their hands and turning in circles and singing their hearts out.

On the way home, I stayed close to Karen so I could tell her how incredible she was. Usually when I was around her, at school or in her home, she was easy with me: talking about her brothers and sisters or our teachers or homework or whatever was happening. But now, for the first time, she seemed shy, and it was only when Olen asked if she had heard me singing, that she acknowledged my presence.

"I heard you," she said, "and in my opinion, you have genuine potential." Then she looked right at me. "So I have a question for you, Mister Take-Any-Dare. Would you like to sing in the choir with us?"

‡ ‡ ‡

For the next few months, when I left my house on Sunday mornings, I took my gym bag with me, my good clothes packed inside as if I was going out to play ball with the guys—and two evenings a week, when I said I was going to meet Olen, I'd go to his house and then walk to church with Karen for choir practice. Our first time there, Karen introduced me to Mr. Pidgeon, the church's Minister of Music, and he sat down at the piano, had me repeat scales he played, and asked if I could read music. I said that I could—I'd had accordian lessons for a few years when I was younger—and he said that was good, and he gave me a folder with music in it. He said I would sing with the tenors, that he appreciated the quality of my voice—its "timbre"—and that (when he spoke the words, Karen showed nothing) I had "genuine potential."

We did a lot of familiar stuff like "The Lord's Prayer," "Ave Maria" (Karen and a girl named Louise Carr alternated on the solos for this), and "You'll Never Walk Alone," along with hymns and spirituals everybody knew like "Swing Low, Sweet Chariot," but the music I loved most was music I'd never heard before—pieces that seemed half-talked and half-sung and where, after you'd gotten through the basics, Mr. Pidgeon encouraged choir members to step forward and take solos if the spirit moved them to do so. Some of these songs were slow and sad and could start tears welling in my eyes, but the songs I looked forward to above all were the ones with a driving, insistent beat that became faster and faster, pounding away until you thought the church walls were going to bust open from trying to hold in the sound: "Don't Give Up" and "We Need Power" and "Packing Up, Getting Ready to Go"—songs that, except for the fact that they mentioned God or Jesus, you never would have known had anything to do with religion.

Mr. Pidgeon worked as a caretaker and groundskeeper for the Dutch Reformed Church on Flatbush Avenue that was across from Erasmus, and sometimes, when I saw him in the yard there, raking leaves or tending to gravestones, he would wave to me and I'd go into the yard and we'd talk for a while, mostly about my progress with the choir. "Control is the secret of beautiful song," he'd always say to me, the way he did to all of us at the start of choir practice, and he'd urge me to remember that passion without control was as useless as control without passion. If I remembered that, he told me, I could become a pretty good singer.

During the first few practices at Karen's church, I found myself in awe of the way other singers could make their voices do these intricate flips and wiggles that verged on screeches, and at how they could pull them back and turn them into soft liquid harmonies, or could move from minor to major and back again without the musical score telling them when to do it, and I was determined to be able to sing like them. I practiced hard and after a few sessions, and once I was warmed up, I found that I could get to the really high notes and could throw in harmonies that made the music richer and stranger—and I also found, with practice, that I could modulate my voice so that, almost instantaneously, I could get it to go from a full-throated howl to a soft whisper.

Until this time, I'd never thought of Karen in the way I thought of white girls I grew up with: as girls one might want to touch, hold hands with, or kiss. Now, though, especially after a practice or a service, I couldn't think of her in any other way. What was cockeyed was that when I was with her I felt incredibly comfortable and incredibly awkward at the same time. And when her Uncle Joshua or the Reverend Kinnard said "Let us pray," and she closed her eyes, lowered her head, and drew in a slow, deep breath, I felt something else entirely: a stillness inside me that was like the stillness I sensed in her. I would clasp my hands and lower my head too, but I wouldn't close my eyes because I loved looking sideways and watching her in profile, and when we were apart the rest of the week, and for years to come when I found myself in difficult times, I would often summon up a picture of how beautiful and peaceful she looked in these moments, and this would help me through.

‡ ‡ ‡

The Friday night before Christmas vacation, we were scheduled to play James Madison at home. They had beaten us on their court in early December—our only defeat so far—but had lost one other game, so that if we beat them this time, we'd move into first place in our division and be on our way to getting an automatic first round bye to the city championships.

This was my first season on the team, but because we were usually way ahead early into the second half, I was getting to play more than I'd expected to. I wasn't scoring much, but I was distributing the ball well and playing solid defense during the five or six minutes a game the coach called on me. Everybody knew how intense I was—in team scrimmages, it was as if my life depended on every single play: if I didn't score, or steal the ball, or if the man I was guarding scored, I *died*!—but what Mr. Ordover, our coach, praised me for—and this, since I'd started going to choir practice, was new for me—was that for all my seemingly madman ways, once I was in the game, I could focus and play under control so that I rarely made a turnover or a mistake on defense.

We broke the game open early on when, during a six minute stretch, Johnny and Olen went on a tear and we outscored Madison 21 to 3. Johnny was having his best game of the year, outplaying the Madison center, Rudy LaRusso (who went on to have a long NBA career after being All American at Dartmouth), and winding up with thirty-two points. Olen wasn't far behind, with twenty-four, but best of all was that with a solid lead the coach put me in before halftime to give Jimmy Geller, our regular point guard, a rest, and when the guy guarding me dropped off to double-team Johnny or Olen, I fired away, hitting four straight shots from the top of the key.

We were a pretty happy crew that night, and in the man-by-man evaluation Mr. Ordover did after every game, he said that what was most important about my contribution wasn't the points I scored—I was third high scorer, with thirteen—but the intelligence with which I played. Intelligence, he declared, was what separated the very good ballplayers from the rest.

Most Friday nights after home games, we'd all get together in a back room at Garfield's Cafeteria, where, when the team walked in, the crowd would erupt in cheers. This week, though, Jane Friedlander, who lived on Bedford Avenue, near Midwood High School, a more middle-class section than ours, had asked me to spread the word that she'd gotten permission from her parents to have a victory party at her house.

As soon as I came out of the gym with Olen and the rest of the team, I spotted Karen—she was across the street with a group of her friends—and I didn't hesitate: I went up to her and told her that Olen and I were going to the party and asked if she wanted to come too. She didn't hesitate either, and after we got to Jane's house and took off our jackets and put down our gym bags, and while everybody stopped dancing and crowded around to tell us how great we were, she stayed next to me.

"So," she asked a minute or so after things had quieted down, "are you going to ask me to dance, or what?"

"Sure," I said, and I took her hand and we walked into the middle of the living room. I put my arm around her waist—the record that was playing was one of my favorites: Eddy Arnold singing "To Each His Own"—and I was so excited to feel her close to me—she let her cheek rest against mine the instant we started dancing—that it didn't even occur to me that people might think it unusual to see a white guy dancing with a black girl.

It was only later on in the evening, when the crowd had thinned out and I was standing around with some of the guys and going over plays from the game, that I realized Olen was gone, that Karen was the only black person left at the party, and that maybe people were noticing she was the only girl I'd danced with all night.

Usually, at parties—or, the previous few years, when I was on our synagogue basketball team and we traveled to other synagogues for Saturday night games-and-dances—I danced with lots of different girls, and most times by the end of the evening I would choose one girl to walk home with and maybe get to make out. But this time I danced with Karen every time they played a slow dance, and each time we moved around the floor (she told me a few times how much she liked having me hum softly in her ear) we got closer and closer until, instead of letting her right hand rest in my left hand, she put both arms around my neck and I put both my arms around her waist.

A few minutes before midnight, Jane's mother came down the stairs and said that our parents were probably wondering where we were and that we should consider the next record the last dance. Jane put on Tony Bennett singing "Cold, Cold Heart," walked up to me and, in a voice that sounded just like her mother's, announced that I hadn't danced with her all night and that I now had the opportunity to correct this significant omission.

So I danced with Jane, and by the time the record ended, Karen was gone. I caught up to her within a few blocks, and when I asked if she was mad at me for not dancing the last dance with her, she hesitated, shook her head sideways, told me not to worry about it, and slipped her hand into mine. We held hands all the way home, and when we got to her house—all the lights except for the porch light were out—she tugged on my hand and led me along the side to the rear door. She let go of my hand then, leaned back against the door, and closed her eyes.

"You can kiss me if you want," she said.

‡ ‡ ‡

Because my parents both worked in Manhattan, they didn't get home most evenings until after seven, which meant that all through January and early February, from the time I got home from basketball practice until my parents arrived, Karen and I were able to be alone in my apartment. We were careful, and would enter my building separately, and sometimes, if the coast wasn't clear, she'd go back to her house and we'd only get to be together for choir practice. Walking to and from church, though, we'd duck into doorways to kiss, and sometimes we'd find a car with its door unlocked and would climb in and make out in the back seat. A few times, too, Karen would wind her way through the backyards and alleys of my block, go down to our cellar, ring the kitchen bell—our apartment was on the fifth floor of a six story building—and I would haul her up in the dumbwaiter.

The first few weeks we were together after Jane's party, we would neck until our lips were almost raw, and I couldn't believe how wonderful it was simply to kiss again and again and again—long, sweet, delicious kisses—and to try out all kinds of things neither of us had ever done before. By the second week of January, Karen was letting me touch her on the outside of her sweater, and a week or so later she let me unhook her brassiere and feel her breasts. After this, we took to lying together on my bed, naked from the waist up, and moving against each other, my leg between hers, or her legs around my waist, until I came. The first time this happened, I panicked and kept saying how sorry I was—"I'm sorry, I'm sorry, oh God, I'm really sorry"—and how this would never, ever happen again, but when I said this Karen just pulled me closer to her, stroked the back of my neck, and kissed me softly on the cheek.

"You are my heart," she said then, words she repeated the next few times we were together. When the same thing had happened about a dozen times, though, she started a new routine where whenever I said I was sorry, instead of pulling me to her, she would start giggling, after which I would insist that I was really, *really* sorry.

"Sure you are," she would say, then add: "But I'll bet it felt really, *really* good."

When she said this, I'd answer that it was certainly *possible* that it felt really, really good, and we'd burst into laughter, and grab and tickle each other until one of us had wrestled the other off the bed and onto the floor. Sometimes, too—one of our favorite things—we would stay there on the floor, face down, one of us on top of the other, pressing against each other as hard as we could for as long as we could.

When we were in Karen's home, or in church, we never held hands or touched, but the first time we went for a walk together when it wasn't to or from church—this was on a Saturday afternoon, in Prospect Park—she suddenly stopped and glared at me.

"Are you my brother, or what?" she asked.

"No," I said. "Of course not."

"Then why aren't you holding my hand?"

I took her hand, and after this whenever we were together, except for when we were on my block, or near her home, or in church—and even in the hallways at school between classes—we would hold hands or walk with our arms around each other.

Because we didn't dare make out in her home, and because our time in my apartment was limited to an hour or so a few afternoons a week, what happened was that we came to spend most of our time together talking. On weekends, and during late February and early March, when my father got laid off and was home all the time—we'd find luncheonettes on Flatbush Avenue, or on Empire Boulevard near the Botanic Gardens and Ebbets Field, and spend hours talking while we drank tea and hot chocolate, and ate toasted English muffins and French fries.

Although everyone at school knew we were going together, and some students and even a few guys on the team began giving us the cold shoulder—not returning our hellos, or crossing to the other side of the street if they saw us coming—and though doing what was considered forbidden back then ("West Side Story" didn't become a movie until a half-dozen years later) may have been part of what made our being together exciting, when we were apart and I thought of being with her again, I found myself looking forward to our *conversations*—to all the things I wanted to tell her—as much as I did to our physical closeness, because no matter how much we talked, when it was time for us to separate and return to our homes, I always felt we'd hardly even *begun* to talk.

Some of the time we talked about ordinary stuff: our teachers, or students we knew and which ones we thought were for real and which ones were phonies, or about the kinds of things Olen and I had always talked about—basketball, college, and what we wanted to do after college. We talked about our families too, but in a different way from how Olen and I had. With Olen, conversations were mostly about how we would do anything to get away and be on our own, and about what we'd do when we got there, but with Karen, I found myself talking more about what I *felt* about my family—about what it was like to be an only child with parents who made each other miserable and who took their misery out on me. I talked about how angry I got sometimes—totally out of control—and how this made me do some of the crazy things I did so that I could get my parents angry back at me and then have a justification for shouting at them or storming out of the house.

I knew my anger was probably a cover-up, I admitted, and that what really bothered me—why I got *so* angry—was because of how sad and lonely I felt a lot of the time. Nothing I ever did was enough for my parents—if I got a 98 in a course, why hadn't I gotten a hundred? If I cleaned up the kitchen and living room while they were at work, why hadn't I cleaned the bathroom too?—so that being an only child who was always being criticized made me end up feeling that some essential part of me was missing—as if, without having given me a brother or sister, my parents had somehow never finished making *me.*

Karen talked a lot about what it was like to be the oldest girl in a large family—to be put in the position of being responsible for her younger brothers and sisters, and to be blamed when they did things that upset her mother, her grandmother, or her Uncle Joshua. She was determined to go to college, but whereas her mother and her Uncle Joshua were *counting* on Olen to go, the idea of Karen going to college was out of the question. Even though she'd always been a straight-A student, her mother had insisted she take a commercial course of studies so that when she graduated she could get a job as a secretary and help support the family.

My parents didn't fight me about *going* to college the way Karen's mother and her Uncle Joshua did, but I wanted—desperately—to get away to an *out-of-town* college, and, because my parents claimed they didn't have enough money to send me, they insisted I apply *only* to the city colleges—Brooklyn, Queens, or C.C.N.Y.—which had free tuition then. "With a brain like yours," my mother would argue, "why should you go somewhere where you'll be a little fish in a big pond, when you can live at home and be a big fish in a little pond?"

When I argued back that if I didn't win a scholarship, I'd work my way through with part-time and summer jobs, they'd become even more upset, my father yelling that you had to be a total idiot to pay for an education that wasn't as good as one you could get for free (and presenting as proof the fact that C.C.N.Y. had produced more Nobel prize winners than any college in the country, including Harvard), and my mother starting in with what it would be like for me to be a poor boy among rich boys at some Ivy League school where I'd have to work all the time, even on vacations, and how all she ever wanted in life was to spare me suffering.

So Karen and I talked about these things, and by acting out antic responses that even I, for all my anger and big mouth, didn't have the courage for—like telling my father the reason he wanted me to go to a place like Brooklyn College instead of a place like Swarthmore or Dartmouth was because it would show him up for the failure he was—we were able to laugh about our situations, and to console each other.

We also talked, at length, about our feelings and about how wonderful it was to *feel* free to talk about our feelings. Sometimes, too, we fantasized about enrolling in an out-of-town college together—a small liberal arts school in upstate New York or New England, or a school that specialized in the arts like Oberlin or Antioch or Bard, where people would be more tolerant of an interracial couple—and how, if we had to, one of us would work at a job for four years and put the other through college, after which we'd switch, so that within eight years, when we'd still be in our early twenties, we'd both have college degrees and, married, we'd be able to start a family of our own. Mostly, though, we talked about how lucky we were to have discovered each other—and about how good it felt to be able to tell each other anything and everything and to feel understood in a way nobody else ever had or, we believed, ever would understand us. We also agreed that the biggest surprise for both of us was not having fallen in love after knowing each other for so many years, but that being in love had turned out to be—the word we came back to again and again—so *easy*.

‡ ‡ ‡

The night before our quarter-final game against Lafayette for the Brooklyn championship, Johnny Lee came down with the flu. He suited up and kept drinking liquids, but he wasn't himself and wound up playing less than fifteen minutes and only scoring seven points. Olen was a maniac under the boards and on defense, and, scoring thirty-three points, single-handedly kept us in the game, but by the time Jimmy Geller fouled out with four minutes left and the coach put me in, we were eleven points down. I played well enough, but the guy I was guarding, Stan Groll, their All-City ballplayer, pretty much did what he wanted with me, using up the clock by dribbling around near half-court like he played for the Harlem Globetrotters. I was able to steal the ball from him once, which, from the look in his eyes, he seemed to regard as an insult, but I also had to foul him three times to give us a chance to get the ball back, and he made all his foul shots. We lost by seventeen points.

With the basketball season over and my father back at work, Karen and I had more time alone in my apartment, where she tried to cheer me up by telling me obvious things—that like, Olen, I'd given it my best, that there was always next year, and that—believe it or not—she still loved me *even if* I wasn't on a city championship team. This helped some, but what really got me out of my doldrums was when one afternoon, as soon as we were in my room, instead of lying down on my bed, she started picking up and examining some of my model airplanes and looking through the windows of a few of the houses I'd made.

"Okay," she said. "Tell me how you make these things. I mean, how does a guy as restless as you are have the *patience*?"

So I started in showing her how I put the planes together, and took a few old ones out of my closet (she remembered me bringing them into class in elementary school for show-and-tell, and flying some of them around the schoolyard at recess) to show her how much more detailed the newer ones were: pinheads on the propellor mounts to simulate bolts, blackened string next to the wheels to represent shock absorbers—and then I showed her sketches I'd been making for houses, and—I couldn't resist—the plans for a house I was designing for the two of us to live in some day.

The house was based on one by Frank Lloyd Wright, its main section cantilevered out over a waterfall, with enormous wraparound windows that would make you feel there was no separation between the interior of the house and the exterior. Karen liked the sketch, but what interested her more than the fact that I'd dreamt it up for the two of us, was how I was going to turn it into a model.

For the next week and a half, whenever we were in my room, we worked on the model, which, because it had huge windows that seemed to have no supports, was more complicated than any model I'd ever built before. I made the exteriors of most of my houses out of sheets of oaktag that came in different thicknesses, and I'd glue two pieces together, which made the finished product surprisingly strong and, unlike the kind of thin wood people usually made models from, had the advantage of never warping.

For the houses I'd made so far, I showed Karen, I began by drawing the main walls and roof sections on a single sheet of oaktag—the way, on the backs of cereal boxes, cowboy ranches, fire stations, or Army bases were made of one piece of cardboard that you cut out and folded along dotted lines—and with my razor blade and a steel straight-edge, I'd make half-cuts along the lines that showed where the walls and roof sections of the houses joined to each other. I'd prick the corners of windows and doors with a straight pin first so that the unneeded pieces fell out cleanly, after which I'd cut out pieces of celluloid a little larger than the window openings, and, with a phonograph needle held in a pin-chuck, I'd scribe in the sashes that separated the window panes, then tape the celluloid to the back side of the openings.

I kept most of my materials and tools (razor blades, nails and pins, files, compasses and protractors, scribers, small saws and hammers, rolls of adhesive tape, jars of poster paint, glue) in an old dentist's cabinet I'd gotten a few years before when our family dentist renovated his office. It had lots of compartments, including three flat slide-out drawers where I kept different size and color papers I'd been collecting for glueing to the outside walls—imitations of brick, stone, wood, and stucco—along with sheets of oaktag, Bristol Board, celluloid and—my favorite—a flexible glass called Perspex.

After Karen and I had laid out and put together the main section of the house (I decided to construct it in two parts, then to join the parts together), I cut out a large piece of Perspex, drilled holes in it for attaching it to floor and roof, and then, with a small Bunsen burner, began experimenting with warming it to different temperatures in order to bend it to the shape we wanted. The great thing about Perspex, which was almost as rigid as glass when it cooled down, was that it could be used for walls without needing any extra supports. The not-so-great thing about it was that it was almost impossible to find and maintain the right temperature for bending it.

About ten days after we'd been working together, on an afternoon when we were as close as we'd been to getting the Perspex to stay fixed (I'd cut out a curved piece of wood to use as a form around which to mold the glass), and when we were trying to set it in place on the model, we suddenly heard noise behind us—the front door opening and closing. A few seconds later my mother pushed the door to my bedroom open.

"What are *you* doing here?" she demanded.

"Helping Alan with a school project," Karen answered quickly.

"Of course you are," my mother said. "Of course you are." She shifted a bag of groceries from her right to left hand so she could wag a finger at Karen. "But let me tell you something, young lady—you don't fool me for a minute, do you hear me? You don't fool me for a minute, you or your famous brother."

After saying this, my mother did an about-face and left. I thought of apologizing for her—of telling Karen that my mother's bark was worse than her bite (which wasn't true), or of following her out of the room and *ordering* her to come back in and apologize to Karen . . . but I knew my mother would only use anything I said to stir things up more, so I just stood there, and after a few seconds, Karen put down the tube of cement she'd been holding and reached for her coat, which was on my bed.

I pointed to the clock on top of my dresser. It was nearly seven-thirty.

"I guess we lost track of time," I offered.

"Yeah," she agreed, and then: "They say that's what happens when you're happy, right?"

Then she put on her coat, picked up her books, and walked to the door. When she turned and looked back at me—her cheeks were flushed, a patchy rust-red—I wanted to rush to her and put my arms around her and tell her that everything would be all right, that I would love her forever no matter what my parents said or did, that we *would* go away to college together and have a home of our own someday, that if we stood by each other everything would work out....

"I'm sorry," was all I said though.

"Well, things could be worse," Karen said. "At least we weren't dry-humping on your bed, right? At least we still had our clothes on."

‡ ‡ ‡

That night, after my father came home, my parents summoned me to the living room to tell me they'd heard rumors about me and Karen—"Love may be blind, but the neighbors ain't," my mother said, repeating one of her favorite sayings—but that they had talked things over and made a decision to let things run their course and not to interfere. They loved me very much, they insisted, and they knew, despite some of the things I did and the choices I made—my "eccentricities," they called them—that I hadn't *intended* to hurt them.

I told them I didn't need a sermon, and my father said that given how much time I was spending in church, I was probably right, and then my mother cut him off, saying we didn't need to be facetious at a time like this and, more important, that we shouldn't have secrets from one another: that it was time I learned something about them—something they should have told me long before this, and that it had to do with how once upon a time she had been in a situation not unlike the situation I was in now.

What amazed me was how calm my mother suddenly was. She was like a different mother than the one I'd grown up with, and when she told me the story, it was as if she'd been preparing to tell it to me since the day I was born.

Before she married my father, she said—this happened when she was nineteen years old—she had become engaged to a Catholic boy named Tommy O'Connor, and when both sets of parents objected and made life hell for them, she and Tommy had borrowed a friend's car and driven down to Elkton, Maryland. Elkton was famous then for allowing marriages where, if you were under twenty-one you didn't need your parents' consent, and she and Tommy were married there.

When they returned to Brooklyn, they didn't have a place of their own—realistic planning was not their strong point, my mother noted—so they had returned, separately, to their parents' apartments, and their parents had taken each of them in. A few months later—without their ever having lived together—the marriage was annulled. Seven months later she married my father.

"It's all true—" my father said, "—it's all true, every word of it," and he added that what they had learned from this—given how their parents' opposition had only served to drive my mother and Tommy into each other's arms—was not to make the same mistake with me. So they had decided that if I continued to date Karen, even though they wouldn't like it, neither would they oppose it.

By this time we were sitting at the kitchen table—my mother didn't want the brisket she'd prepared to get cold—and my father was making a speech I'd heard before, about how the point of it all was that he had married my mother, that they'd stayed married for twenty-three years, that they they were still married, and that they would go to the grave married.

I asked my father if he wanted a medal for his achievements, and he called me a snot-nose who was still wet behind the ears. My mother seemed to snap out of it then, and talked to me the way she usually did.

"Here," she said, picking up the carving knife and leaning across the table, the knife pointed at me. "Why don't you just cut my heart out with this and get it over with now?"

My mother put the knife down, and my father, who was sitting between us, picked it up and placed it in front of me, after which he started yelling at my mother that it wouldn't help things for her to get so worked up and histrionic, and off they went again, arguing with each other about the best way to deal with me.

‡ ‡ ‡

The big news around Erasmus—this happened less than a week later—was that Johnny Lee had chosen Yale, and would be going there on a full scholarship in the fall. By this time it was early April, when most seniors had heard from the colleges they'd applied to, and when it was warm enough for Karen and me to take long walks in the park together again. By this time, too, the park was the *only* place where we could be together by ourselves.

The reason for this was that on the night after my mother found Karen in the apartment with me, she had telephoned Karen's mother. The result was that I was no longer welcome in Karen's home—and when I went to choir practice, Mr. Pidgeon came up to me before rehearsal started and said that it was probably best if I didn't sing with the choir for a while.

Things were just as bad with Olen. Whenever I tried to talk with him, he became quiet and sullen the way he was with everyone else, and when I'd offer to go for a Coke and fries with him and ask if he wanted to get together over the weekend to play ball or do other stuff, he'd say he didn't have time to hang out with guys like me.

Karen said he was being the same with her, but that what was making him this way didn't have to do with us, but with what had happened between Olen and Mr. Ordover, and that what had happened was this: as soon as Olen learned about Johnny's decision to go to Yale, he'd gone straight in to see Mr. Ordover and had demanded to know what was going to happen to *him* next year. Despite the fact that Olen had good grades—a solid B—and had had made first team All-Brooklyn and third team All City—Mr. Ordover told him that the only coaches who'd talked with him about scholarships were from two all-Negro colleges in the South.

Olen had exploded, it seemed, and said he would rot in hell before he'd go to one of those places. That was all Karen knew. She didn't know what else Olen said, or what his plans were, because, as had always been the case with her brother, the more enraged he was, the quieter he became.

The next time I saw Olen, I tried to get him to talk about what had happened with him and Mr. Ordover, but when I did, all he did was to snap at me that if I was so interested in his future, why didn't *I* go in and talk with Mr. Ordover.

So I did. During my free period after lunch the next day, I found Mr.

Ordover in his office and asked him if it was true—that Olen's only choices were two Negro colleges.

"It's true," Mr. Ordover said, "but what you have to realize, is that when a college makes a commitment to a young athlete—the way Yale University has to Johnny—it has to be certain that the athlete will be capable, for his part, of honoring the commitment."

"So?" I said. "So why would that stop any college from wanting Olen to play for them? He's a good student—a lot smarter than people think—and an incredible ballplayer..."

Mr. Ordover praised me for being such a loyal friend, and then, switching subjects, started in about *my* prospects for the following year. He told me that unless some new player came along to beat me out, I would be his starting point guard, and also—excellent news he'd been saving for an appropriate time—that he'd already had inquiries about me from coaches with whom he had good working relationships. Not from places like Yale or Princeton, to be sure, but from some fine Division Two schools like Union College, Muhlenberg, and Tufts, all of which were in the market for a smart point guard.

"But what about Olen?" I persisted. "What's *he* going to do next year?"

Mr. Ordover had spoken with Olen's guidance counselor, he replied, and learned that, mistakenly counting on an offer of an athletic scholarship, Olen had, unfortunately, neglected to apply to any colleges in the traditional way. That was why Mr. Ordover had been speaking with coaches from several Negro schools where admissions standards were a bit more lax, and where arrangements for the coming fall could still be made.

"But he was counting on *you* to get him in somewhere," I protested. "The same as Johnny. Everybody knows that's how it works. The colleges contact you and you set up the rest the way you always have."

Mr. Ordover responded by saying that Johnny, for one, had applied to colleges the way everyone else had, that he thought Olen would do well in one of the schools he'd found for him, and—he rose from his chair and looked at his watch—that he had an appointment. Our conversation, he declared, was over.

"No it's not," I said. "You let him down, coach. He played his heart out for you for three years and you let him down."

Mr. Ordover said again that our conversation was over.

"No it's not," I repeated. "Because do you know what? If you don't get Olen into a regular college, then—" I searched for words "—then I won't be your point guard next year because I won't *be* on your team."

Mr. Ordover laughed. "You're not being very intelligent," he said. "Why forsake your chances because of your friend's obstinacy? That's just cutting off your nose to spite your face. The schools I can get Olen into, where he'll be with his own people, are good choices, and for Olen to allow his pride destroy his future would be foolish beyond words."

"But you can *do* it," I said. "We all know it. If you want to, you can still get Olen into a place that isn't all-Negro. Coach Fisher got Sihugo Green into Duquense, didn't he? And Cal Ramsey's going to play for NYU next year, and Tony Jackson's going to St. John's, so how can you say the only place for Olen is with other Negroes?"

Mr. Ordover sighed. "Please," he said. "As a ballplayer, Olen is not in Green or Ramsay or Jackson's class—not by a long shot—and for you to think he is may indicate that you are less intelligent than I've been giving you credit for."

The bell went off for changing classes then and when it did, Mr. Ordover took me by the arm, led me to the door, opened it, and told me to get to my next class. What he wanted, he said, was to prevent me from saying anything I might regret later on. For his part, he was going to try to forget that our conversation had taken place because he didn't want my passion and aggressiveness—qualities that served me well on the court—to endanger my opportunities. I was, he said, echoing my father, still a young man who was wet behind the ears.

I knew I should have stopped myself then, but it was as if he was daring me to answer back, and when I was out of his office and in the large room where the secretaries worked and the other coaches hung out, I spoke the words that came to me.

"Intelligence?" I said. "*Intelligence?!* Let me tell you something, Mr. Ordover—in my opinion Olen has more intelligence in his little finger than you have in that crap between your ears you call a brain."

‡ ‡ ‡

Word got around the school pretty fast about what had happened between me and Mr. Ordover, but it made no difference to Olen—whenever I saw him, he either evaded me or rejected my overtures—and it surely didn't help at home. As soon as my parents heard what happened, they demanded I give them a full and accurate accounting—which, in my righteous outrage at what had been done to Olen, I was happy to do—and then ordered me to send a letter of apology to Mr. Ordover. When I refused, they told me I was still the immature, selfish child I'd always been, and told me that since I was so free and independent, I could take my meals by myself from now on.

And after that, they pretty much stopped talking to me.

Things got worse for Karen too. Although her mother's style may have been gentler than my mother's, the results were basically the same. Karen wasn't banished from the dinner table, but when she was there, everybody—including her brothers and sisters—ignored her. In addition, her mother and her Uncle Joshua took to blaming *her* for Olen's situation. If she was so smart, and cared so much about her brother, why hadn't she been more watchful—why hadn't she seen to it that he applied to colleges in a proper way? She knew how busy Olen was with basketball, with his weekend job, and with keeping up with his classes. What kind of secretary was she going to be some day if she couldn't even help her own brother with sending for applications, filling them out, and seeing that they were delivered on time? Worse still, they accused her of having neglected her own family in favor of—their words—an *unhealthy infatuation*.

Karen kept trying to get Olen to talk with her, and even went to his guidance counselor to find out if anything could be done about getting him into college for the fall, but the guidance counselor said that the only choices left for him were to go to one of the schools Mr. Ordover had found, get a job and apply again for entrance a year from September, or make a late application to one of the city colleges. But Olen had no interest in attending a school where he couldn't play ball, and because of the point-shaving scandals three years before, when star players at C.C.N.Y. had taken money to fix glames (this after C.C.N.Y. had won both the N.C.A.A. *and* N.I.T. post-season tournaments), the city colleges had all dropped big-time intercollegiate basketball.

From this point on, whenever Karen and I were together, we spent pretty much all our time trading stories of how lousy things were for us at home. We still made out—kind of desperately—when we could find a secluded place in the park or an unlocked car, but although we didn't say it, it was as if we both began feeling doomed, and on walks or sitting next to each other in luncheonettes we'd go for long stretches without talking at all.

When I went down to the Holy Cross schoolyard on weekends for games of pick-up ball, the guys told me how brave and crazy they thought I was to have talked to Mr. Ordover the way I had. But when I suggested they join me—that if we all stuck together and we all refused to play, Mr. Ordover would have no choice *but* to make some calls and get Olen into a good school—I didn't get any takers.

Then, one Saturday morning in early May, for the first time since our season ended, Olen showed up at the schoolyard. He sat along the chainlink fence with the other guys, not saying much and nobody saying much to him, and when he got on the court to play against a team I was on—we'd won four in a row—he was at his best, scoring at will and jibing the guys on my team about how bad he was making them look. But then, his team up nine-to-two in a ten-baskets-wins game, when I was going in for an easy layup, he suddenly left his own man and instead of trying to block my shot, clotheslined me with a forearm to the chest that sent me skidding on the concrete, after which he just stood over me, smiling.

"What are you smiling about, you big ape?" I said when I got my wind back.

"I'm smiling at a guy who just doesn't have it," he said.

"Well it takes one to know one," I said back, and then, pain suddenly shooting through my arm, elbow to wrist—it was skinned raw—I felt tears rush to my eyes. I pressed my eyes closed, bit down on my lower lip, and when I opened my eyes, Olen was still standing there smiling.

"You're an idiot," I said. "Do you know that? You're nothing but a big stupid black idiot. Correct that: You're nothing a big stupid black *fucking* idiot."

The other guys crowded around, told us to go easy, and I saw a few of them get on either side of Olen, moving in to keep him from doing any more damage.

"Shut your mouth," Olen said. "You just shut your mouth."

"Who's gonna make me? *You*?" I stood up and stepped toward him so that the toes of my sneakers were right up against his. "Come on, big man—show us how smart and tough you are—how you always pick on guys your own size and your own intelligence, because you know what? The only thing smaller than your dick is your brain."

I saw fire flare briefly in his eyes, and then he just turned and walked out of the schoolyard. The guys came to me then, offering me their bandanas and handkerchiefs to wipe off the blood, and starting in praising me for how totally out of my mind I was to go at Olen the way I had.

"Fuck all of you, too," I said, and left the schoolyard.

I caught up with Olen and stayed by his side for a few blocks, neither of us saying anything. Before we turned the corner to his street, though, he stopped and looked down at me.

"How's the arm?" he asked.

"Still attached," I said.

"But I mean it—I want you to just leave me be, okay?" he said. "I don't need you holding my hand or sucking around to do stuff for me. It only makes it worse, do you understand?"

"No," I said.

"Then fuck you," he said.

"You and what army?" I shot back.

"And don't always be such a wise-ass," he said, and he grabbed me by the arm, hard, opened his mouth—he seemed on the verge of saying more—but then let go and shook his head sideways, the anger suddenly washing out of him. "Forget it, okay? Just forget the whole thing and leave me be, you *and* my stupid sister, or next time—"

"Next time what—?"

He shrugged. "Maybe next time I drop you down the sewer if I get the chance. Then you'll come out black as me, right? Black as the devil's ass at midnight!"

He laughed at what he'd said, but when I started to laugh with him, his face went hard again.

"You just leave me be, is all, do you hear?" he said again. "Do you? *Do* you? Because you don't know, see. You don't know anything. You just don't know."

Don't know what? I wanted to ask, but before I could say the words, he was gone.

‡ ‡ ‡

I didn't see Karen that weekend—I telephoned her house a few times, but each time whoever answered told me she wasn't in—and on Sunday night, when I was feeling like shit because I was missing her so badly, my mother came into my room, knocking on the door before she did, which was a first, and sat down on my bed. It was killing her for us to be like strangers to each other, she said, and it was hard on my father too. What did I *want*? she asked. Could I just tell her what I wanted from them.

My answer was what it always was: for them to leave me alone.

But they'd been doing that, she said, and it hadn't made any difference. She said that my father believed that often you swallowed your pride and went against your own values, or you even lied—told white lies—to keep peace in the house. *Shalom habayis,* she said. That's what your father believes, and I do too. *Shalom habayis.*

I shrugged, and when my mother changed subjects, telling me she'd had a call from a Mrs. Merdinger, in Belle Harbor, I knew she was getting to her real reason for coming in to talk with me.

Did I remember a young woman I'd met at Temple Beth El named Marcia Merdinger? she asked. I answered that I remembered Marcia, that I'd met her at a dance the year before, after a game we'd played against her synagogue's team. My mother nodded and told me that Mrs. Merdinger had called without Marcia's knowledge because there was a big dance at Marcia's high school—a junior prom—and that Marcia was thinking of inviting me, but that since Marcia hadn't heard from me in a long time, her mother was calling to say that it would be nice if I gave Marcia a call first.

I rolled my eyes, and told my mother to forget the whole thing, but my mother, sensing my weakness somehow—the truth was that Marcia had been one of the hottest girls I'd ever made out with—said that I didn't have to marry the girl, that all I had to do was call her and perhaps go to a dance with her. Where was the harm? My mother knew I was still seeing Karen, and if I didn't call Marcia, she would of course understand. That was my decision. But she *had* promised Mrs. Merdinger she would talk with me, so if I could let her know what I intended to do...

Meanwhile, I wasn't seeing much of Karen. Whenever I asked her about going for a walk, she said she had "obligations at home," and when, on Friday, I pointed out that a whole week had gone by without us spending any time alone together, and asked if she were avoiding me or if her mother and Uncle Joshua were putting pressure on, she got angry.

We were standing in an alcove under the arch at the Bedford Avenue entrance to Erasmus—the school was modeled after a British university, built around a quadrangle with Gothic style architecture—and she kept her books between us, pressed to her chest like a shield.

"Am I avoiding you?" she asked, repeating my question. "Well, you might put it that way. But I'm not doing anything you're not doing to Olen."

I told her I didn't understand.

"You call yourself Olen's friend?" she said. "You call yourself his *friend*?"

"Sure," I said. "He's my *best* friend—"

"Then why aren't you spending time with him? This is when he needs you, and you're nowhere. This is when—"

"But he told me to leave him alone!" I protested. "He nearly chopped me in half last week at the schoolyard and then told me to go fuck myself and to never talk with him again—"

"And you *listened* to him?" Karen shoved her books against my chest, pushing me against the wall. "You *listened* to him?"

"But it's what he *said*," I said. "I tried—believe me—but he just kept telling me to leave him be, to—"

"Talk about stupid," Karen said. "I thought you were the big risk taker—the guy who never saw a dare he didn't like—"

"But this was *different*," I began. "He really meant it, and I just didn't know what else to do..."

"You could have talked with me," Karen said, as if to herself. She took a deep breath, and continued, without anger: "Olen's hurting bad—he's hurting real bad—the worst I've ever seen him, and he's been known to hunker down into some really foul moods. He won't open up to *anybody.* Even when my mother was so worried, she got Pastor Kinnard to come by the house the other night, it didn't do any good. So what's he gonna do? I mean, what's he gonna *do*? Answer me that if you're so smart. You're the only one could reach him, and now you just..."

I tried to put my arms around her, but she pushed me away.

"I counted on you," she said, "and you let me down. You let me down big-time."

"But what was I supposed to do when he said to leave him be—?"

"You were supposed to do *something*. You were supposed to use that famous daredevil imagination of yours. You were supposed to not take no for an answer." She took a deep breath, put her face close to mine, and spoke in a whisper, enunciating each word very clearly. "You-were-supposed-to-be-his-friend."

Then she pushed by me, and walked away. I followed and stayed by her side all the way to her block, but no matter what I said—no matter how I pleaded for her to give me a chance to show her I *could* do better—she just kept telling me to leave her be, to stop following her, and to get on home. And when we got to her house she told me we were finished and warned me not to telephone her or to *dare* to try to see her ever again.

By this time I'd had it, and I let go of the frustration that was boiling up inside me and told her that she was being as stupid as her brother, and to hell with both of them—that it was fine with me if we never saw each other again and if she ever came crawling back asking me to forgive her, it would be too late for her and me the way it was going to be too late for Olen and college.

Karen's grandmother came out on the porch then, along with two of Karen's little brothers, Edgar and Joel, and started yelling at me to leave her granddaughter alone or she'd call the police, and I told her to go ahead and call the police, and then for some reason I started in singing as loud as I could the first song that came into my head—"Oh Happy Day"—and asking her and Karen to join in with me, and when her grandmother went back inside and I kept singing, Karen told me I was truly nuts and that her grandmother meant what she said and that I'd better get out of there.

I thanked Karen for being concerned for my safety, and walked down the street—the Tompkins twins came out onto their porch and made circles at the sides of their heads with their index fingers, which they then pointed at me to show that they agreed with Karen about me being nuts—and I just waved to them and kept singing at the top of my lungs—"*Oh happy day…Oh happy day….* "—but with, I hoped Karen would notice, the best voice control I'd ever had.

By the time I got home I was feeling pretty low, and I telephoned Karen at least a half-dozen times before supper, but each time when I said "Is Karen there?" the person on the other end hung up on me. I walked from room to room of my apartment, then picked up the model of the house we'd been working on and in a sudden fit of frustration almost threw it against the wall, but instead I set it down gently on my desk and caressed it as if it were a puppy, and spoke to it, telling it that everything was going to be all right. All I really wanted was to erase everything that had been happening, and for things to be okay between me and Karen the way they'd been before I'd shot my mouth off at Mr. Ordover. All I really wanted, I knew, was for somebody tell *me* everything would be all right—to talk to *me* with some tenderness.

I lay down on my bed then and, imagining Karen was there with me, I closed my eyes and unzipped my fly. The next thing I knew, the phone rang but I was in such a deep sleep that at first I didn't know where I was or what time it was. I stumbled into the foyer, where our telephone was.

"Hi. This is Marcia, from Belle Harbor," the voice said. "Your old flame."

I said something back about being glad to hear from her, and she said she was only calling because she wanted me to know that she hadn't put *her* mother up to calling *my* mother. In fact, she had no idea how her mother even got my phone number.

"And I'm not calling to get you to go to the prom with me," she added. "I just wanted you to know that I didn't put my mother up to calling. *God!*"

"I figured," I said. "I mean, I figured you had nothing to do with it."

"And also, as long as we're talking, that I followed your team this year. I saw a lot of your box scores."

"You *did*?!"

"Sure. Some girls like saxophone players, but—shh: don't tell anybody—I've always had a thing for basketball players."

"Well, we lost the big one—"

"Lose the game, win the girl—" she said quickly.

"Which one?"

"The girl of your dreams."

"Sure," I said.

"Only listen," she said. "I'm probably embarassing you—which is definitely my intention—but I really did want you to know what happened, and also that if you invite me to the prom, I'll go with you."

"Don't do me any favors," I said back, and when I did she laughed.

"Really, though," she said. "I was just pulling your chain. You don't have to go with me. I mean, it's no big deal. Only—"

"Only what—?"

"I heard you were seeing somebody—keeping company, as my mother likes to put it."

"We broke up," I said. "I mean, we *just* broke up—"

"Oh Jesus," she said. "Sorry and double-sorry."

Then, after she apologized some more for giving me such a hard time, she told me the story of what happened when she'd broken up with *her* boy-friend at the end of the summer—he wasn't black, but he wasn't Jewish either—and about how her parents had been on her case and how devastated she'd been, and I said I didn't think that part of it—being devastated—had hit me yet. When I told her that my best *guy*-friend wasn't talking to me either—I didn't tell her he was Karen's brother—and that it felt good to talk to *someone*—her voice got softer and she said I could call her anytime I wanted to talk. She knew what I was going through, she said, and she knew it helped to talk with somebody who'd been there too.

We stayed on the phone for a long time, talking a lot about how our parents had bugged us, and we wound up deciding that the two of us could probably become Platonic friends—maybe even introduce each other to guys and girls we knew and double date some day, but that until then, where would the harm be if we called each other sometimes just to talk, or if I came out on Saturday night and we went to the prom together? If nothing else, it would make things easier for us at home with our parents so that we'd be freer to do what we wanted to do *outside* the house. I asked about arrangements, and she said not to worry about a tux—it wasn't formal—and that she'd call me back later in the evening with details.

Instead of Marcia calling back, though, her mother called my mother to say that given the bus ride out to Belle Harbor, and given the fact that the dance might end late, I was welcome to stay over on Saturday night in their guest room.

‡ ‡ ‡

So I went to the prom, and Marcia and I danced close all night, with her blowing in my ear sometimes and telling me she remembered what a great dancer I was and that if she remembered correctly, I was a pretty good kisser too. Mostly, though, she seemed happy just to be there, and to show me off to her friends—some of whom had seen me play in Madison Square Garden, and remembered when I'd come out to Belle Harbor before.

After the dance, we went to one of her friends' houses—all the kids from her crowd lived in private homes with garages, yards, and finished basements—and some of her friends passed around flasks of whiskey. There was a lot of necking and slow dancing, with the lights out except for a few candles, and some of the couples disappeared into other rooms. Marcia could tell I wasn't in the mood for much, and when she asked if I was mooning over my girlfriend, I admitted that I was, so after a while, and without making out, she suggested we go back to her house.

Her parents were still up when we got there, and we talked with them about the prom, and about which of Marcia's friends had been there with which guys, and then Marcia said that we were both pretty tired, and her parents said how nice it was to see me again and told me they would see me at breakfast. Marcia showed me to the guest room in the basement, took some stuffed animals and extra pillows off the bed, told me she'd had a lovely time, thanked me for coming, especially given what I'd been going through, gave me a quick kiss on the cheek, and left.

In the middle of the night, though—the clock-radio on the night table said it was 3:22—she woke me, lifted the covers, and got into the bed next to me.

"The bad news is that I couldn't sleep," she said. "But that's the good news too, along with the fact that my parents *are* fast asleep. I hope you don't mind."

All she was wearing was a thin nightgown, and she started caressing me, then giving me these little bites up and down my body that drove me crazy, all the while asking, "Do you like that…? Do you like *that*…? Do you *like* that…?" and telling me that anytime I wanted her to stop all I had to do was say so.

‡ ‡ ‡

On Tuesday of the next week, Karen waited for me after school and asked me to go for a walk with her. We stayed silent all along Flatbush Avenue until we got to the park, and then she told me she'd heard that I'd gone to a dance in Belle Harbor and asked if I wanted to tell her about it.

I shrugged, and asked what was there to tell, given that she had said we were finished with each other.

"So that means I *made* you go to the dance with another girl, right?"

"No," I said. "But it—the dance—didn't mean anything. I mean, my mother was after me—the girl's mother called my mother and–"

"So you were *forced* to go by events beyond your control, is that it?"

I told her that I went to the dance because I wanted to—that she and I were both free to do what we wanted, weren't we? Were we engaged? Were we even going steady anymore?

"I trusted you," she said. "I loved you and I trusted you and in one week, you just…"

She stopped talking, and I could see she was working hard to keep from crying.

"You really stink, do you know that?" she said then. "But do you know the worst part? The worst part is that I still care for you more than is good for me, and I probably always will, so this is what I want to say: If you're willing to try again—no matter our parents, or Olen, or our skin, or whatever—I'm willing."

"So?" I asked.

"So?" she exclaimed. "*So?!* So *are* you? Do *you* want to try again?"

"Look," I began. "I really do care for you, only—"

"Only you just answered my question," she said. "Lord help you. You're breaking my heart, but do you know what? At least I've got a heart to break."

And that was the last time we ever spoke.

Olen didn't go to college the following fall, and as far as I know he never went. But Karen did. In September, 1955, when I went off to college—Hamilton College, in upstate New York, where, even though I stuck to my word and didn't play for Mr. Ordover during my senior year at Erasmus, I was able to make the Hamilton team and became its starting point guard my junior year—Karen took a job as a secretary for a toy manufacturer in downtown Brooklyn.

Whenever I came home on school vacations, and after college too, I'd ask around about her, and what I learned was that after a year or two as a secretary, she'd started going to Brooklyn College at night and during the summers, after which she did the same thing at Brooklyn Law School.

Sometime in the early sixties, I was told, her family moved out of Brooklyn, but nobody could tell me exactly where they'd gone, and none of the guys knew what happened to Olen either. The year after he graduated, he'd worked for a while in the stock room at the new Macy's department store on Flatbush Avenue, and after that there were rumors about him getting a tryout with the Harlem Globetrotters, or with the team of mostly white guys the Globetrotters toured with, but nobody knew for sure.

When, in the summer of 1964, I took time out of school—I was in my last year at the Yale School of Architecture—to work down South helping to register voters, I found myself imagining—hoping—that Karen would be assigned to the same team I was on, that we'd meet and realize that we still loved each other and that there was no force on earth strong enough to keep us from being together.

But we didn't meet down there, and the following summer—in June, 1965—I married Allison Plaut, a Jewish girl from Cleveland I fell in love with when she was a Yale junior and I was working as an apprentice architect for a company in the New Haven shipyards. After living in the New Haven area for eight years, I accepted a position in the design department of an international ship-building company near Baton Rouge, Louisiana, and Allison and I moved down there, where we raised our family—a girl and two boys—and where Allison worked first as an elementary school teacher and later on as a professor in the School of Education at L.S.U., and where, once a year, with our children and then by ourselves after our children went off to college, we'd drive down to New Orleans for JazzFest, where, no matter what other musicians were performing, I'd wind up spending all my time in the gospel tent, sometimes singing along to songs I remembered.

INHERITANCE

W.S. Merwin

At my elbow on the table
it lies open as it has done
for a good part of these thirty
years ever since my father died
and it passed into my hands this
Webster's New International
Dictionary of the English
Language of nineteen twenty-two
on India paper which I
was always forbidden to touch
for fear I would tear or somehow
damage its delicate pages
heavy in their binding this dun
color of wet sand upon which
thin waves come and go at the time
it came out he was twenty-four
they had not been married four years
he was a country preacher in
a one-store town and I would guess
a man came to the door one day
selling this new dictionary
on fine paper like the Bible
at an unrepeatable price
and it seemed it would represent
a distinction just to own it
confirming something about him
now its cover is worn as though
it had been carried on journeys
across the mountains and deserts
of the earth but it has been here
beside me the whole time what has
frayed it like that loosening it
gnawing at it all through these years
it is true I must have used it
much more than he did but always
with care and indeed affection

turning the pages patiently
not harming them as I looked up
what I did not know all that time

PHOTOGRAPHER

W.S. Merwin

Later in the day
after he had died and the long box
full of shadow had turned the corner
and perhaps he was no longer watching
what the light was doing
as its white blaze climbed higher
bleaching the street and drying the depths
to one blank surface

when they started to excavate the burrow
under the roof where he had garnered his life
and to drag it all out into the raw moment
and carry it down the stairs
armload by armload to the waiting dumpcart
nests of bedding clothes from their own days
shards of the kitchen there were a few bundled papers
and stacks of glass plates heavy and sliding
easily broken before they could be got down
to the tumbril and mule
pieces grinding underfoot
all over the floor and down the stairs
as they would remember

fortunately someone who understood
what was on the panes bought everything in the studio
almost no letters were there but on the glass
they turned up face after face
of the light before anyone had beheld it
there were its cobbled lanes leading far into themselves
apple trees flowering in another century
lilies open in sunlight against former house walls
worn flights of stone stairs before the war
in days not seen except by the bent figure
invisible under the hood
who was gone now

The First Days

W.S. Merwin

As I come from a continent
that I saw closing behind me
like a lost element
day after day before
I believed I was leaving it

here surfacing through the long
back-light of my recollection
is this other world veiled
in its illusion of being known
at the moment of daybreak
when the dreams all at once are gone
into shadow leaving only
in their place the familiar
once familiar landscape

with its road open to the south
the roofs emerging on the way
from their own orbits according
to an order as certain
as the seasons
the fields emerald and mustard
and beyond them the precession
of hills with red cows on the slopes
and then the edging clouds of sheep

and the house door at evening
one old verb in the lock turning
and the fragrance of cold stone as once more
the door cedes to a dark hush
that neither answers nor forgets
and an unchanged astonishment

that has never been tamed nor named
nor held in the hand
nor ever fully seen
but it is still the same
a vision before news a gift
of flight in a dream
of clear depths where I glimpse
far out of reach the lucent days
from which now I am made

PENTECOST

—for John Foster West

R.T. Smith

Squint-eyed and cunning, its tongue split
like a wishbone, the canebrake sulls up,
cursive spine and the diamonds in spiral
like genetic code,

and Joby frets the Stratocaster, its plastic
the color of salted ham. A tambourine's
discs shiver, and Brother Pascal wields the Book's
hot gospel like a blunt instrument. This is

spirit. This is bliss. The words from Heaven
would almost strangle you. The Holy Ghost
is a rough customer alright,
and if someone comes for healing touch,

for translation into a mended soul,
a whole body, let him lie beside the altar
all shorn and shocked and willing, sing *amen*, say
grace abounding,

and the current sizzles, the tail beads buzz,
as the road to Zion is not all gleam-gold.
Wind scratching poplar limbs
against board-and-batten and cracked soffit says

stormy heart. You can translate any syllable
into yearning, the Lord's will,
as the rattler agitates, this being winter,
his deep sleep stolen by a prophet's

hands clapping, raw notes of "power
in the blood." He's a mean
messenger, unguessable, and Brother Harvey
Robbins now cradling him

has the look of a man ready for crisis.
Come rapture, come venom,
that double ivory stab so quick you're
not sure at first, then certain. It leaves limbs

chastened, withered. For some of us
in the lantern light, in the Carver's Cove
church house where the floor rattles
like a loom room, a coal scuttle:

we know something is coming.
Snake-shakers, Holy Rollers, Faith
Healers from over in Silva or up in Teague,
we feel the wild muscle contract.

It ain't no cakewalk to dance against
the devil. Uproot and undercut,
and something is coming right
now, something good. Leave your

coppers and dollars in the collection plate.
The moon out there is empty, visible
as a skillet in night sky.
The whoosh of angel feathers is coming.

the snake's hiss, the new dialect
we will sing to spring harvest, hallelujah.
On a good night the serpent will crown
some beloved brow like braided brocade

and idle there, HARMLESS, as we begin
the mortal bargain, breathe the honey air
of limber love and behold
as the jaws open for a half-sought kiss.

Crystals in the hourglass glisten and summon,
the weave of INHERITED BLISS
Sister, keep your eye on the cross, take my hand.

Keepsakes: A Pocket Guide to the Memorabilia in the Room

Robert Gibb

1. *My Father-in-Law's Cigar Case*

A snug and perfect, breast-pocket fit,
The glove leather's tucked in grooves
For three cigars to slip into, like fingers,
The tanned pebbly grain darkened

With the gift of his oils. And the scent
Of tobacco! Great leaves curing in shafts
Of light, brown and biscuit and sorrel,
The whorled smoke waiting as if housed

Inside a bough. Strange how we seem
To saturate the things we leave behind,
Which our lives in passing have touched.
How, like our lives, they are gathered up.

2. *"Early Jazz Greats" Trading Cards*
by R. Crumb

These, even though commissioned,
Came clearly from the heart. Remember
In *Crumb* how he sat in his living room,
Listening in the dark to the music?

"One of the few times," he explained,
"I actually have a kind of love for humanity."
I slip them from the box, portraits
In a pocket-sized Uffizi, face up

And stacked in the order he numbered,
And admire how deftly they're posed
With their instruments—"Fatha" Hines
And Satchmo and a young Sidney Bechet—

Painted as if on the flaps of a carnival tent.
The deck's merely a convention,
Like melody, there being too few musicians
In it to reprise a single combo,

Let alone trade—unless, of course,
You wanted to swap the whole boxed set,
But what would be the sense of that?
In it, they're having the time of their lives.

3. *Change Purse*

A crumpled pocket of clasped black leather
The size and shape of a dried plum,
My grandfather had it with him
When he fell in the mills, back out of time.

It's filled with the loose change he was carrying:
Eight coins that add up to a dollar-twelve.
Not much. Not even the pay dirt of metals
To which the body can be reduced.

I pay them out again, the Indian-head pennies
And Liberty dimes, studying wreaths and faces,
The turn-of-the-century's cusps of dates,
Still actuarial, still trying to square accounts.

4. *Letter Opener*

More curio than memento, this ornate blade,
Flat and handleless, the caravan of elephants
Along its spine like knots of a macramé.

I'm glad it's actually plastic and not the sliver
Of tusk it's been made to resemble—a shiv
Of hand-carved ivory pocketed during the raj.

5. *Pocket Watches*

Three small gleaming glass and metal suns
Passed down in the family,
Each with its circumference of numbers,
The inset, second hand orbit
At the bottom of each face.

5:26, 6:50, 1:05. One side of the meridian
Or the other. Either way
Each is an instance of something stopped,
Though I've tried coaxing moments from them,
Rocking the balance cocks and wheels.

Unfastening the backs, you can see
All the racks, levers, springs, and gears
That once worked together so perfectly.
All forms, I remember, *hold energy*
Against the flow of time.

Industrial Relics, Station Square

Robert Gibb

1. *Brick Press and Electric Furnace*

Here, as if set in threes on cooling racks,
Are the hard, rectangular loaves I remember
Lining the furnace walls, bisque-colored
And featherweight, the balsa of the bricks.

We'd come upon them in waiting stacks—
Gold for the straw of the fire. Or collapsed
In ovens and soaking pits where we'd be sent,
The slabs backing up, and the ingots.

2. *Bessemer Converter*

And up there, above the court, the great
Black egg-shaped barrel hovers on its axle,
Pitted with rust, the slobber of metal
On the vessel nose crusted like barnacles

Or callus on a right whale's head. Welds
And bolts. And because nothing should be lost,
The adz-shaped toggles where the wind box
Was clamped in place, the firestorm caught.

3. *Blowing Engine, Shenango Furnace Co.*

A pair of wheels mammoth as a grist mill's
Functions as the base for the piston
Balanced above them like a water tank, steel
Painted lime against the weather. Switched on,

It once drove gusts from banks of stoves set four
To the furnace, winds hot enough to melt
Down pipe, iron ore churning in the molten core,
The shriek and bedlam of the smelters.

4. *Benches, Bessemer Courtyard*

That sun-dazzle out on the river, as if
A shoal of luminous fish were roiling the surface
Near the Smithfield Street Bridge.
Beyond it the ramps on which traffic's ridged,
In-bounds and out, the wall of the city
Like glass vaults sheared from the sky.
At the end of summer, mid-afternoon, light glints
Halfway down their sides: particles of wind
The cameras catch for us, time-lapsed
On the news—the steady-state of shoppers,
Clouds leveling in above the wharf.
Behind me the last tourists pose, dwarfed
By the relics, then drift off toward the parking lots.
Light on the water webs the bridge's blocks.

Beyond Rubies

Sarah Lindsay

He knew from his studies that some other cultures
adore for their beauty women cross-eyed and fat,
prize wood above gold, or remember and save
every detail of their dreams upon waking;
a missionary in the field must never assume
he knows what people value. One translator
of Scripture had to call Jesus the Pig of God.

The language of the Tlhorh is tonal,
monosyllabic until quite recently,
every syllable depending on pitch for several meanings.
The challenge to its wits is to avoid puns,
to its poets to sidestep rhymes,
to its composers to find themes or motives
that don't sound like mere eccentric speech.

His first sermon was a catastrophe:
He introduced himself as a glorious fish.
Fortunately, a figure of fun
is hard to dislike, unthreatening—
especially when he spends months in his cot
with a local bug his body has trouble translating
and, eventually, with pencils and piles of pages.

When he rendered Matthew 6:20 in Tlhorh—
"But lay up for yourselves treasures in heaven"—
in under one hundred words, without scatological echoes,
tears sprang to the Queen Mother's eyes, and she gave him
a sackful of perfectly spherical rosy agates
polished by the river. He was a millionaire,
as long as he never went home.

The Invention of Comfort

Sarah Lindsay

From the first, in seas and on mucky land,
creatures moved too fast and died too quickly
to notice, but all around them, in them,
novelties sloshed and budded. Eyes, lungs, sleep, fear.
Structural reinforcement
of the vertebrae in a tail, serrated edges
of a carnivore's teeth, a velvet of capillaries spread
over panels jutting from a slow-moving hummock.

Here pillars of flesh pursue mountains of flesh,
scaly necks heave faces with lidless eyes
to the glare overhead, and, dodging underfoot,
something small has grown armor on its thorax,
or a long and flexible sting,
something smaller has worked out camouflage,
something tiny secretes a burning poison,
and something else has a wet and wiggly nose,

but chiefly it has hair. It has been learning
about tangles and mats and waking with squashed
and rubbed-up fur on the side it likes to sleep on, and that with regard
to working the hind spurs as combs there is
one right way and several wrong. This is the ancestor
of a girl in knee-sprung yellow pajamas
hugging her flattened bear. We know because
when at night the creature curls up

to the lullaby of the springy sound in its guts,
it fits its tail around the tender nose
to hoard warmth, but also to smell itself,
and it rubs its downy bellyskin against its feet
in an unnecessary movement to be known as nestling:
a refinement of the urge to avoid sheer misery
that is worthy of admiration,
which will not be developed for ages.

Destruction

Sarah Lindsay

Allsop is fond of quoting Sir Leonard Woolley's
"Excavation is destruction," but he admits
to fantasies of strangling the so-called baron
who spent too much of the nineteenth century
converting portions of Mesopotamia
from sites pertaining to Sumer, Nab and Assyria
into evidence of his whirlwind passage.

They say the Baron von Hausknecht traveled
nowhere without a valet, a chef, and a mistress,
and cursed in nine languages, some of them dead,
which he taught his myna bird. He was stout
and well over six feet tall; his pockets
chuckled with rare old coins. Madly rich
and wildly in debt by turns, he left a trail
of women smitten or well amused,
partridge bones and empty bottles,
rumors of duels, a few of his teeth,
and a newly chic fascination with ancient lands.
He wore black lambskin gloves, they say, at all times,
and had crates of fine wine carried to every dig.

His hands were restless. They wanted filling
not to amass or study, but
to spill, to jingle, to give away grandly,
and if they had nothing else to do
his thumbs would rub at the base
of his middle fingers. Carmelita,
a former operetta-chorus girl who
dabbled in palmistry, pointed out
he was rubbing mostly the mounts of Apollo and Saturn,
a clear indication he should have been
an artist: melancholy, solitary,
in love with beauty in all its forms—
to which he made the correct reply.
No one knew of the malformed Galataeas

he'd carved and smashed to powder; let them instead
admire the bug-eyed, bearded images,
long lost beside the ancient Tigris,
revealed by his new pursuit.
He loomed at the edge of a fresh pit, seized a shovel,
leapt in, and with a single thrust
beheaded a limestone statue of Sililit.

Allsop, seventy-eight years later,
faithfully sifts the unspectacular graves
of Mishgath-Tera, avoiding the gouge
where von Hausknecht did his worst.
He will leave two quadrants untouched, even as
he resists the temptation of pristine Tell Makaira,
just forty miles away. Something must be set aside
for the ones whose coming is foretold:
twenty-first-century scientists with machines,
who will scrape a bowl that once held goat-meat stew
and work out the proportions of honey and fennel,
or tell from a bone the shade of the buried one's hair,
who will reconstruct statuettes from handfuls of crumbs,
and to whom Sidney Sullivan Allsop, he can't help thinking,
will be one more barbarous digger.

THE CRANE AMONG ITS MINIONS

William Logan

Like a chalk-white spire
rising over the Herefords of the Beef Teaching Unit,
the whooping crane stood alone with the alone,

its rackety rattle half whistle, half war-whoop.
Sandhill cranes milled around it like Myrmidons.
Only one man can be an Agamemnon—

everyone else is an also-ran, and still may not survive.
The barbed wire glinted like spearpoints.
The sun blazed like a hammered shield.

Puffy clouds seeped above us like blisters,
the Florida days ten years too long,
Januaries with too much *Sturm und Drang*, or too little.

And there he stood, the great bird with his war crest—
regal, scientific, nervous without nerve—
while the many stood watching an old-fashioned god.

And Now for Something Completely Different

William Logan

In the room, the television blazes
as a fire used to, homely and open to reason.
We peer into it, as a god would—

no wonder I feel there should be a soul.
Cancerous, freckled, no longer a beauty,
her skin like a baked chicken's,

the woman on the screen recalls
the movie she starred in, thirty-five years ago.
I saw it once, when I was nineteen and relentless.

She was just a girl in a yellow dress,
to whom life had yet to happen.
Now it had happened.

If I'd died then, I would have refused to speak
to the living. I wanted to be more than I was.
I wanted to be Achilles.

Dear V. M.

William Logan

You had, like me, to labor for the soul.
If the death's head must be faced, better to face it
without belief, shivering and insensible.
If you could return, my ghost, not that you can,

waiting for grace, cruel as a red-tailed hawk—
forgiving, but not meaning to forgive—
you'd soar in the glamor of your private wars,
beneath the grain the tender glow of things.

Your weakened body grew immune to weather,
the summer hurricanes a memory.
Lying beyond the touch of history,

you know its cold salvations and its sins.
Slipping away the morning you turned forty-four,
you scraped to your mid-forties, on broken wings.

—i.m. Victoria Moore, 1961-2005

JUDGMENT DAY

—after Luca Signorelli

Peg Boyers

Our eager bodies pull through a sea of dirt
to join their tranquil souls—

your father and I
together in the same grave.

The other soul we seek is yours; we can't relax,
we think, on this raft of Afterlife, until we find it.

We notice without shame that we are naked, and that our naked bodies
are hairless (which we like) and sexless (which we don't).

We look everywhere, turn up earth mounds and stones,
but slowly boredom overcomes us, and we stop.

Anxiety numbs, perception clouds:
we vaguely notice that the rubble around us

resembles a Jewish cemetery somewhere,
jumble of gravestones and history just beyond reach.

It occurs to us in our fog that you might be among the damned,
but that thought is too strenuous to maintain,

too heavy for our ever lighter beings to carry
in this erasure of Everafter,

as are all the worries of you, the vitality of
daily fear, the eternal

madness of parenthood which turns out
not to be eternal.

All that is indelible fades.
The oblivion of the saved is their damnation.

SACRA CONVERSAZIONE

Peg Boyers

We're at the gates of the temple.
The arch of the portico, the reliefs on the columns
give away the period.

Your father and I are dressed
in robes of opulent brocade
too elegant, really,

for a carpenter and his wife.
From your place on the steps
you look straight out the picture frame,

brazen and unafraid, chin defiant on your fiddle.
I think, oh, he must be the artist,
doing that Renaissance self-portrait thing.

Suddenly you swing around,
urgent and certain,
I have something to say to you—

But we are talking and talking
as usual while Saint Peter hovers
at the threshold.

His keys' hypnotic glint
catches your eye, beckoning.
You put down your instrument,

say what you have to say,
walk to the other side, step
into the realm where we are not.

Only your echo remains:
I am not like you. I am not like you.
I am not like you.

Ww

Andrew Osborn

As in Azarian's "Winter" woodcut where
The tracks of runner sleds ridden downhill
Then dragged back up initially appear

To wave or otherwise allude to the art's
Essential gesture: the way, were someone
Getting the hang of his tools to have a go

At an anchored block of basswood or maple,
The hand would ride its knife along the grain's
Ingrown urgings in grooves near-parallel.

How many down-warm bedtimes had I read
A Farmer's Alphabet before it dawned
On me how wrong I'd been about that scene

So like the snowy scene December made
Behind my childhood home? Dependably
Asleep before we reach our favorite letter,

My daughters dream of how I'll carry them
Upstairs to cot, to crib. Two double-u's
Dusk red hover above a bleak tree line,

The stag-horn sumac rearing in my head.

Futebol Professional Feminino

Gwendolyn Oxenham

I was spending seven weeks in Brazil, and though I'd known for a month that I was coming, it wasn't until now that I realized I was spending seven weeks in Brazil. I'd gotten out of the cold shower and was lying on the top bunk and there were ants in my sheets and girls speaking Portuguese. I was tired, very tired, and though the daughter of missionaries who sat by me on the plane had taught me how to say various things—I have to go to the bathroom, I am hungry, nice to meet you, how cool, I am sorry—the post-it note I wrote it all down on was in the pocket of the jeans now rolled up in my bag. My teammates came into the room a couple at a time, waving at the passed out American and saying the same thing: "Hello my friend!" I'd roll to one side and lift my hand in "Oi," but my eyes would not stay open and the sounds flying around my head began to fall off until there was no more noise.

I woke the next morning to an empty room and looked up at the ceiling that was close to my head. I had no idea where everyone was or what time it was so I went back to sleep. I woke the second time to the slam of the door and shouting and crying and the reopening of the door. Karen, my roommate, grabbed her bag from above the small curtained box that acted as a closet and began throwing her clothes into piles on top of it, screaming at the girls who had followed her into the room. I stared down at the wild hand gestures, the grief-filled foreheads, trying to make out what was happening. Dear God, I thought, Dear God. Please don't let this be about me. I didn't know why it would be about me but she was sobbing and clearly moving out of the room and I was wondering if she was upset over being stuck with the Americans. Caitlin, the other American, charged into our room, and she too began the wild gesturing and fast, fast stream of noises. I gaped at her, the very blond, very white girl who was clearly fluent. How long had she been here? Seven months? How many years had I taken French? Four? J'aime manger. J'aime le futbol. That was it, that's all I remembered.

Karen wore a cross-cultural look of embarrassment on her face and Caitlin was putting Karen's clothes back in the closet and they were both kind of laughing in that sheepish, post-trauma way. I stared at them. Karen glanced up at me and threw her hands on her head. "Ai-yi-yi," she said as she pointed up at me and the room turned to look, all leaning back at the waist and laughing at the bewildered American who was looking unsurely down at them. And though I was being pointed at and laughed at, it was at least a noise I was familiar with and I laughed too.

"Brazilians laugh and cry more than we do," Caitlin told me as she lathered 45 SPF sunscreen over her face. "Did you bring enough sunscreen down? Ultraviolet rays down here are intense. Anyway Karen just had a misunderstanding with Kleiton, but it's fine now so let's go to lunch." Kleiton was the coach and if I was in the US I would want to know what kind of misunderstanding it was but since I was here and in the dark about most everything, I just nodded and smiled, which I figured I would be doing a lot. I slipped on my Havaiana flip flops, staring down at my feet. Though I wore size eight in women's, these were a men's ten and two inches flopped behind my foot.

"Hope you like rice and beans," Caitlin said as we walked on the dirt pathway to the food. "It's hot dog buns for breakfast, rice and beans for lunch and dinner…sometimes fruit too," she said, making it suddenly clear why she'd asked me to bring her a few jars of peanut butter in my suitcase.

In the kitchen, I ladled the beans onto my plate as the *tias* in blue and white aprons clapped their hands to their face and exclaimed, "Autre Americano!" When Caitlin, a friend of a friend, said her coach in Brazil was looking for an American goal-scorer, I emailed back instinctually, "Yes me, I'm a forward," even though I wasn't a forward and most certainly could not score goals.

"Our next practice is in two hours," Caitlin explained as she sliced a banana and mixed it with her beans. "But you don't have to go. Kleiton totally understands if you want to take the first day off. I did, bad jetlag." Harvard gave Caitlin a grant to run an HIV awareness program in Brazil and she arrived last May, teaching kids in between soccer sessions. So while I was only down here so that I could remember what it was like to be a soccer player, Caitlin was fighting epidemics.

"That's ok, I'll practice," I said as I finished off my beans. I wanted the first practice with a new team out of the way. Right now I had that lump in my chest, that knowledge that nobody knew whether I was good or not. Though I'd played Division I ACC soccer and gone to US national tryouts, these unknown Brazilian faces had me more nervous than if I'd been playing in front of Anson Dorrance.

"It's a forty-five minute walk," Caitlin said as we started out towards the field. "But lots of time we can hitchhike." As we made our way through the streets, Karen and Jani sticking out their thumbs and yelling "Corona!" to passing cars, I guiltily thought about my mother hugging me tightly and warning me about the girl missing in Aruba.

No cars stopped and we walked through the town of Itanhaem, past small *casas*, ugly dogs, electronic stores, a steepled church and the city square, people waving at the girls in oversized Umbro gear. The square was under construction and while you could see traces of cobble-stoned streets, it was now a gulf of orange clay. We ducked beneath fluorescent tape and wobbled along a remaining bit of sidewalk, passing beneath an old railroad track and eventually reaching the field. Beneath the cement overhang of the municipal athletic center, the rest of our team leaned against a powder blue punch buggy with missing wheels. Caitlin tossed me a roll of gauze as we walked up. "It's for your ankles," she said. "The fields suck." We sat down, wrapping the gauze tightly and periodically brushing away the ants that tried to crawl beneath our soccer shorts.

As I put on my shin-guards and cleats, I looked out at the net-less goals that book-ended the field. An old man stood in front of the one closest to us, a stepladder by his feet. He unfolded the net like a favorite blanket, carefully, familiarly. Slowly, his hands wove the squares of the net up the white posts. He stood on the stepladder to maneuver the net over the crossbar, then stepping back to the ground. When the net draped softly down the posts, gathered in a slight pool on the field, he picked up his stepladder and walked to the other side of the field.

Practice began with prayer, twenty or so girls gathered together in a circle, holding hands and bowing heads. Kleiton led and with closed eyes, I listened to the sounds as they traveled up and down, my ears occasionally resting on Hey-zeus. I peeked frequently, worried that Kleiton would stop praying without me knowing. The fourth peek, I looked up into open eyes and Kleiton smiled, the prayer over. "Wendolyn," he said, pointing at me.

"Gwendolyn," Caitlin corrected.

"Gggwendolyn," he repeated. The team laughed and turned to each other, trying out the sound, jin, jen, gen...the Gw- sound as easy for them as the rolling of *r*'s was for me. They began introductions, going around the circle giving their names, not moving to the next girl until I tried to repeat it. They'd say it again, slower, and though my name was mush in their mouth, they didn't understand why I couldn't say theirs. I smiled embarrassed after each botched attempt. Potch, the girl next to me, patted me on the back. "Sem problema," she said with a wave of her hand.

Kleiton gave more instructions and everyone headed out to the field so I followed. "We juggle for a half-hour at the beginning of every practice," Caitlin told me as we walked out. "I'd do it with you but Karen and I are always partners."

"That's fine," I said, and there was a hand on my arm. "Loriena," the girl in front of me said, touching her chest. She held up the ball then pointed to her feet and my feet and I said, "Yes," and she said "Sim." As she flipped the ball up to her feet, juggling it several times without spin, I knew immediately that I was in trouble. I glanced around me, at the sets of partners scattered over the field, balls levitating peacefully in the air, moving in graceful arcs from one player's foot to the other player's foot. A girl to my right was juggling with her shins, actually bouncing the ball up and down on her shin bones. I received a pass from Loriena, my feet spinning it shakily up into the air. I tried to get it steady, back to the graceful, spin-less up and downs Loriena had the ball use to, but it wasn't happening. Since I was twelve-years-old, I'd been avoiding this moment. While I had learned quickly how to juggle on my thighs, doing it after school for a half hour each day until my record was 147 in a row, I never learned to juggle continuously with my feet. At ODP tryouts, when we juggled, I hid on the far outskirts and revolved around the coach's back. I worked on foot juggling for years without seeing much progress so I moved on to other, more game-relevant aspects of soccer. I practiced my dribbling and receiving constantly, assuring myself that this would sufficiently develop my touch and make juggling unnecessary. But now, here I was, juggling with Brazilians, the best jugglers in the world.

"Desculpe, Desculpa, Desculpa," I said to Loriana when I pegged it at her chest or made her lunge to keep it up.

"Não tem problema," she said, smiling.

Suddenly Kleiton was speaking again and everyone was moving and I just followed. "Não," Kleiton said, putting his arms on my shoulders and turning me around, then gesturing and speaking to Caitlin.

"He wants you to jog for twenty minutes to get the plane ride out of your legs."

"Sim," I said.

I began the jog around the field. While the center of the midfield had devolved into smooth, flat, sand pits, the surface of the wings was a cross between a minefield and an egg-crate, and my ankles rolled out from beneath me every other step. I wobbled around the field, my twice-rolled extra-large shorts sneaking higher and higher up my waist, my extra-large shirt draping lower and lower down my legs.

Eight rough laps later, Kletion called Wendolyn and I jogged towards the group. He pointed me out to the wing towards Potch. "Vêja," Potch said, holding my shoulders and then pointing at her eye. I stood behind her, watching as she sent a serve into the box. Two players ran onto it, volleying it perfectly into the goal. The next service came from the other side of the field and another forward volleyed it into the side-netting. Potch sent one more service in and then pointed towards me. "Você."

I dribbled a couple steps and tried to set up my cross, but the ball bounced and I struck the ball awkwardly, my serve launching out of bounds. "Ope-ah," Potch said from behind me. Once again she patted me on the back, "Não problema."

We continued in this fashion…Potch sent it perfectly into the box, I sent it perfectly out of bounds, the ball usually deflecting off my shin-guard.

I was an outside-mid. I was a crosser of the ball. If nothing else, I knew how to move down the wing, get end-line and send the ball into the box, making sure to keep it away from the keeper and to pick out a player running on. In college, though our crossing and finishing drills usually went poorly, I wasn't the one to screw it up. But as I watched Kleiton direct Potch to put it on a player's foot or head or chest, I realized that the Brazilians took service precision to another level; that even if the field had been flat, even if I'd had the playing surface I'd been used to, even if I weren't spraying my balls all over the field, I would not have been able to cross as well as these girls. They put the ball on a platter and the forwards finished; again and again they finished.

I wished I'd pleaded jet lag and stayed in bed.

When the sun started to go down, practice ended and we headed for the spigot in the corner of the field, filling up the Gatorade bottles or lapping the water directly into our mouths. We started the walk back through town, walking slowly, swinging our cleats through pink sky.

‡ ‡ ‡

The Santos Futebol Club is famous. It is home of Pelé, the greatest player in the world, and men throughout Brazil wear replicas of his Santos number ten jersey, whether they are waiting for the bus or going to a game or selling fruit at the Saturday morning market. Now there was Robinho, slated to be Brazil's next Pelé, and the eighteen-year-old played forward while a stadium of people held "Fica Robinho" banners. Stay Robinho, stay. Real Madrid, the team of international superstars, wanted him in their frontline, and the summer I was in Brazil was the last season Robinho was to play with Santos. The SFC men were sponsored by Umbro and Panasonic and they received huge salaries that kept them in exclusive apartments at the top of the city. They did not hitch-hike to practice.

Most people did not know a Santos women's team existed. We did receive brief moments of large-scale attention. The National Brazilian television station did a double feature story on Leo, the men's left lateral, and Joyce, our left lateral, who was 5'1 with large green eyes, the facial structure of a porcelain doll, and the same scrappy style of play as Leo. Caity and Lori Lindsey, the Virginia star who had come down to train for two weeks before trying out for the US national team, were asked by a reporter on television if they had learned how to Samba, and they did the jerky American version with smiles that were broadcast across the country. A camera crew came to our dormitories and did a special story on Caity and me, the two Americanas, before then turning their attention to Néné, our leading scorer. But who knows how many *casas* were paying attention to their television sets during our thirty-second clips. We did not stay in Santos, so the city didn't see us much in person either. Panasonic did not sponsor the women, nor did anyone else. Though once, when the men's team rejected a make-up company's sponsorship, the company briefly considered putting their emblem on our jerseys instead. But it never happened and without the funding, Kleiton was only able to pay two or three players, the salaries amounting to less than twenty American dollars a month.

We stayed in the rural beach town of Itanhaem, where Saulo, Kleiton's father, owned bungalows and agreed to fund the room and board of twelve girls at a time. Bungalow, I discovered, was a romantic word for cement room with cots and bunk beds. But the dirt pathways attaching the branches of bungalows were always kept well raked and the green, leafy plants bordering the sides were watered and weeded by a gardener every morning. A larger room to the left of the dormitories housed the local Itanahaem teachers between classes. In front of the cafeteria, there was a large blue fountain and while the paint was now peeling and water no longer ran, you could tell it was once a proud, pretty focal point and the flowers growing around it were still kept up. Outside the rooms, various people sat in white plastic chairs. Our team and a men's semi-pro basketball team were the long-term residents, but over the summer, the bungalows also lodged passing Brazilian boxing stars, gypsies, rodeo cowboys, and athletes from the Indian Olympics.

On Saturday, my second full day in Brazil, we had our first game of the season and the basketball guys high-fived us as we made our way to the front of the bungalows to wait for the city mini-bus to pick us up. A small TV was in the front of the bus and Néné leaned to the front of the bus and tuned the dial to a music channel; we rocked the mini-bus from side to side to sounds of Shakira as we rode to the game. Pulling up beside the field, half the team spilled out of the bus and headed for the pushcart man who sold chocolate popsicles for three *reais*, and half the team stayed in the van to see more music videos while we waited for it to get closer to game time. As it began to rain, Kleiton ushered us into the locker room, a cement room with a wooden bench along each wall. Stacks of folded jerseys had been placed along the benches and the team turned to a piece of paper tacked to the back of the door to see which jersey number belonged to them. While in the US, the numbers are fixed for a season, Brazilians based numbers on the position you played. The eleven starters received jerseys numbered 1-11, depending on their field position, and five subs also dress out, and as I reached for the number fourteen jersey the paper said I should take, my face felt hot. I'd been in the country for one day and knew that I had no right to a starting spot, but excluding a senior day game my freshman year, I'd started every game I played in since I was thirteen-years-old. And here I was, having traveled to another country to sit the bench. I reminded myself that I was being ridiculous, that I'd practiced only once with the team and had done horribly, that I could earn a spot in the next week of practice, and I tried to focus on the jerseys. We received hand-me-downs from the men's teams, and while our practice jerseys were clearly bottom of the barrel Umbro merchandise, these game jerseys were like silk. The Brazilian soccer federation emblem was stitched in the center of our chest, the SFC emblem to it's left, the Umbro logo to its right. For the first time since I'd been in the country, I felt like a professional soccer player. Even the socks were top notch; accustomed to socks with holes around the toes, extra material bunched up around the ankle, and an elasticity problem near the top, these stretchy, fitted socks with the SFC emblem across the shins made me feel like a ringer.

Around me girls got dressed and I stared, startled, at the players as they assembled their get up. First, they tucked their shirt all the way into their shorts, then blousing these beautiful jerseys out until the girls resembled fashion ads from the eighties. Next, they put on their shin-guards. In practice, we wore no shin-guards so I hadn't been prepared for the massive ankle-guards cluttering up the bottoms of their legs. After pulling up their socks, they shoved both the shin-guards and the socks as low as possible on their legs, leaving several inches of skin between their knees and the top of their shin-guards. They did their hair next, gathering it up into a ponytail at the nape of their neck. Stricken, I turned towards Caitlin.

"I know," she said, as she pulled her socks all the way up to the bend of her knee.

Swigging on a water bottle, Potch pointed at me, looking me up and down, and shaking her head, hitting the cap of the water bottle back down. "Americanos seja loco." She bent down to feel my ankle and pretended to kick the stretch of shin unprotected by the small shin-guards I had taped up high on my legs. She held her fist to the top of her head and wiggled around, apparently imitating my high ponytail. She reached for my waist and tried to blouse my jersey out, and when I held her hand away, she pointed to it and said, "*Feio*" with a grimace. She turned towards Caitlin speaking in rapid Portuguese and then turned back to me, "Ugely," thinking that I just hadn't understood her.

Kleiton entered the locker room and spoke for fifteen minutes on tactics while I let my mind wander, making a mental note that Brazilian coaches talk for just as long as American coaches. After a team prayer, we formed a jumping circle, all (but me) chanting words that sounded exciting. We headed for the field and divided ourselves into starters and subs. The subs stood juggling in a circle as the starters went through a routine of jumps, stretches, high knees, and other preparatory movements led by the man who'd been introduced to me as our weight trainer. Since only twelve girls were sponsored in the bungalows, there was a dramatic drop off in talent from the starters to the subs. While the twelve bungalow girls came from all over Brazil, some from Bahia, some from Rio, some from Natal, the rest of the team was made up of local girls who played in Kleiton's Futsal program. Carol and Fran were locals who had played with Kleiton since they were five and six and they were good, so good in fact that this weekend they were away at the under 19 national camp. But most of the other local girls were trial players who came and went. We subs just stood there juggling, fans lining the fence along the sideline.

Even in the light rain, people stood two and three deep along the fence, the bleachers off to the right crowded. While American fans at women's soccer games usually consisted of parents and twelve-year-old girls, these fans were mainly male. They were disheveled-looking locals with facial stubble, old t-shirts, and worn baseball caps and they leaned their arms casually over the fence. As they watched the starters warm up and us benchwarmers juggle, they appeared truly delighted, like it was the best thing they'd seen all week: *meninas* playing futebol. While the United States was accustomed to the groups of girls swarming soccer fields, while 100,000 fans filled the Rose Bowl Stadium and millions more watched from their TVs as Brandi Chastain celebrated her penalty kick, while *People*, *Time*, *Newsweek*, *USA Today*, and *Sports Illustrated* featured the women's team on their cover, while women's soccer in the US was common knowledge, Brazil knew nothing about it. The Brazilian superstars—Marta and Sissi and Pretinha—were better known in our country than their own. Men along our sideline held their sweaty, faded baseball caps to their chest as they tried to process the futebol feminino taking place on the town field.

After the starters lined up along the half-line and waved to the crowd, the game began and I sat along the bench watching twenty-two Brazilians play the game. By now I knew that I'd underestimated them, that the Latin American *machismo* hadn't kept the national passion away from the women as much as I'd expected. These girls grew up playing in the streets and the beaches with their brothers and the neighborhood boys and though mothers and fathers would guide them back inside toward the housework and the cooking, they'd always find time to escape out to a game and sooner or later their mother or father would pass on the sidewalk next to the street where they played and they'd stop: watching *beleza* come out of their daughter's feet.

So I sat back, ready to watch the same art I'd seen in practice, but as the rain fell harder, I realized that the game unfolding before me was *feio*. And while I thought at first that it was just the horrible way they wore their jerseys making me think so, the more I watched the more I knew this was ugly soccer. The other team toe-blowed the ball and ran in clusters and just kicked it up the field and while our team would occasionally pull off a clever passing combination or skillful dribbling streak, for the most part, we reverted to their playing style and participated in the kick and run.

At half-time, I started stretching out my ankles, sure that it would now be my time to go on, but while the starters were taken back into the locker room, we subs stayed outside. I had started to follow the starters but Priscilla had grabbed my arm and said No, as though I was a toddler who wanted something not allowed. I realized with horror that the subs were segregated, that we did not get to listen to the half-time speech (not that I would have understood it anyway.) I tried to imagine that kind of exclusion happening in college soccer—-Robbie saying, "Nope," as he steered the subs back to the bench. "No half-time tactics for you."

While I'd been trying to be positive and introspective, I was now distinctly annoyed. As the game started back up, I sat on the bench thinking *here I am in Brazil, sitting on the bench in the rain watching sucky players toe blow the ball out of bounds.*

"Brazil, why Brazil?" Casey had asked me.

"The whole futbol as religion thing," I said.

"Why not Iceland with me? We get 2000 a month, a car, a cell phone, and a plush apartment."

"I've been in South Bend. I need heat."

"Well let's send emails to see what the hell we've gotten ourselves into. Hope your sunshine is worth it."

As the soggy wood of the bench seeped into my shorts, I started to compose the email in my head when Kleiton signaled for me to get up. Our physical trainer took me to the corner of the field and ran me through the warm-ups as the fans laughed and whistled at the Americano with the high pointy-tail as she did butt kicks. With twenty minutes left, he put me in at left lateral for Potch. The Brazilian style of play does not have outside mids and the closest thing to my position (which they discovered quickly wasn't forward) was left lateral, similar to a US left back who got to go forward a lot.

So I made my defensive debut in Itanhaem, Brazil and while I tried to convince myself that it was just like playing outside-mid conservatively, Karen and Jani were calling me back to mark the forward which undeniably made me the last line of defense before the keeper. A short Brazilian with hair that stopped above her ears dribbled at me, her foot crudely chopping at the ball, her toes pushing it forward and when I went to take it away from her, she tricked me: she leaned backwards, seeming to fall, and used the very tip of her cleats to nudge it through my legs. Stunned, I turned around to clean out this girl who was trying to scuttle by me, but as I gently rested my hand on her waist, the ref blew his whistle and wagged his finger at me. My God, I thought as I ran into the box to mark my player. All half I sat there watching girls slide-tackle and kick the shit out of each other's ankles without consequence, but a gentle hand on the waist gets a finger wag. One play later, the ball was resting in the grass in front of me and as I and another girl ran towards it, I used my body to check her. She flew and the ref came towards me, whistle back in his mouth. "It was a hip-check. Body to body. That's not a foul," I explained to a non-comprehending face. "Bastard," I said to him, once it was clear that he couldn't understand.

When you're accustomed to playing for ninety minutes, twenty minutes on the field is not a long time and before I'd gotten more than three or four touches on the ball, the half was over and I was walking back into the cement locker room. Kleiton's face was disappointed and after his speech, I didn't need to ask Caitlin for a translation. We stripped off our jerseys and set them in neat piles on the floor, changing back into our pre-game outfits and heading back to the music videos on the mini-bus.

Back at the bungalows, we crossed the street to the beach and waded into the water in our sports bras and soccer shorts. The girls from Sao Paulo and other interior cities did not know how to swim but there was a four-foot drop off they could stay inside of right past the shore, waves lapping around their chests. "Last week, Cris, the keeper, almost drowned," Caitlin told me as we waded out. "She's one of the ones who doesn't know how to swim and she got swept out and Dado had to save her." I stared at Cris, the

6'2ish female using her palm to push water at Nene as she bounced deeper into the water, apparently undisturbed by her recent scare. I dunked my heads backwards, the salt of the Atlantic Ocean making floating easy and I breathed in the familiar smell of a beach.

After rice and beans and a shower—they'd taught me the trick to make the water warm—I climbed up to the top bunk and lay in bed flat on my back, discovering what it felt like to miss someone—*saudades* they called it here, Portuguese the only language in the world that can say 'I miss you' in one word. In South Bend, our last night, we lay there, his Portuguese expressions book open on my right arm, his body up behind mine. I tried out the sounds, forgetting them as soon as I said them, my voice sleepy and shy, my finger tracing down the columns as he showed me the way the words could sound. When I'd told him that I was going, sitting there at his desk and reading Caitlin's email about bungalows and beaches and futebol, he understood, knowing the pull of the country that any soccer player in the United States has always wanted to go to. His junior year of college, following his Notre Dame soccer season, he went, spending the spring and summer abroad in Rio de Janeiro. Now that it was my turn, he dug in his closet and tossed me his Havaianas. "You'll want these." Then he'd added, aware of my frightful deficiency, "And you'd better learn to juggle."

‡ ‡ ‡

We had all of Sunday off and we spent the morning swimming in the small river that met up with the ocean in a cold crossing of water. Caitlin was dating Dado, the Brazilian goalkeeper who trained our keepers when he wasn't trying out for professional teams, so today she was with him and my translator was gone. But there was the beach and a couple boogey-boards, and my skin—South Bend white—felt warm. We spent the day pointing to the sky or the bird or the man and using a stick to write the translations in the sand, making fun of each other as we sounded out words.

Around four, I headed back to the bungalows to meet Caitlin and Saulo, Kleiton's father, for a tour around the city. As we drove past the centre and over the small bridge that rose above the river we'd waded in, Saulo told us that Itanhaem is the second oldest city in all of Brazil. Itanhaem means rocks that sing, the Indians having thought the waves crashing against the boulders sounded like singing. We stopped at a beach tucked into a cliff and Katie pointed to the stretch of sand Santos frequently trained on, a beach featured in *National Geographic* as the largest sanctuary for baby sharks. "But don't worry," Caity assured me. "It's safe." We continued driving, climbing up the cliff. At the top, we got out and walked along the nooks and pathways the waves had carved into the black rock. I stepped questioningly over a paper plate with white marble-sized balls that looked like eggs. "Oh," Caity said as she too moved past it. "Yeah, you'll see those. It's just flour and water rolled up. There's a tribe that believes the devil will eat your soul if you don't leave him food. So they put it up here, at the highest point possible." I walked to the edge of this highest point, looking down at Itanhaem, its shoreline curved liked the arch of a woman's back.

Once the sun dropped down, we headed back to the bungalows. In the cafeteria, girls sat but most did not eat and Rani, the only one who could afford to go to a private school long enough to pick up more than "hello my friend" in English, said, "There is festival tonight. You come with me." Rani's brother was a Brazilian soap-opera star before he was killed in a car accident. "Muito bonito," she told me matter-of-factly as she showed me his picture.

Around seven we walked to the town centre. There was a stage to the right of the church and people samba danced to upbeat Christian music. Christmas lights were strewn over red and white striped tents that served food—three *reais* for crêpes, espheas, or pastels. Fried dough softly scented the street as we browsed the jewelry stands set up by traveling hippies. The team tugged me around by the hand, introducing me to the locals through pointing to me and saying, "Americano!" "Fala," they'd tell me. And I'd say, "Oi." They shook their head, said, "Nao, fala Inglês." I said, "Hi, I'm Gwendolyn," and everyone giggled. Around ten, we licked gelato and walked back to the bungalows. I crawled up to the bunk, lay on my side, brushed away an ant, tried to beat my pillow to softness, and went to sleep, remnants of Portuguese words floating confused in my head.

‡ ‡ ‡

On Monday, I fell into the training pattern. We left the bungalows at 7:45, walking to the fields for morning practice. Around noon, we walked back, ate rice and beans and spent an hour taking it easy in our rooms or lounging right outside our rooms. The basketball boys owned a boom box and they played loud American hip-hop throughout the day as they sat in the plastic patio chairs singing "Your pride is what you had baby girl, I'm what you have," their mouths making the sounds without knowing the words. Some days they played Pooradooh, Brazilian funk, and Flavia and Thais joined them, sitting on the concrete with a tambourine and drum, moving their hips to the beat. At three, we walked back out to the fields for afternoon practice and fitness. On Tuesdays and Thursday we lifted weights, physical training done to the beat of more American music, the girls loving anything from Red Hot Chili Peppers to Ja Rule. In between bench press sets, Flavia and Loriena tried to teach me to samba, and we watched our reflection in the wall-sized mirrors as they moved my hips and feet.

It was winter in Brazil which meant rain was frequent and when too much water collected on the fields, we trained on the beach. On days when conditioning was the focus, we just crossed the street to the beach by the bungalows, running suicides in the sand. On days where we did drills that required more room, we headed to the main beach. As the ice-cream push cart man wheeled by, we did high-knees over hurdles made out of cardboard folds, periodically grabbing them when the waves came too far up. As surfers got out of the water and couples strolled by, we ran through various circuits before beginning our scrimmage in the sand. On days it stormed, people cleared out and we had the beach to ourselves. While the US has machines that read for lightning and officials that halt all practices and games when there is a storm within 30 miles, in Itanhaem, lightning and storms did not alter our training schedule. Whipping winds similar to the pre-hurricane winds I'd seen in Pensacola made big white caps on the water, lightning decorated the sky, and there we were, doing headers of all things, wet sand caking our foreheads. On days where both the fields and the beaches didn't work, sitting puddles on the fields and high tides at the beach, we did agility work on the pavement of the main highway, our bodies taking up a lane. As I slid from cone to cone on the wet cement, cars actually splashing me as they drove by, I thought about all of the torn ACL's in the US, injuries occurring despite manicured training surfaces, and I wondered how in hell these Brazilian girls could work on cutting and turning on wet cement without having a single player out with serious injury. (Their lack of kindness-to-body was a recurring theme: there was no concept of energy preservation—while in the US, day before games meant soccer volleyball and tactical walk-throughs—Santos ran fitness. And while in the US we drank only water starting the day before the game, Santos pounded down cups of coffee an hour before game time.)

After both practices sessions were over, we hand washed clothes in the alleys between the bungalows. We used the outside water basin, plugging up the sinks with plastic bags and pouring in detergent as the water ran. Flavi taught me how to use the rough cement side of the sink to scrub out the dirt from the jersey. And on mornings when I discovered a dirty jersey, having apparently forgotten to wash it the night before, Karen took it from me. "Stupido," she told me and quickly washed it for me, then putting one end of the shirt in my hands and one in her own, wringing it out and yelling at me when I didn't twist it tight enough. Karen's mother was a maid and while Karen didn't mind living with the Americans, she did mind when the other girls on our team came into our room and said "Sujo" while making a face. The other girls took everything in their rooms outside every other day in order to scrub the floor with hot, wet rags. And while Katie and I made sure to keep our clothes in neater piles than we ever had before, changed sheets every day, and always swept after eating crackers, we rarely mopped our floor. Every day Karen would sit down on the corner of her bed, making a scrubbing motion with her hand, and tell us, "Amanhã, we lava," her English developing better than my Portuguese, her two languages mixing into an effective patois. But in between sessions Katie and I wanted to nap and after sessions there was dinner and games to watch or some other reason to put it off. "Sujo," the team said as they passed our door with a laugh.

"Ai-yi-yi," Karen would say, flopping backwards onto the bed.

When someone wore Nike, they also said "Sujo," wiping at the swoosh as though it was dirt. Then they laughed, put their hands on their hips and said, "Outro Lenivel..." And in Brazil, Nike was another level, cleats pricing around four or five hundred *raies*. Rani showed me her Nikes, a plastic model no college player would be caught dead in, polishing them thoroughly as she cradled them in her arms. "Que lindu," she said, holding them up for me to admire.

Every few nights, when my legs could handle another walk, I made the trip back towards town. As I left the bungalows, the old-man guard always stopped me to talk. We couldn't talk, as we didn't know each other's languages, but I said Oi and he said Hi and then petted his dog while he spoke slowly to me in Portuguese. I said "No comprendo," not realizing that "No comprendo" is Spanish and that I needed to be saying "No entaindo." I waved Tchau and pressed play on my walkman. Wearing my headphones and listening to a Brazilian mix Luke had made me, I took side streets up to the main road where there was a computer hub. Teenage boys sweated from the heat of the computer screens as they played video games, and I emailed Luke, throwing in the new words I learned, but as I knew them only verbally (despite the occasional scrawling session in the sand), I free-styled the spelling. He emailed back " 'muita' baby, not 'mewta'" and "Good work *minha gatinha* but try to look in a book once in a while." I also emailed my parents and friends, cutting and pasting large sections of how-it-is-in-Brazil information onto multiple email drafts.

I, Gwendolyn Oxenham, am playing left back. They call it left lateral but that's just code for defense. Rocky first game—here, by the way, taking out someone's legs is fine but if you try to use your upper-body, even a little bit, the refs come over to give you a warning. The second game we're playing some cruddy team and I'm overlapping up the sidelines, picking balls off, winning all fifty-fifties...pretty much thinking that I'd missed my calling, that if I'd played left back in college my entire career might have been different, national team would have been beating down my door. Our next game, we play against these tricky little forwards and of course, my mark is a Brazilian track star. I'm running like hell trying to tail her...meanwhile the rest of the defense is screaming at me in Portuguese, "SIGH, SIGH." And I'm thinking they're saying "Get Back, Get Back," so I'm a nervous-sprinting-wreck whose trying to get goal side. Really "Sigh" means push up, and the rest of the defense is trying to set an off-sides trap. As I see a flash of a forward streaming towards goal, my body keeping her on, it becomes clear that I have misunderstood. My lack of comprehension results twice more in near goals and Karen and Jani are gesturing angrily to Kleiton and shouting "Americano" and I'm just thinking My God, what am I doing in this country. Getting yelled at in Portuguese, playing defense, marking a Brazilian track star. At half time, Karen and Jani use magnets to diagram it and get the half-coherent Katie, who suffered a first-half concussion, to translate "SIGH" and we're good for the second half. After an eternity of sprinting at full speed—and after a month of nothing but rice and beans I'm light as a feather and fast, but not as fast as this girl and every ball played has me scared—the game ends and we get on the bus. Ok, off to watch the Brazilian semi-pro basketball game, though they're no better than a mediocre American high school team. It's clear why this country plays futebol.

‡ ‡ ‡

Futebol games play on television all day and there are always basketball boys and Santos girls gathered around the TV in the cafeteria between practice sessions. At night, the big games are on and after showers, the cafeteria tables are divided by loyalties, everyone cheering for the city they came from. The Paulistos and Paulistas are the biggest group and nights Sao Paulo play they crowd the front, hands on their heads when the ball is in their defensive third, hands clasped in front of their chest when the ball is in their offensive third. The grass is like carpet, the stadium is two seas of contrasting colors, the noise forces the announcers to shout out the play-by-play, and our team watches the broadcast as though they are studying a dream. They gasp, hands banging on the cafeteria tables when a player does somebody up or rifles off an unexpected shot.

The US women's team is better than the Brazilian women's team, but these girls are sitting in front of the TV, the only TV, and they are taking note of every ball, lay off, and cross-field switch. They are students of the game. Though soccer games are being broadcast in the US more and more frequently, coming across a game on TV still makes you feel as lucky as finding twenty bucks in your pocket. Most US players grow up playing but not watching. Here they do both and as I look at Fran, fourteen-years-old and Santos's starting center midfielder, a Jehovah's Witness whose long hair bounces on her back as she glides into spaces no one else sees, I know they will catch us.

As a team, we went to one men's Santos FC game, a treat following our first game. A visiting Christian soccer team from the US paid for a bus that took both teams the two hours to Santos. An afternoon game against a fairly poor opponent, there were still twice as many people than I'd ever seen at a soccer game, but Kleiton assured me that this was nothing. We sat in the stands studying the men who played our positions. Robinho—the player whose picture we cut out of newspapers and taped to our bungalow walls—scored two goals that game, one of them off a breakaway created after he rainbowed it over the last defender. We sat there stunned, all grabbing arms whenever he got the ball. Yet Caitlin and I were the only Santistas, the other girls already attached to home cities, and later in the summer, when Santos played in the Liberadores Cup, Kleiton snuck the two of us away. A mile within the stadium, we saw the flares and the fireworks, the blue smoke bombs pinging down alleys. Sausages and chicken barbecued on sidewalks, ice chests full of bottles of beer sat in the middle of the street, clothing vendors pedaled knock off replica jerseys to anyone who passed by. And men, swarms and swarms of men with number ten or seven on their back and SFC flags in their hands, men forming swaying, chanting throngs, and men sitting in cafes with red and white checkered tables and TVs, men striding quickly for the stadium. While games are normally at ten, giving men time to get off work, this Liberadores game starts at nine, and people are hustling through the streets. We make it to the gate, Kleiton gives a familiar nod to the man and shows our Santos passes. For three *reais* we buy hoagie sandwiches and eat them at the snack bar, then walking through the stadium opening and out into the air. Kleiton and Caity watched me as I took it in, as the sound hit me, as I saw the fireworks rising up from the fans and thousands and thousands of faces who waited in line for hours at venues all over the city in order to get these tickets. There are cheap seats and there are good seats and we sat among the upper-class as business men smoked cigarettes and listened to mini-radios that give score updates of the other cup game. When the game started, I watched the right-lateral, tracing where he moved and when he got back and when he went forward. And every time Robinho got a touch I waited to see if he could shock me again.

There were moments in practice, by the fourth hour on the field, dirt clouds in my face, ankles sore, my oversized jersey ballooning around my body, that I didn't feel like being there any more. Times when I looked at them—(that's what we did in college when we got fed up, we exchanged looks that let you know you weren't the only one tired of being out there)—but here, hours and hours later, they're still absorbed and I'm just the American who can't feel the love. But in the stadium, with the sound and the color and the people and Robinho, I get it: I too want the seventh hour on the field. I am squeezing the bleachers and thinking, put me back on the field, let me be out there, let me play this game. The Santos women want inside this throb of national passion. So they can do it, they can play eight hours a day even though they don't get paid and don't have a good field and don't have a country who know women play.

At the end of every Friday practice, Santos play *brincadeira*. There is no direct English translation, but Caity tried to explain: "It's just for fun," she said, shrugging. "It's a scrimmage, but it doesn't count." It's for experimenting, for messing around. You're not allowed to tackle and you only get two touches and the idea is that you try things. You go for the rainbow, the meg, the continuous, down-the-field juggle. You try out your tricks and when the lift works or the bike scores, your whole team erupts, doing flips or sprinting in sharp zigzags down the field or beach. Here, at the very end of the week, after four days of two-a-days, when legs were beat, I saw the fundamental difference between me and the Brazilians. I didn't want to mess around, I wanted to save my legs for the game day tomorrow. And I didn't understand. What did they mean it doesn't count? What do you mean you are playing just to play?

‡ ‡ ‡

Most of the girls on the team have not gone to school past eighth grade. Three-quarters of the team do no have dads who are still around. Potch's mom wants her to come home, needing her to help make money for the family. She puts her hands on my cheeks and points to her chest, "Eu muita, muita triste." Nene, our leading scorer, grew up in favela, the government-shunned areas that don't show up on maps. When her brother was stabbed, she identified his body in the morgue, knife still in his neck. She just now came back to soccer, having given it up to work in a factory painting happy meals toys to make money for her eleven brothers and sisters. (We have a *Finding Nemo* fish next to our bunk beds.) Flavi's been working since sixth grade. Loriena is from a small island without cars and running is her mode of transportation. She hurt her ankle at the beginning of the summer and though they put her in a cast, they did not give her crutches and she made the transition from jogging everywhere to hopping everywhere as though it were the most natural thing in the world. Susanne's brother is in prison for drugs. The day I am sad, the day after I emailed my mom asking what size Havaianas I should buy Nolan, the day she emails back that he won't need Havaianas for a long time, Susanne puts her arm around my shoulder and says, "Meu irmao tambem." Priscilla lost her uncle in a car crash the day before our last game. Joyce's mom has had two abusive husbands. The average age on the team is eighteen. While there are days they seem younger than me, days when they steal my fruit and tug on my hair and shout in my ear and dance and dance and dance, there are also days when they are older—days when I see Carol or Karen across the street from the bungalows, sitting alone on the peeling blue bench by the water. When I walk by, and say, "Tudo bain?" they smile, wipe their eyes, and say, "Não."

‡ ‡ ‡

When I arrived in Brazil, Caity told me that she was actually leaving three weeks before I am, having to go back to the States for a while to see her family. My eyes got wide and I imagined my Portuguese-less self without *autro Americano*. But I had a month before that happened and, though she was frequently gone, either spending time with Dado or running the health empowerment programs, she was able to keep me filled in as we lay beat in our bunk beds. Now though, the month was up and Caitlin was hauling her suitcases to the taxi and heading towards Boston.

I waved Tchau and turned back to the bungalows, saying, "Ai Yi Yi" to Karen. We looked at each other, our translator gone. Karen, though captain of the team, is always the late one, and as I could plead clueless Americano, I just did what she did. Most days, we left for practice later than everyone else, tossing cleats into our bag, locking the door, and taking off in one hurried swoop. We set off down the road, Karen saying, "Girl, Girl, ai-yi-yi," and pointing to her watch. We held out our thumbs, looking for rides, and she mimicked me, apparently poking fun at my thumb-holding technique. After a week though, I had it down and I made the same funny smile she made, the one that made cars think: "Why on earth wouldn't I give these two girls a ride?" They pulled over, we gave each other high-fives and ran for the car. I discovered quickly that the nice cars fly right by but that the shitty ones—the ones with missing doors and hubcaps and rusty frames and unidentified-animal-fur on the seats—are always willing to help you out. Karen sat with her elbows propped on her knees and kept up a continuous thread of chatter with the driver, stopping only to wave victoriously as we passed our walking teammates. I'd learned that if I kept my mouth shut I could pass for Brazilian, but when the driver looked questioningly into the rearview mirror at the mute girl in the back, Karen just slung her thumb at me and said, matter-of-factly, "Americano."

In practice, I was a sheep. I did whatever everyone else did. I followed, followed, followed. Sometimes they put their hands on my shoulders and pushed me in whatever direction they wanted me to move. I was fine with this at first, but eventually, I get annoyed at being manhandled and said to them, earnestly, knowing they wouldn't understand a word, "Stop pushing me, I will move if I feel like moving," and they laughed. Kleiton could speak a little bit but he didn't like to and he let me pretty much figure it out for myself, telling me "Boa," once I'd got it. At the end of practice, before we started our walk home, we played the ear-flicking game…juggling in a circle until someone screws it up. The one who botched it got the tip of their ear flicked, and there's something surprisingly frightening about five or six girls coming at you with their finger poised in the air. Usually I, the sucky juggler, dropped the ball and sacrificed my ear before we started home.

Outside of practice, I was also a sheep. I got on buses having no idea where we were headed, I followed girls to town, no idea why we were going to town, I put on whatever kind of clothes Karen put on, and I learned to appreciate the surprise factor, finding it exciting, or at least sardonically amusing, that I never had a clue where I was going or what I was doing.

I emailed home:

Stuck between a two-month long Portuguese pre-season and a giant, never-ending game of charades. I've devolved into a toddler: making giant over-wrought faces to convey emotion. And never want to see another bug in my life: ants in my toothbrush, my underwear, my sheets. Bug growing inside our goalkeeper's thumb. Carol—bit by a bug that left burn marks all over her body. Karen—my roommate—covered in mysterious white splotches. Can't say Karen's name right—can't roll the R—and when I ask, "Dande Karen?" none of the girls understand who I'm asking for, no matter how much I try to make that growl noise. Oh, and offsides, this aspect of the game I've never really had to concern myself with—the one I'm now trying to figure out in Portuguese—won me a sexy, Brazilian nickname. Cris, our keeper, is frantically trying to get my attention and when she tried to shout my name, she came up with Gremlin. Gremlin. Yes, same meaning in Portuguese. But while Brazilians have different standards for joking material—for example, they call one of the girls Lorieana, which means Blondie, not because she's blond but because she's so black they think it makes a nice irony, and when we drape these black rubber bags of sand thingies around our shoulders to do resistance jumping, they point to the bags and then Cris and make it clear that her arms and the tire rubber are the same color—they've apparently decided Gremlin is over the line. In the cafeteria, they surprised me; they all learned how to say the Gw- noise and they made a song to the same tune as Jingle bells. Gwen-do-lene, Gwen-do-lene, Gwen-do-lene, lene, lene…and now they sing it all times of day, Karen hums it as we fall asleep, the team sings it on the bus to games, on the walk to practice, etc.

Tchau,
Gwen-do-lene, aka, Gremlin.

P.S.

Flavi comes into the room one day carrying a small silver pole in her palm. "Vôce quero?" she asks and points to my belly. "Nao entandio," I say, my go-to expression. I don't understand, I don't understand. She walked out of the room and brought in KaKa and pointed to her pierced chin. "Nao entandio," I repeat. She walked out of the room and brought back Thais and showed me her pierced stomach. "Você?" she asks. "Nâo! Nâ*o*," I say, wrapping my arms around my tummy. "Nâo!" The silver pole is apparently an at-home stab-machine that is being passed around the team. Six girls have new piercings, two eye-brows, two belly buttons, and two chins, one un-sterilized piercing tool. I say, "You guys wash floors every day, change sheets every day, have ungodly levels of cleaniness, yet you have no problem stabbing each other with dirty pointed objects." "Nao entandio," they say. (I did let them take me to a pharmacy where a shirtless hairy man pierced my ears.)

‡ ‡ ‡

Karen discovered my Radiohead and lay every night with her face flat on the sheets, saying, "Love music, Love, my room sister." In between sessions, I wrote and she thought it was weird and she cleaned and I thought it was weird. Now that she was no longer out-numbered, she'd become a cleaning Nazi, dusting my toiletries. I grabbed my face lotion from her hands and gestured madly, "Você é loco!" She plucked it back and said calmly, "Brazilians, we clean." Then she pointed to my computer and my books. "Americanos...voce think," she said, tapping my head and then taking my hand and leading me back to my computer. She talked to me in Portuguese and I talked to her in English and sometimes we pretended like we understood, nodding and smiling. Other times, when she was clasping her hands in front of her chest and speaking in the steady stream of noises, I cut her off: Nâo fala Portuguese! Nâo comprendo! And when I spoke at her in English as we fell asleep, she just put her hands under her head, closed her eyes, smiled and murmured a soft refrain of "No speak English, No speak English, No speak English" until she fell asleep.

One night, I was freezing and shivering, having shunned the orange, ratty blanket that was more disgusting than any hotel blanket I'd ever seen. I woke to Karen retrieving my blanket from the closet and wrapping it around me as she whispered to herself, "Stupid Americano." I pulled it around me, mumbling, "Love room sister, love."

When our gestures and patois didn't make things clear and some circumstance demanded that we figure it out, we looked it up. The dictionary was also used recreationally, and Flavia, Nene, and Loiena liked to come into the room and we used it and the Portuguese expression book Luke gave me as we sat on the bed with our legs crossed Indian-style. They pointed to my locket, flipped through the pages and asked, "Namarado?" Si, boyfriend. "Voce fiel?" Flavia asked, while digging her fingernail beneath 'faithful.' Si, I said, and on the rest of our walks from practice back to the bungalow, when a Brazilian guy talked to me, Flavi walked over and thumped my locket.

Loriena engaged in a full conversation through constant back-and-forth passing of the dictionary. Why aren't you on the national team? she asked. Because I'm not good enough, I said. *Porque*? She asked. I didn't know how to answer this in English or Portuguese, so I look up I don't know. *Não sei.* I asked her if she is on the national team and she says no. I asked why, she shrugged, *Não sei.* She looked up the word for dream and tells me that her *sono* is to play one day in the Estados-Unidos. To come to Estados-Unidos. They all want to come to Estados-Unidos.

Six games and seven weeks later my time in Brazil was up and I was going back to the Estados-Unidos. Good-byes, tchaus, are hard, and before the day in the cafeteria in the Itanhaem bungalows, I'm not sure I've ever really made one. Nothing's ever really a good-bye because sooner or later faces turn up and reunions occur and you see people again. But when I hugged these girls and looked at these faces, Carol, who drew words with me in the sand, Potch, who used touch and facial expression to try to make me understand, Loiriene, who always always said Hello my friend!, Loiriena, who hopped or jogged everywhere she went, Cris, who christened me Gremlin, Susanne and Rani, with their sad, older eyes, Flavia and her Samba, Karen, my room sister…I knew this good-bye was probably real.

"Americano. Gwendolene," Karen said, heaving my suitcase into the trunk. "I. Miss. You." She hugged me and wiped at her eye and laughed and then frowned, and I hugged her and laughed and then frowned. I got into the car, *saudades* already in me.

Soccer and futebol are not synonyms. Soccer is a system—we run and pass and run and shoot and run. Futebol is an art. In the United States, we focus on being technically sound. We learn the moves—the step-over, the Ronaldo, the V—but in Brazil, nothing's set, dribbles bleed into one another and a player's just moving her feet, inventing, creating, no idea what's going to happen. She's after the surprise. I didn't learn how to Samba—twenty-two girls couldn't teach me to listen to the music without forgetting the beginner's 1-2-1 step—but I did learn to bring sway to my game. On the bus, with tambourines and drums, at practice, with water bottles and a thump of the hand, in the alleys as we washed clothes and in the town square on Saturday nights, there was a beat, and when I played, I tried to follow what I felt—like Fran and Karen and Robinho, I waited to see what would happen, which way my hips would move, what kind of thrill I would feel.

But during Brinkadeira, those just-for-fun games, I knew the truth—I played to beat people, to tackle, to go full-out. But they just played to love it.

Three to Get Ready

—for Brubeck at 85

Michael Anania

i

someone let it slip, as though
a small metal object had been dropped
and rang out as it bounced across the floor,
the sounds of solidness at play, the world's
clarity, I suppose, commending itself to us,

as accidental as anything compelled by
gravity might seem, a leaf yellowed and curled
against this December morning's light snow,
twigs stiff and broken in the driveway,
one more loose sentence to puzzle over

ii

waltz is invariably concave, its spaces
stitched into the still air like pine needles,
sunflower hulls and thistle husks, the finches
grayer each day, shadows, merely, graphite
moving just there across slate-colored clouds,

all that you might imagine, a lilt passing
like breath amid the ordinary swirl of things,
caught, as though in song or rather in song's
conditioned anticipations, counted out as
though its syllables were yours for the taking

iii

where was I?—waltz, song, sentence, gray winter
morning lifted like a scrim, birds, seeds, snow
stitched loosely across loosely woven cloth,
bright leaves and broken branches, things unexpectedly at play, the sudden ring of objects

falling, how crystal resounds within crystal,
brass against brass or steel wound around steel,
struck just, as they say, in time, time itself
flaking, then spinning away, its bright shapes
sudden and curled outward from your hands

WHO'S YOUR FRIEND?

Kevin Ducey

—Max Michelson, Imagist Poet 1880-1953

The Imagist fades away out of the metro
and into the Seattle mist of 1918. He finds
the soldiers and sailors there
'less patriotic' and speaks with 'contempt
of the bugaboo of death.' In a year
those soldiers of Seattle were out in the streets—
the red bandana on their arms. An image
thrown against the coming storm. Images all
come with baggage.The lumber barons
were lynching these soldiers
before the decade was out and the
Spanish influenza blew in on the train with
the demobilized. Max was packed off: 'rest,
diet, catharsis, hydrotherapy.' A time
of plague and Palmer Raids.
Imagine
a country with an unpatriotic military
(there's an image wavering in the
current heat).The Post Office in Chicago
refused to deliver any Union material
and Heywood fled the country.
And Max—
in the Seattle Sanitarium—demanded
a new hearing. "I had nothing to do
with the conspiracy to blow up that
Post Office. It's a dirty story..."
The image is a variety of letter
bomb after all and Max's insistence
on an IWW lawyer reconciled politics
and the imagination better than the rants
on usury sung out of St. Elizabeth's.

FROM THE FACTORY IN WOLFSBURG

John Peck

There is no beauty in New England like that of the boats: George Oppen.
There is no beauty like that of weapons: David Jones,
who tested that proposition.

Both things as old as Phoenician trade, as knapped flint.
A B&B Anchor-etched m/m 25 drop-forged chisel
seats itself in oak coifed with a brass noose
to accept the tapping hammer.
For years I have left its right leading edge snapped off
to acknowledge the nicks left in Diné pottery
for the egress of formal energies. *Exeunt omnes.*
That blemish brings the near-eternity of the tool
within range of ourselves paint-slashed for the axe.

It was the later 'sixties, night flaring along the Bay
as we drove Jake Ander of the Kingston Trio
to San Francisco's airport. The People's Car, the Bug
which preserved the seed-form of Hitler's prototype,
gradually lost speed and would not respond to the pedal.
I got it into the breakdown lane and we coasted to zero.
Jake and his Martin guitar were due in Chicago
so we lifted the rear engine hood, clicked a flashlight, and stared.
Hailing a trucker and clasping the matte-black Bette Davis shape
of his Martin, Jake was swallowed by the cab.
Then headlights behind us: another Beetle, a blond strider with black bag.
I cawm frawm ze factory in Wolfsburg. Fhat year iss it?
A 'sixty-three, known for its fickle fuel pump.
Jhoost a minute, then a short-sleeved clink-chunk twist-tighten.
No charge, ziss vun iss on ze factory! and he was gone.
Had Jake stayed he would have crooned his refrain:
Noooo, that didn't happen!

Forty years on at the Group-of-Eight Summit a drawl stays on-mike
as six-hundred-thousand Lebanese flee north from Israeli planes:
Gotta go home. Got something to do tonight.
Go to the airport, get on the airplane and go home.
How about you? To Hu Jintao. *Home? How long does it take you to get home?*
Eight hours? Me too. Russia's a big country and you're a big country.
To someone else: *It takes him eight hours to fly home!*
Eight hours. Russia's big and so is China.

Fed by rich land-mass runoffs
cyanobacterial slimes turn the brains of sea lions
who chew on their pups and strand themselves onshore.
The species die-off by the end of this century will halve the kinds.
The stud-sail sprag resources of their rig pranks.
Kinds, the grandfather word for *species*. It takes all kinds.
It will take us a long time to get home.
There is no car from the factory pulling up behind us.
There is no one and nothing to get us out of this.

Not the weapon, the boat: immersing in conflict, to steer
mind and heart through it and, leaving, to leave no dent.

For who can defeat us? spirits veiled in matter, mantillas of fine pained stuff,
endlessly distracted yet tooled for completion, crazed yet aimed,
out of time while knowing that it will take a long time.
Beneath craze knowing the past

is not just deadly alive
in the present but both are pushing
off into possibility
continually, their wave
its own airfoil, clutching
each other half tangled, half free,

that the field of time wears a nick for love
which unconditioned works just to one side of time,
love dressing its tool with the rathe oil of action

as long as the octane cocktail
of consciousness lifts and wreaks
the traffic. In Eritrea
spartan warriors kneel
to the sunrise with scorpion casques
though the great write them off as error.

Patience

Laton Carter

That responsibility could be fear,
the bedroom wall never enough to mute it,
woke me, or kept me awake.

My father's speech garbled by the weight and stupor of sleep,
every word tipped away from me,
too inchoate, encrypted.

They rose to howls and broke their own spell.

I pretend this knowledge does not exist.
It is enclosed, repeats, and can be put away.

So little of my own body made for sleep.
Vigilant, I break words,
watch their letters dislodge, anagram:

hangs is *gnash*; *renamed* is *meander*.

Can I remember everything?
If I could, it would do more to explain
the fastidiousness, the slowness of my ways,

this recognizable ache for do-over.

* * *

Parochial, temporal,
the psyche recorded hears only its own voice.

—to cut that self away,
talk with ease, see plainly.

You want me to say, but the you is I.
You want me to say *let it breathe,*
treat it gentle, give it song.

You do not want that.
You want to know past the short crust of what
today you know.

If you can, without I.

* * *

Just once my skull
touched the grit.

Furred cap of the fallen oak seed,
tassel of lichen, there was
world enough.

I couldn't know nor see,
was never bored.

As it did with nearly everything,
the weather would see to me.

In the moment before, in its own transience,
a hastening of wings.

Vengeance

John Hennessy

How qualify love for a God who'd wager
with Satan, prop Job—childless, penniless,
riddled with boils he scraped with potsherds, salved
with ash—between them? Who stranded Ruth to numb
her fingers barley-gleaning among strangers?
Whose nightingale trill stumped Abraham, put Isaac
on the block at knife-tip? Fear, respect,
due any desert patriarch, come easily.

But think how sweetly I loved my father when
he saved me in the alley from Dog-Star Freddy,
his troop of runners, sadistic thugs who'd just
as soon grope as punch you, drag you to the basement,
for once not letting me fight my own fight, Dad's
fists coming down like waves on Egyptian cavalry.

CALLING

John Hennessy

He crosses slag heaps behind the laundry, new
Neolithic, face hidden by mud and hair,
one dirty denim shirt-sleeve gone, signaling arm
bruised, covered with welts or sarcoma. What am I
doing back here in mail-order flannels, leather-soled
shoes? I can't name the impulse that took me off
the train to the city, but this is no dream. He holds up
the shell of a cell-phone plucked from the river
and asks if I'll buy it. Anything can happen.

I'll lead with my left, aim to split the skin
below his eye-socket with my wedding ring.
Or I can scrabble over a stack of pallets,
head for the alley, shortcut to our old street.

He waves the phone so it catches the sun.
It's silver, clean from the river—for a second
I'm blind—but he forces it into my hand. From where
we're standing we can just see the rusted dome
of Rahway Prison. Last I heard, Freddy was there
or buried under it. Sure, I'll call *him*.

Or Curtis, who nearly bled to death from hit-
and-run while crazy Frieda sat and watched.
Or Ball who broke my nose once, heart twice.
Or smart-ass Eddie who left for MIT
and stirs the Persian Gulf in a nuclear sub.
Or Paul whose scrip—perverse black bag—hauled East
to east, beyond stark Golgotha's squared-off teeth,
to some fermented eagle's nest hung above Seoul.
Or silent Keesha who thanked me for *Gateless Gate*—
I thought the book would make her moderate.

The salesman's gone already, disappeared
down river with the rest, past muddy clumps
of skunk cabbage, pigweed, spiderwort,
a gutted pickup chassis, still holding my change.

WALTZ

Matt Bondurant

It fills the gaps in suddenly, remarkable,
the possibility of a father, a child.
Massaged like the hand-held heart,

these walls reflect the sharp mustard folding
of wood-grain and common sense,
the scent of thirty-year carpet,

cigarettes, the touch of greasy needles,
Café Richeleu, Paris. 1995.
The fine strains of a far off waltz.

Last night she said: *We all heard the moon fall, even from America.*
Dover, I said, I want to churn the chalk
and stones like Matthew Arnold,

holding the phone between two extended
fingers, picking the paint from the third wall.
I think this might be it, the real deal she said,

knocked up, and this flat four-iron of logic
makes the rosy floating babe appear,
then years later, now faithless and squinting,

both of us long lost, left on an old
couch in the sagging suburbs of Roanoke.
Baby powers a Chevy down a white knuckled exit

to the Old Virginian Truck Stop,
coffee, biscuits and sausage gravy,
strangers; they will fall in love at least.

Over the filmy gravel of Interstate 81
the night sky funnels and erupts
like oil paint on water as baby lights

a cigarette and curses the eternal midnight.
But here, *C'est incroyable!* they say
watching the soccer match,

while I drink tepid Stella Artois
and kick at the curling carpet,
one hand over my heart, holding on tight.

Poem For a Woman You Never Knew

Matt Bondurant

This is not about the beautiful
young woman, Buffalo, New York, 1956
stepping onto the sidewalk

and lighting a cigarette,
hair and lips the same deep red
of the blooming tulip, freshly cut.

This is not about the illness
that broke about her like a garland,
how a remark or look brought

hours or days of lamenting and worse.
How? One day she turns the last page
of *Madame Bovary,* a quick drive

downtown, a cigarette and the drugstore,
and all the world turns to endless sea.
This is not about you:

just a boy who didn't know better,
a dime in your hand smilingly proffered,
years after she rode passenger side

to Niagra, Syracuse, Alexandria, Mt. Vernon,
towns that thunder with phantom trials.
No, this is about a woman you don't know,

one you've never seen or felt lonely for,
a woman who turned her collar up,
and walked into the wind alone.

Elegy for Anthony Piccione

Shane Seely

Out by the lake, the graves of soldiers
lurch in thaw.

Their bodies
are uneasy with the weather,

and their souls—
I cannot tell you where their souls have gone.

If the grass
shaded by this gravestone

is a song,
then who will hear it?

I do not speak
that tongue.

We suspect the dead are singing.
A high pine

sways inside the wind.
There are hollow sounds in the eaves.

If there is singing
after death, and souls gone somewhere

past the great thatch of cloud
above the lake

can pitch a tune,
why sorrow for the dead

and all their poems?
Their poems live, even

when their song is wind—
but here, we spade fresh dirt

onto a grave
and tunnel deeper into our lives.

I suspect the dead don't sing
and can only hold their heads

in disbelief
at what they have become.

Letters of Blood

—for Jesper Svenbro

Göran Printz-Påhlson

"Here I am, an old man, being bled by a nun"
Would be one way of starting this poem,
Unless it sounded too much like a quotation.
But in this a poem, or a book, or a parabola
Of the arrow, are at one: it doesn't matter overmuch
How it starts, it is the end, although
Predictable, which is at stake, the founding
Of the monastery, the killing of the fallow deer,
The blowing of the horn, and all heroic antics.
And where that arrow falls there is a
Legend: "Everyone is entitled to have
One puzzle waiting, if he is
Arrogant enough." Phlebotomy
Was for a long time the only
Regimen of the *pharmakoi*:
Scapegoats stochastic at their checkered sports.
History has many canny spoors.
Nowhere else is syntax so close
To the angry syllabics of the track,
Patterning the snow with countless decks
Of playing cards, first black, then red.
This is the patience, the true game of patience
Of the wolves...

New Poem of Sappho

Jesper Svenbro

World War I will change our perception
of this kind of military parade
but on this day of May 1914
it is still possible to think that His Majesty's Mounted Regiment
is "the most beautiful thing on earth" in Egypt,
as it advances at a slow walking-pace
on one of Cairo's main streets.
How the sun shines!
Cavalrymen in dark blue
with dazzling helmets.—Back in England
it is an infantry battalion
which, drawn up for delivery in front of an immense barracks,
seems to others to meet
the standard of uniform beauty,
while we ourselves barely perceive the echo
of a distant shout of command:
"Attention!".—Others claim
that some units of the British Mediterranean navy
returning to Malta
at the speed of 20 knots in the westerly breeze
are more beautiful than anything else.—And now this woman claims
that "the most beautiful thing is what you love"!
She has an entire column at her disposal in the *Times* for May 4, 1914.
Is it possible in the Greek sense to "love" the cavalry?
The infantry? The navy?
The woman is at least said to be Greek,
She certainly *speaks* Greek,
ancient and dialectal.
Her words are rendered in print
and are accompanied by an English translation.
The sun over Cairo is stronger.
She is "darkskinned" and her family comes from Asia Minor.
She and her relatives have been called "kakopatrides"
on the island to which they have emigrated.
It means roughly "of undistinguished origin"
but no such information is provided

in today's issue of *The Times*
although a second column
is devoted to other facts.
This is what has happened:
archaeologists Bernard Grenfell and Arthur Hunt
have unearthed a new papyrus in Egypt
containing fragments of Sappho, Book One,
which, according to a statement at the end of the text,
is supposed to have consisted of 1,332 lines.
Supposing that we are dealing with quatrains
this means that the book contained
333 Sapphic stanzas,
of which we have the first seven
plus seven others which belong in three different poems.
To this can now be added at least five new stanzas
of which the first and the fifth
are perfectly intelligible
and appear in today's paper!
The cavalry regiment comes to a halt
in the Egyptian sunshine.
There is silence under a mother-of-pearl sky.
"The most beautiful thing is what you love."
Anaktoría!
I whisper breathlessly.
Grenfell and Hunt are sitting thoughtfully outside their tent at Oxyrhyncus,
everything is khaki, yellowed canvas and desert sand.
They are just over forty,
both of them from Oxford,
trying to imagine the face of the girl in the final stanza.
(They hardly notice
the word "chariots" a few lines below.)
How many British infantry soldiers from Oxford and Cambridge
later brought the clipping to the front?
How many agreed with Sappho
before they died in a chaos of barbed wire, exploding shells and mud?
The sun is shining over the palms of the Nile valley.

Grenfell and Hunt have given the floor to Sappho.
Two days later the House of Lords votes
against a bill
proposing women's suffrage.

—Translated by Lars-Håkan Svensson

The Centerfold

Jude Nutter

The semaphore of sleek flesh among the wrappers
and coffee cups, and at first I think there is something alive
among the garlands of rubbish. She is even the size
of a fetus or a small baby and I wonder
about the narratives that might lead backward
from this moment, about how she came to be
here inside the bin of a public toilet in a rest stop
somewhere on the coast of North America.
She was once alive for the person who placed
her here: a girl, perhaps, who felt hidden and diminished
after discovering her lover's stash and then
found herself driving as far as her mood and the hour
would allow to dump the evidence; or a man,
exhausted and sick of his own addiction for whom
she is always a fact that must first become a fiction
before she can seem real to him. It's what
detectives do—create myths out of facts. At least
on TV. And she does look a bit like one of those bodies
at a crime scene that lie contorted in a puddled,
rubbish strewn alley or flung against the dark
and mottled background of a forest floor with a few
cunningly placed leaves and scraps of fabric. I know
why no one burned her: such gestures have a most
terrible history. Bodies going into the fire.
I look at her, redolent there among the dated
papers, a worn wiper blade flung down
across her torso and find myself wishing that I
could discard my body like this, toss it without
regret into a bin at a rest stop or a train station, leave
it in the dust by a fruit stand in a foreign county.
The body has always been a problem and I think
we invented the soul to explain it.
And she has that smile: the one
that's been the trademark for a woman on display
ever since da Vinci painted his Mona—how
to use the mouth itself as a promise

of entrance into the kingdom that lies
beyond the gates of the physical world,
and I think of that photo in last week's paper—
the one of the beautiful gunner crouching
down behind the shield of his armoured machine gun
who had a picture of his wife or his lover
stuck to the plating just to the right of his shoulder:
his woman, smiling and demure
as a Russian icon; his woman, on display
in the line of fire, but inviolate,
beyond harm, her smile a blessing falling
equally on all things as he
hoses the civilian neighourhood with bullets.
And here we are, then: the soldier
and the soldier's lover, Mona Lisa and Leonardo,
that nameless, naked centrefold and me—all
of us held together for a moment in the pale
soak of sunlight coming through the fiberglass
roof of a public, unisex toilet until

I cover her up—her work, whatever we call it,
done; until I walk forward and the door
snaps shut behind me and there is the Pacific
with its bright, precise grammar of sails
and the wind peeled free from the water rattling
the sabers of the eucalypti; and here
is my lover, the man I have chosen, one
among millions, waiting, with his hands
in his pockets and his back to the wind. Alive
in this world. And still smiling.

The Lover

Jude Nutter

He takes the seat next to mine on the overnight
flight to Chicago, holding a single rose in a plastic,
leak-proof vial. He's in uniform and I can see
he's been weeping. But it's not what I think. Yes,
he's on his way to meet a woman, but a stranger,
simply because she believes him to be
the person her lover spoke with as he lay dying; he feels
he's joined an odd tribe of people who have taken,
from others, the one moment love prepares them for
all their lives. He feels like a thief, he says,
and has nightmares and sleepwalks, waking
often with his hands locked around the throat
of his fiancé; sometimes he's holding a manila
envelope of childhood photos, trying hard
to walk backward into the life he had
before this one: to himself as a boy with a glass
jar of fireflies; to the calf he raised that grew
into a bull then slept every night of its life
under his window; to the great wedge of its head
and its nose like a polished boot toe.
He wishes he had those proverbial
last words; that he could hand those final
moments to her, organized like a box of quality,
handmade chocolates with an insert
to inform her that the Heart is a Bittersweet Truffle and the Sailboat with a White Stripe
a Raspberry Crème. But it wasn't like that.
There were no last words, just noise and the whole
street wavering and twenty yards ahead,
that man, the lover, lifting and literally
coming apart. Fragments and pieces and a coffin
weighted so it felt and sounded
as if it contained a complete man. He calls him
the lover, he says, because it gives his death
a mythical grandeur. Who can say what he saw?
The roil and the rubble of the street as he was carried

upward? The shadow of his own young body
dismantling? He has the lover's death speech
all prepared, he says, so it sounds a bit like Hamlet
dying in the arms of Horatio. Of course it's a lie,
he says; he's never once seen a man actually die
like Hamlet. *But war is war*, he says, turning
his face to me for the very first time, *and we're all*
so very tired of loss and must build whole worlds for each other
out of what we lack.

JILTED LADY, GOLD-HAIRED LOVER

Trent Busch

I felt the usual things when
he left—of course at the time I
didn't think they were usual—

then rounded out the baby part
of a year that ended with a short
man sweating and a wife in braces,

the woman across explaining
a desk full of papers that
precluded first words and visits,

normal stuff that takes most
of us down to empty beaches
and a sky full of screaming gulls.

You might say, though, if you've an ounce
of spite about you, things for me
turned out opposite and gladly.

Naturally, I am older, but I
have a late breakfast, the ocean,
a slew of dresses in my closet.

Maybe the wife was only civic
minded, her short man become
a giant in a land of aisles,

maybe one stood from her basket
and nakedly and naturally
entered the world of apes and wolves.

STABBING

Trent Busch

Three or four cows and a house
make a farm when you walk
in Brohard, painter-wise.

Never mind limestone rocks
covered with loose dirt for
stalls in barns—or the flies.

Three or four purple flowered
weeds and a butterfly
make a field, never mind

the basket on a mussy
quilt thrown beneath a tree
on poor grass—or the fence.

The woman who stabbed her
lover and his wife must have
said, Never mind the blood;

three or four moments of
silence and a sigh make
the mind paint, killer-wise.

THE BELL TOLLS

Raymond Perreault & R.D. Skillings

Beyond the mountains
more mountains

Today is a funeral only a mother will attend. I'm sitting at the café, trying to make sense of the tragedy. The horror of his small body sprawled on the grey sands of the town beach haunts me. Wherever I look I see his blue lips and staring eyes, his contorted mouth with its missing tooth. That black gap devastates me. How can a man of twenty—still only a boy in size—have done so much evil and met such an end? It chills me to think back to 1978 and my first encounter with Ti Mou Mou.

I was sitting at this very table, on the patio of this, my favorite place on earth, Marie-Thérèse's Chez Moi, so truly named, so rightly acclaimed by her adoring patrons—peasants, bourgeois, elite and blans alike—facing the Iron Market, the eternal marché, with its ceaseless voices and bustle, and only a block from l'Église Ste. Anne, where the Mass will be read in less than an hour.

It was late afternoon, rain was threatening—how distinctly I remember. The sky darkened suddenly, gusts of wind swirled up, and I prepared to go inside.

The Madam Saras, those irrepressible traders of produce and gossip who come from nearby villages on foot or by mule, were hurrying to pack up their goods. Piled with green plantains, the spooked mules were kicking over stalls, scattering the fruits and vegetables, refusing to leave the shelter of the overhanging roof. I stayed on, drinking my Barbancourt, enjoying the spectacle.

Strangely the rain never came. The day declined in dim peace, the marché grew empty and quiet, the light failed, and finally I headed home, down the long hill with its stair-stepped street. A fine, scintillating mist made my skin feel like millions of cool kisses, though everyone I met still seemed intent on taking cover.

A tiny hand grabbed my wrist. I looked down to find a dirty, raggedy boy, about seven I thought—in fact he was ten—with the saddest, most plaintive eyes I'd ever seen. Otherwise he wasn't particularly attractive, as Haitian street waifs go; he had large, bulbous, cracked lips; his left cheek and the upper right part of his neck and chin were discolored, and his dusty, reddish hair spelt malnutrition.

The children of the Caribbean are charmers and con artists, and any strolling blan can expect to have his hand adopted. Who can resist their soulful eyes, their winning smiles? Who can avoid being moved by their rags, their grimy hands rubbing their hungry tummies? All those young lives devoid of hope.

I took his hand and drew him down the hill to my house. I helped him undress, put him in the shower and scrubbed him well. Then I gave him a pair of clean pants and a Cape Cod t-shirt from the five or six boxes of good used clothes I collect in Provincetown and bring to Haiti every fall. Then I fed him from my infamous pot of stew that always sits on my stove, and welcomes all who come. He begged some for his mother and I gave him a bowl and a top that fit, and made him promise to bring them back. And I gave him a bottle of vitamins.

The next day he reappeared while I was waiting at my window for Madame Philomène to pass by. I invited him to sit down, but to my surprise he insisted I give him money, as well as food; he was quite aggressive. That was when I really noticed how short he was, how small.

I said, "My dear young man, you don't say, 'Give me money,' but, 'May I please have some money?'"

He shrugged and didn't turn on the charm, as others would have done. He never tried to be ingratiating, after that first day, and always seemed determined to show his worst side. Again I was struck by how small he was, how ugly; I felt sorry for him and his beautiful eyes. I had nothing in mind. I do not prey on children. I am discreet. I do not wish to offend the people of this town that I love, as certain piggish persons do, to the shame of the rest of us.

I told him to meet me at noon the next day at Chez Moi. He came. I bought him a sandwich and a Coke. His name was Maurice Bouchard. He knew the alphabet and printed some stick-like letters on a napkin proudly. He wanted to go to school, but his mother was too poor. His father? Who ever knows where a father is?

The following day I consulted with Marie-Thérèse, and then, despite her misgivings, I enrolled him at St. Martin's, the best school in Jacmel. She warned me to beware. He was a well-known source of trouble, and all too soon I saw the proof.

He was Ti Mou Mou Ti to taunting, bigger boys, who stole the pennies he made by washing cars, and he acted in kind to younger children, women and the old. Eventually I learned that he had only stayed in school one week, then quit, taking the tuition. It was only eight dollars, but it was a lesson. I once gave a woman $25 to get her teeth fixed, but of course she never did, not in a country where the daily wage is two dollars and a half.

Meanwhile I reproved Ti Mou Mou when I witnessed his belligerence in the street. Instead of showing remorse, he always demanded money, but I always refused. I was hearing stories about him; he was always getting beaten up, or doing the same to someone else, and though he kept growing he was always small for his age, always Ti Mou Mou Ti.

He became a thief. I saw him assault a lady with a basket of chickens on her head. He assumed she must have sold at least one, and have some money on her. She protested she had none, then ignored him. With a ferocity it frightens me to recall, he knocked her down from behind and tore at her bosom, where Haitian women keep their cash.

She screamed and three Madam Saras rushed from the marché. Two held his arms while the third whacked his face back and forth with the palm and back of her hand for what seemed an eternity, but must have been only a few seconds.

When they finally let him go he went wailing away, lips and nose bleeding, screaming obscenities, swearing to get even.

A day or so later he was still livid with fury, stamping about—he was quite light-skinned and I was amazed to see how drawn and pallid his face was, how adult his expressions could be—and then he vanished, and next I heard he'd been put in jail, the first of many times. He always came out unchanged, or rather more spiteful and violent.

Till the chicken lady I had felt sorry for him. Everything was against him, his size, his looks, the hazards and hardships that beset all but the elite; but his cruel meanness finally killed all feelings of pity in me, and everyone else in Jacmel, except his mother, who never could believe anything ill of him.

Once he had learned I would give him no more money—or food either, unless he asked politely, which he would not do, extortion being all he understood—he left me alone. Yet, now I remember, he was always lurking like a shadow in the back of one's mind. Along with exploits of pure, malicious vandalism, which got him nothing but beatings, he relished kicking or taking a stick to dogs or mules—animal abuse is almost a national vice, perhaps because they must eat too—but he seemed to have a grudge against all living things. From time to time I heard of some new outrage or of another week in jail, the regimen of which one hesitates to depict.

No one could stand him. Marie-Thérèse chased him away instantly, at sight. He would climb up and lean over the railing and snatch bottles off the tables to sell or leftover food from people's plates. He would chew up fish or chicken bones till he could swallow them, meanwhile cursing one and all. He even tried to grab money out of the basket at church, but the parishioners pounced.

Worst of all was the enmity he developed toward my dear friend, André, for it was partly my doing. André was a seventy-two year old peasant, whose spindly legs—obviously he had some malady—could barely carry his weight, and with a basket of garbage on his head he gave the appearance of one trying precariously to balance himself on stilts.

André prided himself on never having accepted charity. He earned his living by hauling baskets of fatra from nearby residences to the neighborhood dump. He always came to my house after four, when I had finished the day's cooking. I would give him a bite, a biscuit or a bowl of stew. Once he went off with my salt and pepper shakers. He thought I said, 'Did he want them?' I meant Did my stew want more seasoning? I had to go after them. His humble apologies, which I could neither accept nor restrain, were most painful to me.

André liked his little nips of clairin, raw peasant rum—oh yes—and why not? What other pleasures did he have? He hobbled in and out of Nado's all day. The kids made fun of him, but Ti Mou Mou was relentless in trying to trip him up, especially with a basket on his head. After a few nips André wobbled like stilts upon stilts, but he was too kind ever to get angry at jokes. He was always gracious and formal, bowing beneath his load, saying, Bonjour Monsieur, Bonjour Madame, to everyone he met.

He had a dark, lined face, saturnine in repose, and a broad, flaring nose, was completely toothless, and when he was not working he wore an old, hay-colored, conical hat with a blue band. He slept, among others who also had nowhere to live, on pieces of cardboard, on the circular porch of an abandoned café, at the bottom of the hill, once the liveliest nightspot in town, overlooking the Customs House and the bay, which for a time, before Randall died, it had been our ambition to revive.

When I first knew André he lived in a little shack under some palm trees near the beach, but his wife, a much younger woman who sold vegetables, died of tuberculosis, and then his fortunes fell and he joined the pa gin kai.

One afternoon—I was sitting right here, as usual—Ti Mou Mou came prowling. He was like a gangster with no gun, but as he grew older he made do with menace and threats, plus his reputation. "Masisi," he said, roughly faggot, "give me some money."

"My dear young man," I said, "in the first place my name is Achille. You may have forgotten. Secondly, you are well on your way to becoming a pariah. Thirdly... "

I saw I had caught his attention at least and cast about for something useful to say. The admirable André was just passing with a heavy load. "Do you know that old man?" I said.

Ti Mou Mou said, "Yes, and I don't like him."

I said, "That's your prerogative. However, you could learn from him. He prides himself on not begging, and at his age still works all day so he can earn enough money to eat. Everyone respects André.

"You on the other hand have no pride. At your tender age you prefer to steal and beg, when you could be running errands or washing cars for the tourists. You refuse to go to school. At this rate you will never be half the man André is."

I turned away and sipped my drink. Still he stood there by the railing with his small stature, like a thwarted L'Ouverture—and then those beautiful eyes and that marred face with its unappeasable lips—and suddenly, violently wishing him gone, I said, "No, no, Ti Mou Mou. If I have money to spare I'll give it to André, not to you."

He stomped off angrily toward the marché, then sprinted after André, who was tottering under his load. Ti Mou Mou turned to see if I was watching, made a defiant face and lunged at the back of André's legs, plunging him into the stalls and strewing his garbage amidst the piles of mangoes and bananas.

I jumped up, ready to kill the little bastard, but Marie-Thérèse held on to my belt. The Madam Saras gave cry and chase, but he darted away down the hill with the most astounding agility.

We all helped André pick up his garbage. I invited him back to my table, and bought him a chicken plate and a good rum. We were thankful he wasn't hurt, and André, incapable of blame, only kept answering our imprecations with a songlike, mournful murmur, "Ah, he's a bad little boy, yes he is, poor Ti Mou Mou, so bright and so crazy, poor, poor Ti Mou Mou."

The outcome I will carry to my grave. Ti Mou Mou waylaid André one night on the porch of the deserted café, when no one else was there, and demanded money; André refused. He still had a few gourds from his day's earnings. Who can guess what he said, the mild André, to the furious demon before him? Who would willingly envision what ensued?

Mou Mou got a rock from the street the size of a good melon—there are rocks everywhere in Haiti, rocks and debris—and then he advanced on André, holding it above his head—he was fourteen by then—and when André stood his ground—what else could he have done?—Mou Mou knocked him down, and then, lifting the rock in his thin arms, brought it down on André's legs, shrieking obscenities, demanding money, until André lost consciousness.

His fellow tenants found him, roused someone with a truck and got him to the hospital. When the Madam Saras heard—by then it was morning—they rushed to my house and I went right to the hospital.

André's legs had multiple fractures. He never walked again.

Living in the hills above Ti Jacmel, Maurice Bouchard's mother knew only good of her son, her only child. At the marché, where she seldom came, she was deaf to what the Madam Saras shouted at her, and endured their insults stoically. Ti Mou Mou—it turned out—gave his mother the money he stole, saying he'd earned it, gave her snitched things, as things found. She denied all wrong-doing on his part, and people forbore to condemn her.

Nonetheless Maurice Bouchard was arrested, tried overnight—he was too notorious to warrant much in the way of formality—and sentenced to two years in jail.

Every day his mother took him something to eat, as only bread and water are provided. An inmate without a Samaritan is in dire straits.

While André was in the hospital I brought him cookies and snuck him clairin in a mayonnaise jar, with a chicken heart floating in it, his favorite treat.

The first time I saw him after he got out I almost cried. Someone had made him a flat cart of boards with tricycle wheels and he dragged himself along with a pair of ridiculously oversize gloves. There was a rope on the front, and people would pull him up the hill, but it was a long way—and often a long wait for some kind soul. Going down was tricky and he was always getting spilled, but he never complained.

He sought work, but no one could employ him: to do what? Now he was always filthy from the unpaved streets, who had once kept neat and clean.

The Madam Saras fed him, and the vender who was always open always had her eye out for him. Marie-Thérèse and I discussed renting him a place to live, but we never did. Everyone helped him. Marie-Thérèse gave him a few gourds every day or sent him a sandwich, and he did not lack for his little nips, oh no. I saw to that.

He would stop at my house—it was halfway between the marché and his abandoned café porch—I would hear him and go out. He would never come in any more; it was too arduous, but he would rest on my bottom step, and I would bring him a banana or a mango.

He never spoke a word against Ti Mou Mou. It was always, "Ah, poor Ti Mou Mou, so bright and so crazy!"

Life went hard with André. Still, it can be said that he never had to beg, nor ever went hungry or thirsty.

Ti Mou Mou was not welcome in Jacmel when his term was up. He was sixteen by then. But he was neither humbled, nor circumspect in returning to his old ways, only more ruthless and rash, and we braced to see what would happen next; but fortunately he went to Port-au-Prince and stayed a good while, living on the streets. Occasionally someone from town caught a glimpse of him begging, but everyone shunned him.

He came home from time to time. He tried to get on the better side of me. He was hustling sex by then, but I wanted nothing to do with him, and neither did anyone else, who knew what he was.

I used to wonder how he felt when he saw André dragging himself along on his cart. Perhaps I should have asked him—it could have done no harm, perhaps, perhaps—but I never spoke to him again. We had all turned our backs on him.

One year there was a terrible drought. By late October, when I arrived, the flowers were coated with dust; feet in the unpaved streets raised a powdery haze; you gagged to swallow. Food was costly and scarce. There was no water; there were constant blackouts. The sky stayed blue by day, blazed with stars all night. Eyes ached from sun lancing off the white houses trimmed with yellows and pinks. Shade baked, breeze abraded, green was a dream. The heat was like a beast. Everyone was parched, edgy, at each other's throats. The harsh voices kept rising frighteningly long after they would normally have cracked in laughter, and each day reached a new limit of endurance.

How wonderfully, how blissfully it ended! Only later did I think how evil came of good. It had been a somber evening, absolutely still and dead. We were sitting here as usual, drinking our Barbancourt, too weary even to talk, when I noticed Mme. Manouche was acting strangely in Gerhart's doorway. That was her place every day from 5 p.m. when he closed, till the square emptied out, on towards dawn.

People thought she was crazy; kids threw things at her because she wore a plastic bowl for a hat and ate out of it when anyone gave her food. It was faded blue and fitted perfectly over her kerchief. She never entered my house but would borrow a spoon to take with a bowl of my faithful stew. She always brought it back clean and always brought me something in return—a piece of hard candy, a book of matches, a pin. She was very proud; she never begged for anything but cigarettes; she loved to smoke; I always gave her three or four. She was a tough old bird, rumored to own properties in Cayes Jacmel.

But at that moment she resembled an aroused cobra. She zigzagged into the street, holding out her palms, her bowl-capped head turning intently this way and that.

"Pli à veni," she called softly. "Pli a veni. Pli a veni."

Around the tables on the patio the patrons one by one stood up and put their hands out over the railing. Tiny invisible drops fell at tantalizing intervals while everyone held out their palms and looked up. Whoever felt something gave tongue and a quick leap of the feet. People inside the café crowded out to investigate. Pli à veni could be heard everywhere like a whisper of wind, hopeful, interrogative, disbelieving. Mme. Manouche was kneeling in the middle of the street, holding out her bowl.

The ghostly drops diminished and coalesced in mist that seemed not to fall but stop still in air, then agonizingly, tentatively, slowly thickened and descended, slowly, slowly increasing in density, became virtually a sprinkle, slowly became rain, heavy, steady, unmistakable, then the splattering deluge.

Everyone fell down on their knees, crossing themselves, praying, clamoring. I joined in. It didn't seem strange to me—I hadn't been to Mass since I left Maine forty years ago—to kneel in the muddy street. We screamed with happiness and hugged each other. Marie-Thérèse had Zof turn the music up, and the whole café began to dance.

The street, deserted before, quickly filled with ecstatic Jacmelians. Best were the kids, racing around with their shirts off. No one minded getting drenched; it was as if the rain were washing our sins and sorrows away, cleansing the dusty leaves and our weary souls.

Amid the joyous throng teeming about the café was Ti Mou Mou. Some saw him. I didn't, or if I did I don't remember. Why should one have taken note of him at such a time? From his porch André no doubt watched the silver splashes on the water within the faint circle of the lone streetlight by the old Customs House. I wish I had gone for him.

But everyone else was there to celebrate. Tears flowed in harmony with the heavens. Gerhart got his guitar and sang some songs. The Commandant was there, brooding, courteous and distant; the Huberts were there. Madame Violetta came and we drank and we danced and we wept. Marie-Thérèse, ordinarily elegant in a long dress, for some reason had on a godawful t-shirt and dungarees, and she swivelled among the tables with the greatest suavity, reminding her friends of their invitation to her long-planned, grand party in honor of her parents' Fiftieth Wedding Anniversary, two weeks hence.

Mou Mou overheard. It was sure to be a sumptuous affair, though he could not think of going, could take no pleasure in the hope of hearing about it from anyone who did. To him it merely seemed a chance, an idea which took possession of him—and him alone—amid the boisterous rejoicing.

Within the hour a loud-playing, grinning band aboard a truck arrived from Ti Jacmel, and a wild celebration ensued. Never, before or since, have I felt such pure, rapturous gratitude for everything in life.

When Marie-Thérèse closed down at three a.m. a gentle rain was still falling. It stopped even before I reached my door. I remember marveling at the wonderful smell that seemed to emanate from the earth, how well I slept, how refreshed and cool I woke.

For the next few days Mou Mou furtively cased the town, laid his plans, finally, shrewdly picked the Huberts, very rich, elderly people, who lived in a secluded house on the outskirts of town. They were sure to go to the party; there was sure to be money in their house, and jewelry.

The Huberts were beloved in Jacmel. M. Hubert's father, risen from the common lot, had bought up land, and his son had kept his affinity for the farmers. Madame Hubert had a considerable coffee fortune of her own, and devoted herself to good works. They let the peasants farm their land rent-free. They gave each of their tenant families a hundred pound bag of rice and two turkeys every year. They put peasant children through school. Their benefactions of every kind were endless and wide-spread. Like many prominent families they were publically pro-Duvalierist, but opposed in private, which caused them to send their children abroad, lest their true colors attract vengeance.

On the destined day, at the hour of eight, the much-anticipated party gaily commenced in Marie-Thérèse's magnificent garden, on three levels, overlooking the bay. She had strung lanterns from the arbor to the trellises and swings, and the air was rich with mingled fragrances. A banjo, guitar and Creole bass played and cocktails were served. The elite prefer Scotch. But not Marie-Thérèse; she loves her Barbancourt, yes, she does—the best rum, let it be said, in the whole world.

Everyone was there, the bourgeoisie, the elite and the white community—French professors, Lebanese and German merchants, retirees from Canada, escapees from convention, devotees of Jacmel from every corner of the earth, an odd and fortunate assortment—plus relatives and friends from the hinterlands and Port-au-Prince, seventy-five or eighty in all, an elegant, high-spirited gathering.

The Mayor and the Prefect and their wives, the Commandant and the Director of the Alliance Francaise, the two priests, everybody who was anybody to the family Fournier was there with the sole exception of the

Huberts, who were missed by all. Marie-Thérèse went about greeting her guests with the doleful news that Madame Hubert had called to say that M. Hubert had spent the day in the fields, had developed a dizzy spell, was not feeling well enough to come. Mme. Fournier was especially disappointed as she and Mme. Hubert were like sisters, being both from Cap Haitien.

Marie-Thérèse's parents were an exquisite, silver-haired couple in their late seventies, she in a long, lavender dress, he in a dark blue suit, his seigneur's countenance always inscrutably benevolent and grave.

About nine o'clock Marie-Thérèse took their hands and like a child led them to the middle of the tiled floor of the arbor, a slightly-elevated, gingerbread structure, lushly overgrown with bougainvillea, spacious as a small house itself. Trays of delicate cups of good luck soup, giroulmon, were passed among the guests, and Marie-Thérèse toasted them, wishing them fifty more years of health and happiness together.

The younger priest gave place to the older, who stepped forward and blessed them and said a short prayer while all bowed heads.

He withdrew and the band started up. The Fourniers were the first to dance, the epitome of elegance. Then Marie-Thérèse danced with her father, while her teen-aged sons danced with their grandmother. Then everyone joined in.

Presently two chairs were set by the steps of the arbor, and Marie-Thérèse brought out the gifts from the sun room. With ceremonial attentiveness M. Fournier handed Madame Fournier each one from the opulent, gaily-wrapped pile at their feet, and then laid them out for all to see. When she opened mine, a modernistic, almost-transparent statue of the Virgin Mary I had bought in New York for this day, she held it up and kissed it, which made me very happy.

The help had laid a fine buffet around the unfailing central platter of rice and beans—tomatoes, cucumbers, griot, cuts of goat, chicken, timalice, a spicy cole slaw, mangoes, kiwi and the like, cake and strong, black coffee.

As soon as the band had gorged itself the music resumed. Handsome Sergot, looking quite like a wise monkey, was in top form, and his glorious, powerful voice soon had everyone up and dancing again.

At ten an intermittent mist came off the bay and kept the guests circulating in and out, but had no displeasing effect and merely increased the dazzle of the evening. The children played happily off by themselves on the small swings, and the guests of honor, looking ever more limber and light of heart, gave every evidence of planning to dance until dawn.

Nonetheless Marie-Thérèse felt a presentiment. She smiled and smiled at her parents, and kept returning to them, while she lovingly attended each of her guests, but her caresses had an anxious, imploring touch, and once she glanced at me almost grimly it seemed.

The mist that shone in such brilliant haloes around the lanterns of the celebration of the Fournier's fiftieth wedding anniversary made Ti Mou Mou's hands clammy and froze his sweating face. All this horror I have since pieced together from hearsay, testimony and endless, helpless imaginings. His feeble flashlight had to be jiggled just right to make it work, and even then it sometimes faded to a glow that lit only itself. He had brought his mother's knife, to jimmy the latch.

The flashlight belonged to Artur. The shopkeeper had put it down for a moment and the passing thief had picked it off. At first it had thrown a powerful beam and the boy had been enthralled at how quick and far it reached in his hardly-moving hand. Then it had grown erratic and seemed to be dying, and he begged it to last through this night. The knife, slim from years of patient sharpening, he knew well, in his mother's deft, deliberate hand.

The Hubert house was monstrous in the dark. He went in the open gate to the garden and crouched by the bushes, listening, sniffing the air. There was no light in the house, nor sound.

To his surprise the kitchen door was not locked. Within he stopped to listen. Hunger bit at him, but he gave no heed to the tomb-like refrigerator that ground its monotonous rhythm in the darkness. His planned to ransack the bedroom, where the money must be hidden, nor would he encounter anyone, as he had been careful to ascertain that none of the Hubert servants slept in.

He had never been in such a house before, six rooms, two stories, modest by bourgeois standards, but still mysterious, menacing, cavernous.

From the living room a stairway led up into denser darkness. He started up, one step at a time, trying to get the flashlight to stay lit. It winked and failed and winked, casting its weak glow, then leaving him blind. He shook it quietly, exactingly, like a sacred rattle, and the beam leapt about like a burnt tarantula.

In the bedroom M. Hubert could not sleep. His wife breathed lightly beside him, comforting and still. He heard the batteries knocking together in their chamber, dull lead and rubber, unnatural, ominous, unlike anything he had ever heard.

He listened. The sound came closer. He touched his fingers to his wife's temple till he felt her eyes open. Then he slipped out of bed and tiptoed to the open door.

Ti Mou Mou, gaining the foyer, stopped in fright at Madame Hubert's questioning murmur, and tried to shut the flashlight off, but suddenly it beamed brighter than ever, burning more intensely every instant as if it meant to explode, and though he muffled it against his chest it made his torso glow. The switch went smoothly back and forth, with little clicks, beneath his futile thumb, but he dared not jiggle it for the noise.

Stepping softly into the foyer, M. Hubert saw the inexplicable light, halted, blinking, and bent a little forward, the better to see, heard a gasp and suck of breath, half-sensed the mamba-like, lunging strikes, more and more numbly felt the searing rents in his neck and chest, died as his knees buckled.

Madame Hubert hurried to the doorway, thinking he had tripped and fallen, saw an almost-familiar shadow, one of her grandchildren come unexpectedly, unaccountably in the middle of the night, called out her husband's name, got no answer, nor did the dark phantom speak, nor move, and then she cried out the names of her sons and daughter, but still no answer came. Then she began to hear a suppressed, desperate panting and grew fearful and quiet.

Mou Mou threw the flashlight furiously away, smashing a mirror, then hurtled headlong down the stairs, banged into walls and furniture, found the kitchen door, escaped into the night. In the cool sheen of the garden he knelt to breathe and clean the knife in the leaves.

Mme. Hubert turned on the lights at last, and finding her husband in his still-spilling gore ran out on the balcony and screamed and screamed and screamed for help.

Passing through the garden gate, Ti Mou Mou turned to look, soothed by the ceaseless agony lengthening out, himself the cause, and felt the strength swell in his chest. He came under a lamp and Mme. Hubert recognized the tipped-up, gargoyle-like head with gaping mouth and mottled marks of kwashiorkor down cheek and neck.

She called the casernes.

Maurice Bouchard was intercepted, knife in hand, before he got home.

The party was plunged into pandemonium when an officer burst in, shouting for the Commandant: "Ti Mou Mou, Ti Mou Mou a tué M. Hubert, M. Hubert est mort."

Music, dancing, laughter—all ceased. European manners turned to Creole cries. Madame Fournier broke down completely. Her husband tried to comfort her, but abstractly, with a remote hand upon her back. He would not sit down but stood staring into the now empty garden. In the early Sixties, his brother, a colonel in the army, for a disloyal mien, was made an example, dismembered in front of the National Palace in Port-au-Prince, and left in a jumble, with the head propped in the middle, like some vèvè of limitless evil.

Violetta wept and raged on my shoulder, "They should have shot him years ago."

Mou Mou's name was hell-fire in every mouth. No one was surprised to hear new ill of him, only that he had finally done the unthinkable.

All had opinions of why the boy was so vicious, each recalled some particular savagery, and the same lament spent every tongue: If only the Huberts had come to the party, if only, if only...

After first throes had passed Marie-Thérèse drove to the casernes to learn what she could. She felt too maddened to let anyone come with her—ghosting in slow silence through the sweet, unpeopled night she became convinced that it was all impossible, some sort of mis- communication, but the moment she saw the low, orange, block-like barracks she heard the high-pitched voices of the milling crowd, gaping in windows, poking brave heads in the door, urgently debating what should be done to Ti Mou Mou.

Inside the deputies were drinking coffee, making menacing gestures toward Maurice Bouchard, who stood handcuffed in one corner, his stark face dreaming some gruesome carnival of the doomed.

Marie-Thérèse pushed through the hushing, familiar faces, which made way for her. She had come to speak to the Commandant, but upon glimpsing the scene within she faltered and turned back, her determined demand loathsome on her own tongue—to make him slave like a zombie night and day, feed him dirt, never let him sleep or die. Her weary, woeful shrug when she returned told those of us still waiting there with her parents that nothing could be done to bring M. Hubert back to life.

The Commandant was a man of culture, greatly respected in town, thoroughly and proudly Gallicized. He had long looked forward to taking his family to see Paris, but as conditions had never permitted he solaced himself by reading Balzac and Montaigne. He played classical clarinet, could often be heard whistling in his office, and went when possible to the infrequent concerts in Port-au-Prince. He never performed investigative tortures himself, but had them done by underlings. During interrogations he played Brahms tapes to intimidate the guilty. Always immaculate, once burly, still handsome and distinguished in manner, he was now beginning to shrink a little with age. Strangely enough, his head bore an uncanny resemblance to that of our late Dictator for Life, that immaterial being, Papa Doc Duvalier, and he wore large, black-framed glasses to enhance the effect, withal was a gentle, kindly man who, like M. Hubert, loved the peasants and strove to ease their lives.

Maurice Bouchard, brought once again before his desk, showed no recognition of the Commandant in festive dress. The boy's blank stare repudiated everything, past, present and to come. Un-handcuffed, he was held at strict attention by two enormous guards, who twisted his arms in their sockets or bent his elbows back, and whose ready eyes never left their boss's face.

"Sit down, Maurice," he said. "We need not long detain one another. I know you will be able to corroborate Madame Hubert's statement."

He lifted the page, read her few words, laid the page down, and looked at the butcher.

"Pas moi," Mou Mou said.

"You have blood on you. Madame Hubert saw you. Do you say she lies? This is a mere formality," the Commandant said.

"Pas moi," the boy said. "Pas moi."

"You did it," the Commandant said. "You will confess."

They were old antagonists. The Commandant watched the boy's fight against fear, tempted to dispose of him at once, contemptuous of this denial, for he had never before sunk to a claim of innocence.

He questioned Mou Mou relentlessly for ten minutes, but the boy admitted nothing. The knife had not been found; the blood he refused to acknowledge as M. Hubert's. He knew this day might end in death, unless he could escape, and he steeled himself, incensed that the Huberts had not been at the party.

Reason unavailing, the Commandant called in the First Deputy and said, "Do with him as you must."

The three marched Mou Mou into another, smaller room with no furniture or windows, and the two guards took turns beating him with a mop handle.

The Commandant sat under his shaded bulb, smoking Gauloises, his face gleaming with sweat. Presently he fetched a pitcher of water and a glass. It sat on his desk untouched while he listened to the muffled noise beyond the wall. The Hubert's were great friends of his; no Brahms played.

In a few minutes Mou Mou sat before him again, his own blood staining that of the murdered man. Half conscious, he was kept erect by the two guards who leant to observe his swollen face with salacious glee. The morose Chief Deputy stood by the desk, at parade rest.

"Are you ready to confess?" the Commandant inquired.

The boy answered, blood bubbling on his lips. One of his ears was torn off, the Commandant noted dispassionately. He bent to hear, but could not understand, though wide-eyed murder clutched the Chief Deputy's face.

"Give me water," was what Ti Mou Mou was saying.

Rage nearly overcame the Commandant. He hated to sweat; it made him feel uncivilized.

"You will confess," he said. "But you will have no water."

Mou Mou refused to admit anything, spoke only the same implacable words: "Give me water."

Both knew he would be convicted whether he confessed or not. It would be a meaningless submission, but one which the Commandant without remorse would sooner see his prisoner dead than waive, as a matter of professional pride, and feeling for the Huberts.

On the verge of applying more refined measures, he was informed of Madame Bouchard's arrival and had Mou Mou removed from sight. Awakened in her bed and brought to the casernes, she was escorted through the suddenly silent crowd, crossed the threshold, glanced fiercely from face to face of the lounging deputies, subduing them, too, halting their gestures in mid-air.

The Commandant opened his door, and helped her to a clean chair.

She too was no stranger to him, a gaunt, very black, severe-looking lady crushed in her pride, who had always defied opinion and defended her son, but now hunched trembling where he had been slumped only two minutes before, and wept, head bowed nearly to her knees.

"So many times, I heard so many blames," she said finally, slowly straightening up with resigned dignity. "He was such a good son, I believed whatever he told me. He always swore he did nothing wrong, that everyone tormented and lied about him, even André. He said he didn't remember anything, some loa must have ridden him, because he could never have harmed an old man like André. How could I not believe him? And perhaps it is true?"

"Madame, I grieve for you," the Commandant said, "and plead for your help. Maurice denies everything, though there can be no doubt of his guilt. Perhaps you can talk to him. I know I need not tell you how essential it is for him to acknowledge his crime."

"I can't," she cried. "I'll look in his eyes, and then I'll believe every word he says."

The Commandant gazed pensively at Mme. Bouchard's own eyes, a startling blue, come down no doubt from the fabled contingent of Polish conscripts in Napoleon's army, which defected and fought beside the former slaves to help maintain their freedom. Honor to the Poles! he thought with emotion, then remorse—eerie those eyes, no matter their origin.

In youth he had rigorously striven to suppress his rural paganism and adopt the teachings of the Church. In maturity he had sought acceptance of an absolute materialism, but the strangeness of this blue still struck him as stigmatic.

"I should have known when André was hurt," she cried, shaking her head so hard the tears flew. "I heard what people said, but I didn't believe them."

The Commandant folded his hands upon his desk, remembering the times she had protested her son's innocence.

"He was always a good child," she said, looking away, "always, always, but he was so small, they always beat him up, and I kissed him and wept over him. Ti, Ti, Ti, that's all he ever heard. I took him to a houngan to find out why he didn't grow, I fed the gods, I paid and paid. Many times I took him to the Waterfall and saw him bathed in mud. How he loved that, but no loa ever danced in my head. I prayed to the Virgin of Grief, but she never answered. Someone I offended must have put a spell on him or Jesus is angry with me," and she writhed in her wretchedness. "What have I done to deserve this? What? I demand to know."

"Madame!" the Commandant said sharply. "Écoutez-moi. I know every instance of your son's unhappy life. He is completely devoid of humanity, I say this to you in all candor: he was born evil, une âme damnée. It would not have mattered who raised him, nor in what country he was born, ni en France ni L'Afrique Guinin: he would have been the same."

The woman sat dumb with misery, for not ten years before, in desperate need, she had appealed to Madame Hubert, who for some months had hired her to do housework, in truth a made-up job, as the Huberts already employed a charitable excess of help about the house and gardens. Madame Hubert would always ask after her Maurice, heard his humble praises sung with evident satisfaction, never neglecting to congratulate the mother on her treasure of a son.

"The same!" the Commandant insisted. "No matter where or to whom he was born, he was destined for such a fate. To ask why is merely idle, or blasphemous, if you prefer. You are his final victim, the one who must suffer the most. I regret to trouble you further, but perhaps you can persuade him..."

The mother sighed and sagged, as if giving up the ghost.

"You are the only one in the world to whom he owes allegiance," the Commandant persisted, more coldly than he intended, "the only human soul he might oblige."

An awful repugnance welled in the mother's throat. "Pas connaise," she cried, violently washing, slapping, brushing her hands in the peasant disclaimer of knowledge or interest or blame, "Pas connaise. Pas connaise."

The Commandant rose resignedly, laid his palms upon his desk, bent toward her. "Please do not concern yourself further," he said kindly. "I can promise you that Maurice will confess."

Madame Bouchard's head snapped up, her back straightened, her jaw dropped open. "You must not beat him!" she cried, stern and obdurate.

The Commandant gazed down upon her with wonder. He had had Mou Mou beaten more times than he could remember. Had the boy never told her? How could he have explained or concealed his bruises?

"No, no, you must not beat him," Madame Bouchard warned and wagged a finger at the Commandant, to whom she suddenly appeared to have grown old, much, much older, old enough to be his own mother, or grandmother even, too wise, too dignified, too matriarchal to contradict, and that tone—that peremptory tone was Ti Mou Mou's.

"No," she said, "beating him will not help. Because of his size. He was beaten many times by bigger boys, but he would never let them see him cry nor ever flinch from their blows. Fists will only make him more defiant."

The Commandant grimaced in silence, incredulous and impotent. Mou Mou lacked the ingrained Haitian fear of authority that could normally have been relied on to bend even the brashest malefactor. Admirable in its way, the Commandant had to acknowledge, though it did not in the least weaken his resolve to exact a confession. Permitted his choice he would have killed the boy like vermin owed no consideration from gods or human law. Neither did he wish to prolong Madame Bouchard's ordeal, nor further incur her imperious powers, so eerie and unsettling.

"My son is very brave," she said dreamily, proudly. "There is only one thing he is afraid of: the dead. Take him to the morgue," she said with terrible stridence. "There he will tell the truth, whatever it is."

Taken by the thought, the Commandant bowed, came around his desk and helped her to her feet, escorted her to the door, which was opened instantly by the Chief Deputy, who had been standing outside with his hand on the knob, and now snapped to rigid attention.

"Drive her safely home. Report at once," said the Commandant, then turned on his heel and bowed once more to Madame.

"Let nothing harm my son," she said.

"Si Dieu vlé," said the Commandant sincerely and withdrew into his sanctum.

The Chief Deputy cupped Madame's elbow in his huge hand and, surrounded by his myrmidons, forced a path to the jeep through the mob, which this time jeered and hooted and howled maledictions, brandishing fists and making ferocious faces at the murderer's mother, who held her head high, staring impassively over the windshield into the shadowy branches of the massive mapou tree that shaded the barracks by day, hid wicked or complicit spirits at night.

The Commandant sat at his desk in white muslin. "Has the evening been a success? The evening has not been a success," he catechized himself. Presently he rose and went to his locker, strapped on his holster and pistol, and sat down again to wait.

Angry voices came through the windows, through the concrete walls. They had the pitch of anarchy, of spirit borne down past all endurance. Beneath the harsh bulb the Commandant's bitter, disdainful features took on the cast of martyrdom.

When the Chief Deputy returned, Mou Mou was brought once more before the Commandant, who said with quiet menace, "After all, is it truly not you, mon vieux, to whom we owe the loss of our dear friend, M. Hubert? All Jacmel awaits your answer."

"Give me water," Mou Mou said.

"You will confess," the Commandant said, "but you will have no water."

Maurice Bouchard yawed his eyes away, seeking relief, and the Chief Deputy, ever alert, gave his hands, cuffed behind his back, such a zealous wrench that Mou Mou cried out and buckled at the waist, his head driven down against the edge of the desk.

The Chief Deputy instantly yanked the dazed boy upright and watched without pleasure as a veil of blood rose to the swelling bruise above one eye.

"You will have no water," the Commandant reiterated. "Fetch Corporals Justin and Emanuel," he enjoined his Chief, who without a word flung Mou Mou back like a sack of charcoal into the heavy, metal chair and went to get their two most imposing subalterns.

The telephone worked, to the Commandant's grim surprise. He spoke briefly, sharply with Bernard at the morgue, and hung up. He surveyed Ti Mou Mou without interest. The boy was getting a respite, slumped forward, hardly conscious, clothes torn, face smeared red.

"Mon vieux, I fear you are sleepy," the Commandant said with reproach, "but rest comes at day's end, which awaits your confession, and then you may sleep as much as you wish, until the first cock crows."

Mou Mou heard but did not lift his head.

"Maurice, I give you one last chance," the Commandant said. "I trust you will think it only wise to spare M. Hubert an occasion for charging you himself. He will not be pleased to find you in his presence yet again. Upon this you may count."

Mou Mou's wary eyes turned up, the whites redly riverine.

"The dead have their methods," the Commandant said negligently. He lighted a Gauloise, placed the match on the edge of an ashtray with fastidious fingertips, inhaled a numbing lungful, held it for two, three, four seconds, compressing his thin ascetic lips, and at last vented the spent fumes from his nostrils in diminishing streams.

The boy had not grasped the import of the terse phone conversation; the name Bernard meant nothing to him; the morgue was merely an ornate facade he had walked past all his life but never given a thought, one among many parts of the bourgeois world which did not exist for such as him. But now something new and ominous loomed.

The threat's effect gratified the Commandant. The boy suddenly looked like a lost child in need of its mother. "You have only to tell the truth," he offered softly, "then you may go to your cell, where you have sojourned so often, and avail yourself of this, your last chance ever to enjoy its tender hospitality."

But the Commandant's phrases fell dead before Mou Mou, who was too battered to feel more than familiar dread. The Chief Deputy and two hulking soldiers entered, filling the room with murderous eyes, and Mou Mou's defiance revived. To confound his tormentors was all he had left to want, mere survival would be victory enough, had he not killed M. Hubert?

The guards, so huge they nearly hid their small charge, dragged him after the Commandant and Chief, through a frenzied surge of shrieking mouths and shaking fists to the jeep, heaved him bodily into the back seat, and sprang in on either side. The guards glowered imperiously and the Chief smirked, for no matter what heights of anguish and fury were reached, none would dare lay a finger on Ti Mou Mou. All they could do was fall silent, glare massed hate at the terrified boy, who crouched on the floor between his guards. The Commandant revved the engine till it roared. When still none moved to make way he pulled his pistol and fired into the mapou tree.

The murmurous crowd swayed back, opened a way, gulf-like and sullen. Bits of leaves flittered down on their heads as the jeep jolted across the rough parade ground, careened onto the boulevard with its wide sweep around City Hall, downshifted with a screech and skid, turned up the long, steep, dusty hill, engine straining.

We heard it coming, huddled here on the patio in our party clothes, having fled the Fournier household when Madame Hubert was helped through the door, and fell wailing into Madame Fournier's arms.

The jeep raced past us, leaving a veil of dust in the bright moonlight, and stopped at morgue's door, which opened to the Commandant's staccato knocks. The limp little figure dragged within could have been no one but Ti Mou Mou. We rushed to the railing cursing, shouting our assent—right for him, we thought, to be dispatched at once at that most expedient place, like a basket beneath a guillotine. Or perhaps, we theorized, it was only to make him look upon what he had done, though who could have hoped Ti Mou Mou would feel remorse, much less call to atone?

No, no, we wanted him dead then and there, preferred him dead, would gladly ourselves have bludgeoned his head to mush or hacked him to shreds with machetes if chance had offered, I almost believe.

Then the freighted minutes held us in thrall, but soon we grew appalled in spite of ourselves, the morgue's blank face voiceless of what transpired within. We fell to querulous mutters, wanting we knew not what, but no sign came as time went by, and we sighed finally, half with relief, and drank anew, with more purpose, as if everything possible had been done and rum were kind, till gradually we bowed, sagged, dozed, wagged our heads, one by one toddled homeward, stumbling down the long, steep hill, still too sober for sleep in that dawn greeted by countless cocks, which seemed to swell with hideous vitality.

It was some while before I knew how the Commandant had been deprived of the confession his outrage and pride demanded. The priest had hastened there before him, to be sure that M. Hubert was truly beyond Extreme Unction, and then had lingered in prayer for the soul of this good man. He was a stiff-backed Français, last of those not appointed by Papa Doc, also a personal friend of M. Hubert, now supine upon a metal gurney, chest and lower throat caked with blood jelly, as if the heart had exploded.

Exposed to the waist, the gory corpse—no rare sight in these years—lacked the uncanny presence the Commandant had intended it to have, propped in a chair, face to face within arms' reach of the chair Ti Mou Mou himself would be handcuffed in, a single inch of candle guttering toward extinction on the floor between them, alone close together in the flickering shadows, the room loudly bolted, while the Commandant, calmed by deep drafts of nicotine, awaited entreaties for release, or death by fear, whichever came first.

But it was not to be. The resolute priest brought to bear all the sophistry of Christendom upon the machinations of voodoo. He could offer the murderer hope of eternal life through purgatory for his confession and a sincere vow to seek forgiveness in the name of the Savior, never, upon pain of perpetual agony worse than anything he had ever experienced, or could ever imagine, to betray that quest for a single moment during what remained of his earthly existence. No doubt for Ti Mou Mou to escape the toils of hell virtual sainthood would be required. Yet nothing was impossible for God.

"Nor man," said the Commandant, who had striven to rid himself of all religion, perhaps the only native in Jacmel who had imposed upon himself such a challenge.

They fell to disputing precedence of civic and ecclesiastical law, and deferentially, at cross purposes, debated the existence of spirits, the pantheon of African gods and the Heaven of Christian Saints, the priest an implacable and frustrated adversary of voodoo, precisely the Commandant's proposed means of persuasion, which the priest regarded with the utmost abhorrence.

The Commandant now found himself, out of perverse and painful pride, defending the moral virtues and comforts of Haiti's aboriginal paganism. As a rationalist he had lately conceived of a new loa, a pitiless one akin to the European devil—born perhaps in Cité Simone, source of so much evil—that waits on no houngan, mamba or ritual, but mounts its victims secretly and makes them its slaves and servants of misery and destruction. He knew it for an idle syncretism, faced with fastidious distaste the intractable fact that he could never wholly uproot voodoo from his own psyche. He was thrown back upon the position that the living gods of Haiti might have no real existence in the eyes of the Church or science either, but nonetheless acted for the good of all their devotees, mostly.

M. l'entrepreneur de pompes funèbres, the elderly Bernard, who somehow gave an impression of great blackness and pallor both, stood aside and kept his peace.

The two men grew ever more pedantic, acerbic and cold, until tempers flared and they shouted in high hauteur at each other across the corpse of M. Hubert as if they were contending for the soul of Haiti itself, until suddenly coming to themselves they gaped with remorse and sorrow, the only sound their labored breathing.

"Unto Caesar," allowed the priest finally.

"Unto God in due time," said the Commandant.

"We must never despair," said the priest.

The Commandant bit his tongue on the last word.

Almost forgotten Mou Mou swayed in numb thirst, half napping, incurious about his captors' strange blabber-jabber, the mysterious code of a world that meant nothing but harm to him, that possessed only money, all the money there was. The corpse caused him neither pity nor alarm, only amazement at what he had done, recalling his pleasure in Madame Hubert's screams that avenged him somewhat for their not being at the party where they should have been, spoiling his plan, landing him in this trouble, with the certainly of more to come. Worst of all, he had lost his mother's knife. What would she use now? It might be years before he could steal her another. He could not think of that, just yet. He was glad to be left alone, and not long after we had all gone weaving homeward down the hill he found himself back in the jeep, off his feet at last.

Zof who was opening the cafe saw them drive away, very slowly, absent-mindedly it seemed to him.

The Public Prosecutor delivered a summary verdict. The judge concurred. Never to confess anything to anyone, Maurice Bouchard, age seventeen, was sentenced to life imprisonment in the National Penitentiary in Port-au- Prince.

That was January, 1985. We never expected to see Mou Mou again, but nobody ever forgot him, and nobody forgave.

‡ ‡ ‡

Ah, Haiti Cherie! The first time I ever saw Jacmel in 1973, what a magical day that was, what a relief from the putrid sewerage and refuse of Porto-au-Prince, not that I didn't love it there too—this was before there was much of a road. We went by tap-tap—camionettes, little, decrepit, open buses made in Japan, sometimes just flatbed trucks with benches and a top. All painted with local scenes in bright colors with names or sayings like American Airlines Jet, Plaisance, Sauve-qui-peut, Honor and Respect, Feed the Invisible, or Goute Sel, A Taste of Salt, which is supposed to awaken a zombie, also now a plea for literacy. This one had Crayon bon Dié pa gain gomm, God's pen has no eraser.

It was a tremendously loud gear-grinder with everything under the sun on top, wicker cages of poultry, baskets and bags and old suitcases with belts or rope around them, miscellaneous collections for trade, one guy had a guitar, there was a baby goat and a piglet down with us, the man beside me had a bottle of clairin, I burnt my throat, people were laughing and joking the whole way, maybe ten of us. And the fantastic hibiscus and bougainvillea. The non- road often ran along a dry riverbed, jostle and jolt the whole time, but nobody minded. Boat was the only other way, and what a boat! No thank you. I went straight to Chez Moi. I knew hardly any Creole, just some Maine Canuck.

Marie-Thérèse has good English. She took me in at once and made me welcome, smoothed my way everywhere. I immediately became one of her best customers, I spent my days at Chez Moi, watching the marché and drinking my Barbancourt, and my nights too—it was good to be on the other side of the bar—and her food was excellent. I wanted nothing more. Everybody came there, passed by, or dropped in for a minute every day. The top of the hill was like a large, busy stage, the center of everything. I do love opera.

Provincetown has color, but nothing compared. Jacmel is also an end-of-the-world place, there's no further a blan can go. Marcel—I'm afraid I'm to blame for him—I told him to come and see for himself what paradise is—his first day he tried to seduce Marie-Thérèse, then got mad when she ignored him. Even after he found out who she was he'd still take his cock out when he passed the bar on the way to the WC. He's not a nice person and only gets worse down here. He'd would roar in his bad English, "I am French, and I will never ever learn one word of Creole." I never knew a nastier sense of humor. When he laughed you had to shudder. He'd been at Dien Bien Phu and escaped from a North Vietnamese prison camp. He was a very tough guy, though you'd never guess it, with his red nose and distended belly in a filthy, yellow, golfing shirt with a little frazzled collar too small for his flabby neck. His one attitude toward everyone and everything was lecherous, lascivious contempt.

Nothing bothers Marie-Thérèse. He was simply beneath her notice, and he treats her now with respect, the only person here he acknowledges as Somebody. She has a beauty salon two doors down, where she sells her ceramics. The only thing she's not is an intellectual. I know she was surprised but not so surprised when I adopted Philippe. He's the most beautiful, smartest, nicest boy in town. He thinks he's about fifteen. I think maybe less. When he smiles at me I'm filled with pure hope and purpose, I'm glad to be alive. I'm going to see that he gets to college, one way or another. I send him checks in the winter, sometimes he calls me. I tell him to call me collect, but he never will. He has his pride.

Now look who comes—that Canadian whore Odette, she hired a broken-down tap-tap to do her business in, she even tried to privatize her little piece of beach. She did help Wolfgang open his bar and ball-room. The Macoutes shut the bar down, and beat up his crew, but they let the ball-room go on, for a fee. Then they found out he had AIDS and deported him to Santa Domingo, where he died. That was before anyone really knew much about it.

When my friend Randall had his heart attack the Jehovah's Witnesses were the kindest people to me in my grief. We were going to re-open La Chouchouboulette. I drank so much I had to quit for a while. That was the year I bought Fresca by the case. I couldn't face the thought of another rum-sick day of the shakes, and then Librium. That's when I adopted Philippe. And that's why. I'd be dead by now without him.

Oh, yes. And Madame Violetta. What would I have done without her? Marie-Thérèse says she will never marry a Haitian, which leaves her few to choose from. But how she does love flamboyance and carnival! When Ruby Brown comes down they carouse together. Ruby has to behave herself in Provincetown, where she's a grande dame and must live up to her—what shall we call them—her social limitations. In Jacmel she can gamble and swill and let her girdle out.

And ZiZi, my other love, feisty little bitch. In her way as magnificent as Madame Philomène. She couldn't have weighed more than eighty pounds, with the prettiest little titties you ever saw. She never let me photograph her though, she was scared of cameras. She beat up Ti Mou Mou one time. He was always doing something vile and then streaking away, but she caught him. She was the only one who ever did, once he had a head start. She beat the bejesus out of him, and no one was anything but glad. That was one of my first lessons in the reality of Haiti.

For a while she lived with a retired Swiss named Jules. He came for a month, met ZiZi and stayed three years. I saw her slap him around too, for what I don't know, but he didn't defend himself. The next day his face was swollen purple.

Then he decided to get rid of her and disappeared into the Dominican. Then he realized he loved her and came back, but she wouldn't have him any more, her disdain was quite picturesque. Marcel was mad for her too, he never gave up. He'd say, "Come, little flower, come to my happy bed," and his face would kneel, so to speak, in absolute humility.

So Jules disappeared again, then he came back crazed, went nude in the street, threw rocks at people. One night, quite drunk, he came by with his arms stretched out and his head on one side like Christ crucified. He shuffled around the whole square, then he pounded on the church doors till he hurt his hands and began to curse. Then he lay on his back with his ankles crossed and his arms out wide.

Mou Mou went right for him and did a little dance, then went for his pockets, which made Jules try to sit up. The Madam Saras gave chase, and away he ran with his handful of gourds. It was all rather strange and funny.

After that he began taking himself to Georgette's. Once when all her rooms were full one of her best customers came and his favorite girl was in bed with Jules. Madame rousted him out, draped his pants on his pecker, and told him not to wait. Then he disappeared again—blans come and blans go, from where to where nobody knows, nor why either—I doubt he's back in Switzerland though.

Not long after that I heard ZiZi was in the hospital. I had no idea how bad off she was. She wasn't that old. I'd brought her a nice bouquet. I was shocked. She was all skull and eyes, like she'd aged twenty years. I don't think she knew she was dying, or if she did she had no concern at all, that I could see. The flowers made her so happy I almost wept. She soon lost awareness of me, and I just sat by the bed holding her hand.

In the next ward apparently an old man died, and women began lamenting, louder and louder. Suddenly ZiZi gasped, and struggled to sit up. I thought it was her death throes, and tried to calm her. She kept repeating something. She wanted me to go next door—I realized she'd heard the name—then I remembered her bemoaning her first love, whom she'd had as a girl, and lost, the favorite of all her many amours, and still pined for. Her last words, to me at least, were to take the flowers and put them in his hands.

This I did with as much formal feeling as I could express—strange apparition I must have been, trying to explain in pidgin Creole. Finally I just beckoned and backed away. As I turned to go ZiZi's door was crowding with intent, tear-streaked faces, which for some reason all seemed to resemble Madame Manouche.

Ah, memories, my memories. Back in the days. The Tonton Macoutes were no joke, going around shooting off their guns. I'd had enough of that in Korea. One had to be careful. I had a real scare. Cric. Crac.

Patrice. Patrice was always outspoken. He talked against Jean-Claude in the park. Marie-Thérèse was always yelling at him, "Shut up, shut up." He was very black and very handsome. He'd learned English somewhere, and spoke it without an accent. And he couldn't get a job. He predicted the fall. "Oh, no," he'd say, "we're not afraid any more. We have nothing to lose." Meanwhile everybody else was still saying, "M'fe pa politik," peasant for I'm not interested in politics.

One day I saw him talking to some men on the steps of an arcade—relic of colonial days, with stained, cracked stucco—where women were sitting with wide-spread legs sorting coffee beans. There might have been a dozen men, all peasants I would guess. Suddenly a group of Macoutes with their white t-shirts, jeans, red neckerchiefs, sunglasses and guns came around the corner—you can't imagine the sinister, hateful sight—the men melted away like drops of ice in hell, all but Patrice and one old man who ignored them till they were surrounded.

The peasant was wire-thin, knobby and gnarled, the kind you see just sitting around like totems of time. He had on a straw hat so huge he nearly disappeared under it. I was caught between wanting to witness, and wanting to sneak away, no claim on my dignity, let alone honor and respect. I hardly dared to look at them—you must never, ever meet their eyes. Of course you can't see through those dark-glasses, so you don't dare let your eyes stray anywhere near them, but while the others were occupied preserving the sacred order of the state one of them seemed to be staring right at me. I glanced away, and then back at him briefly, then again. He was like a mirror, glancing from me to Patrice and back, as if he were mocking me, and—how well I remember—I shivered in the noon heat.

Corrupt zealotry wears an ugly face, but Patrice and the peasant stood their ground. The one with the Uzi said, "S'a'k pasé," meaning "What's up?" A casual greeting, in his mouth all menace.

"The usual," Patrice said, "Pèzé-sucé," which is the name of a popular frozen treat, also slang for Squeeze & Suck money from the peasants.

I was terrified. I was sure Patrice was as dead as the last Carib. The Macoutes were as stunned as I. The Uzi barrel rose, another gripped his pistol butt.

Patrice said, "What're you going to do, kill me? I have a wife and children I can't support. I don't even have a job."

The peasant said, "They lie me, they lie the whole country."

At a sign from the boss a third Macoute knocked him down with one obedient swipe, then kicked him, a real good boot, that might easily have killed a man his age. He sprawled in the dirt groaning piteously.

Patrice with great gentleness pulled him to his feet, and they walked away very, very slowly, Patrice half-carrying, half-dragging him. The Macoutes shouted threats and derision at their backs, but they weren't happy, oh no, they were used to perfect servility.

One Macoute who had kept a foot on the peasant's huge straw hat dusted it off and put it on over his own straw hat. After a blank moment—he did look ludicrous—they all broke out in hilarity like spiteful children and went their way, laughing and joking.

I spent the afternoon at Chez Moi telling Madame Violetta the whole thing, including my fears. "They wouldn't dare touch you," she said. "They won't touch a blan."

But I was still scared. Murder is unheard of here, apart from politics—Mou Mou proves the rule—but maybe this was politics. Maybe I'd seen too much. Or maybe this particular Macoute just hated me at sight. I should never have met his eyes. They're touchy as well as gross, the Macoutes. My dread wouldn't go away. I could feel I was being watched and followed, especially in the busy street.

One moonless night I got an awful foreboding and didn't want to go home, my flimsy door with its little bolt could hardly keep a child out. As I sat there I felt my tenuous immunity as a blan—even one well known at Chez Moi—simply evaporating. Finally I was the last one left and Zof was closing. All the way down my hill I kept stopping to listen. Several times I glanced back and thought I saw someone in the shadows. I got home but didn't turn on the light. I let down my blind, I was going to peek through, but I was too late, already there came a stealthy tapping at the door. I felt the terror of inescapable fate and opened it, the bravest thing I ever did. Without sunglasses, he looked scared to death. It was my Macoute, and joyfully I pulled him in.

I don't know what became of him. Only the bad Macoutes were harmed. The general ire was growing, drums thrummed all night in the hills. Nation-wide, huge demonstrations ended in massacres. Rebellion raged in the countryside. Chains of blood vengeance killed many every day, no one knew the true numbers. No news was reliable. The phone lines were cut. Rumors kept coming that Baby Doc was on his way out. The tension became unbearable. All Haiti verged on explosion. Then, on January 31, 1986, by short-wave radio Haitians heard the news that the Duvaliers were airborne for parts unknown. Euphoric delirium seized the country. Within hours Jean Claude spoke on Radio Nationale. He had not flown away. He was President for life. He was not going anywhere, never, ever.

Joy turned to rampage. Macoutes were mutilated, butchered, neck-laced with burning tires, their houses pillaged, destroyed. The police and army made themselves popular for once, and didn't intervene to save Macoute skins. The Commandant drove about in his jeep with a bullhorn and blocked total chaos, but for weeks smoke and stench fouled the air.

On February 7 Jean Claude and his filthy family finally flew into luxurious exile in France, and Madame Philomène ceased her twenty years of mute mourning for her murdered family in Jérémie, and danced the banda in her red dress before the cheering throngs right here at Chez Moi, a story I've told many times, will never tire of telling, will tell till the day I die. It was the privilege of my life to be present at that.

Oh, yes. It was grisly. The Dechoukaj, the uprooting, got underway in earnest, is still raging in Port-au-Prince, will go on forever it seems. But I must not let these horrors make me forget the good, the ordinary days, how the women carried pails of water on their turbaned heads, casual and easy, never spilling a drop, or balanced a flat of high-piled oranges or mangoes. Once I saw an Amazon with a huge basket of feathered tumult, which, when she took them out and lined them up in the alleyway before the back door of a restaurant, proved to be thirteen young turkeys on a string. Out of their basket they presented themselves with pride and decorum, and she tapped them sharply on the head with a stick if they crowed or flapped or pecked each other.

The Levantine proprietor bent to inspect them, gave each one particular praise, but today, alas, alas, he had no need. She looked terribly disappointed, but she got them back in their basket, and then with one eloquent swoop settled it on her turban. I will never forget how she stood, stately, nonchalant, hands on hips, turning at the waist to look this way and that, like the regal spirit of the island, perfectly conversant with the frenetic buffetings and guttural, indignant squawks overhead.

On March 5, only a month after the fall, when all political prisoners had been released, the National Penitentiary was opened, and 238 murderers, rapists, thieves, convicted criminals of every kind went free. Naturally we were apprehensive at the realization that Ti Mou Mou—he never escaped that Ti—was among the freed. Some said he would surely come back, others scoffed that he would ever dare set foot in Jacmel again. One or two wondered if he had been chastened by life behind bars, or if the national revival had given him a patriotic pride and call to reform. We shrugged, a bit sadly, at that.

The jubilation was short-lived. The big crooks were well-entrenched. The unending frenzy paralyzed the Namphy government, which promised democracy with one mouth but fought each other for power. Officially disbanded, the Macoutes soon made a comeback, they were so desperate, so well-armed. There was a horrible crime wave, total turmoil. Food was scarce, hundreds of thousands of jobs were lost. The charismatic churches, Protestant and Catholic both, launched campaigns to suppress voodoo and harass the houngans and the mambos, and make them give over the sacred objects of their rituals.

The election scheduled for November 25 got put off four days, then turned into Bloody Sunday, and no vote. You had to wonder what had changed. The politics of faction and mob-rule produced constant paroxysms of frustration and fury in the slums of the renamed Cité Soleil. Violence would spiral, subside, then spiral higher.

It was all most depressing. Jacmel was blessedly without curfews or further strife. We blans at least could resume our pleasures in peace, which is why we are here in the first place. Now and again someone would report seeing Mou Mou in Porto-au-Prince, but no one ever went near him and he certainly could expect no better from any Jacmelian than a curse or a kick. At those first sightings I felt quite bitter, but then I—we all—accepted the new situation. And in fact what has changed? Nothing. Nothing is new, really, ever, in Haiti. From time to time he would be spotted near the Port-au-Prince bus station, lurking about to snatch from the unwary a few gourds or something to eat. He was always still only Ti Mou Mou, Ti Mou Mou Ti, and so he would remain.

‡ ‡ ‡

Oh, yes. There is no end of misery, no end of carnage. Until three days ago I had never seen a cockfight. From the day we met Madame Violetta had made it her business to introduce me to Haitian culture. She took me to a voodoo ceremony. At Gros MaMa's. Once was enough. They bit off the chicken's head with their teeth. The bloodless ones with fake trances and sexy dances are produced for tourists, who understand that they're expected to leave big tips.

All this winter I've been hearing about Violetta's cook's husband's prize rooster, just come of fighting age. He had worked hard preparing it, and now it was ready for its baptism of battle. He had fed it clairin-soaked raw meat and hot peppers, toughened its skin with ginger, massaged its neck, feet and rump with mahogany bark, with infinite affection and meticulous care had raised it from a dominant chick to a fierce, brave, aggressive cock, which he counted on to bring him many lucrative, proud victories.

As a lifelong foe of violence in any guise—politics, sports, crime, family, hunting—I had till then managed never to attend one of these cruel, human contrivances.

Violetta, having first tried my house, found me at Chez Moi Moi—that strange refrain, started as a joke, now stuck in my head. Because it was such a lovely Sunday afternoon, and it was her family cock, so to speak, I finally gave in to my dear friend's irresistible charm.

Having won my assent she excused herself, a bit mysteriously, and left me sitting here. In no time she returned, transformed from a neatly-dressed, well-coiffed, middle-class lady, into a peasant woman with tattered dress, turban, clogs and all, not wanting to draw attention to herself at what is almost exclusively a male domain.

I congratulated her on her disguise, put aside my misgivings, abandoned my Barbancourt. Smiling gaily she took my arm, and we set forth in the hot sun to the gaguere, a small arena in an open space of dirt, circled by handmade, wooden benches, not far from town.

The familiar aroma of wood-smoke welcomed us amid great excitement. Loud, sing-song voices chanted in rhythm to the pulsating drums.

People stood in line buying their weekly share of hope: a bet on their choice of cock.

Bottles of clairin passed from hand to mouth to hand. People crowded about and overhung the two squatting coriadors, the owners, who were arming their cocks' claws with sharp spurs. Avid men pressed close, hoping to catch some shrewd assessment or divine hint before placing last minute bets.

Clutched in their coriador's hands, the fierce gamecocks were thrust together, beaks clashing, till both reached a frenzy of bloodlust, and were tossed free, instantly to spring at each other, tear, slash and buffet, while their backers cheered and the coriadors bellowed their cocks' fighting names.

It was exactly the sad savagery I had expected. The over-looming ring of straw hats hid the faces, and I gave up trying to get close enough to watch the terrible birds enact their fates. As in all things Haitian, even cruelty, money is most at stake—and brief diversion from constant want and woe. As for the cocks, the victors often don't long survive the vanquished.

The crowd was completely engrossed, except Violetta, who, because her cook's husband had yet to arrive, remained apart. She didn't want to watch either, she just wanted me to.

As I moved to rejoin her a wild-eyed, sweat-faced man came running, panting, reeling, as if he couldn't keep his feet a moment more, and burst into the gaguere, shouting in such hoarse exhaustion, at first we didn't understand, "Ti Mou Mou là. Ti Mou Mou là."

The close-packed men stood to popeyed pandemonium and rage. "Là, là, là," and a pointing finger was all the response they got from the panting messenger. The coriadors snatched their fervent birds, and looking straight ahead strode through the mob. One, then another and another ran after them toward town, till everybody took off running, even the elders, quick-limping behind. Madame Violetta and I hurried after them, too full of dread to speak.

We had long since slowed down to catch our breath, gasping in the heavy heat as we joined the stream of people rushing from all directions toward the beach. At the water's edge a crowd had gathered. Twenty yards out several skiffs and swimmers with inner tubes circled about, peering into the depths or diving.

Mou Mou had snuck into town in a big straw hat and out-sized dark-glasses—had been recognized, a hue and cry raised whichever way he turned, while a taunting crowd converged from everywhere. With all ways of escape blocked he ran for the beach, and then, faced with an advancing wall of murderous faces, he waded as far as he could, then dog-paddled out, going where no one could imagine, and sank, kept sinking, thrashing, flailing up, sinking again, because he couldn't swim, or not very well, waving his arms and calling for help—while the crowd watched in silence—calling for his mother, swallowing water, coughing, horribly gurgling—so we were told by those first on the scene. But no one had moved to save him, and only after a good, long wait of gratified suspense did leisurely efforts to recover him get underway

He had by then been down a long time. No one left and newcomers kept arriving and were told what was known, reasons guessed at according to witness or hearsay, and when an excited shout came from one of the boats and the body was brought up into view, there were ooohs and ahhhs from the throng like the grand finale of fireworks on the 4th of July.

A murmurous quiet fell while he was rowed in and dumped naked upon the sand under a spreading mango tree. Then hesitant groups of threes and fours edged forward and bent, as if to inspect a viper that might yet strike, then turned away, making room for others, muttering or shouting triumphal voodoo vengeance or blessings on the justice of Jesus, Mary and the Holy Ghost. I took my turn to look. Violetta would not go near. We remained until the police finally came, affably dispersing the crowd, and a burly corporal bursting out of his too-small uniform picked the corpse up like nothing at all and threw it in the back of the jeep with an awful, double thump.

Violetta and I were still speechless when we set off up the steep, stair-stepped street of elegant, decaying, colonial houses that leads to the center of town, Chez Moi Moi, and needful Barbancourt, this night sans Coke. As we were turning to leave an elderly man standing nearby, who still farmed one of M. Hubert's properties, bowed and said softly, "My life would have been incomplete without this day."

That was Monday. I'm still numb with shock. Today is Wednesday. The bell of l'Église Ste. Anne has been tolling now for some time. Doleful, dreadful, final. But I'm not going anywhere, I'm not moving, I'm sitting right here, having before me another Barbancourt, many Barbancourts, as many as I like, from now till the day I die.

In my mind's eye though, I can't shut out the sight of Maurice Bouchard sprawled on his back on the grey sand. He was completely naked, no shoes, no shirt or pants, no sunglasses, no straw hat. I haven't seen Mou Mou naked since that day I took him home and gave him a bath and a bowl of stew. Those soulful eyes of a child—I never saw them again, gone overnight it seems now—but the patchy skin, and the reddish, frizzy hair of persistent starvation, they remain unchanged.

He had only his mother to feed him, and me, once or twice, in all the years I knew him. He was always alone. I never saw him with anyone. He never had a playmate, that I ever saw, never had a friend. He never did anything but steal, and failed monstrously at that. He never swam naked with the other boys, while I watched by the hour, imbibing their freedom and beauty. He ended his days on the sand like a piece of refuse. His penis lay there so shriveled and meek, I had to wonder if he'd ever known love for anyone but his mother, whom at this moment, of all human beings on earth, I pity most.

She lives—or used to live—up in the hills, where there's hardly a blade of green, much less shade. How she lives, or used to live, I do not know. The trees have gone for charcoal. It's all rocks and barren ravines. From the plane sometimes you can see a brown ring of topsoil around the coast. One day there'll be nothing but rocks, and the Haitian diaspora.

Haitians fought in our revolution, won their own independence in 1804, which neither we nor the Vatican recognized until 1862. We should have done—we should do—better by our neighbors, allies, friends.

Now, finally, here she comes—Madame Bouchard—who else can it be? The bell is tolling, tolling. The whole horror grips me again. I can hardly look at her, I 'm afraid of her eyes, but she passes slowly by without a glance for the Café. Looking straight before her she passes the iron market and the frozen, silent Madam Saras, gathered to watch—a bent, little, black woman, dressed in black, weary from toiling up the endless hill. At the church steps she stops to rest, before starting up, a lone, stark figure, who reminds me now of Madame Philomène, perhaps because I've never seen her before. Everyone seems to look like everyone else to me these days.

I suppose all is now known, as much as it ever will or can be. Did he come to see her? What then? Who knows? Perhaps he missed the streets of his youth or meant to resume his life of theft at home in Jacmel. Perhaps he felt amnestied as well as freed. Would he have been permitted to live if he'd returned as a penitent? Did he think he could remain incognito? I don't know. I know nothing. Nothing.

But this, now this—this passes all belief—André on his cart rolling by, rolling by, pushing himself along with his gloved hands. His arms have grown stringy with sinews since Maurice Bouchard broke his legs—can it be only six years ago? He's dressed in rags, grimy with dust. And now he's climbing the steps, backwards, hoisting himself to sit from step to step, and now like a decrepit crab he drags himself sideways across the portico and through the tall door into darkness.

My heart is broken beyond help. Tears rain in my rum. I get to my feet.

I was sure there would only be one at the funeral, the mother, two with the priest, but since André has come, dear André, myself will make four—

I should shout, In the name of all we have witnessed, and all we know, surely with so many of us patriots, here and everywhere, how can we dare to abandon hope for Haiti?

The sky reels. I start unsteadily toward the gaping door. The bell tolls.

—1988

Of Monarchs and Hope, an Epithalamion for Ivana and Jason at their Reconvergence

Peter Michelson

There is a laedie who speaks in season, Where
there is hope, she says it is said,
there is life. It is often said reverso.
Yet the truth is as she says it.
Come celebrate, she says, the triumph of hope.

Again is it even as she says.
Experience, which is its own reward,
is no obstacle. Hope is the thing
with wings, a fluttering lively thing that bounces
upon the air and flings itself to the winds,

always its delicate wings brilliant and buoyant
as sails before or athwart the breeze.
Beginning in the ever fickle northern chill
in Colorado or Saskatchewan or
Virginia, Dalmatia or Tashkent,

it will shed its skin perhaps four times,
facing predators, parasites, and opportunists,
surviving not on honeydew
nor on meringues of paradise
but on the milkweed thistle's nectar

before descending toward the highland tropics.
No creature else so slight and pending goes
thus far to find its portion, its only goal
by way of pheromones to lure to each
a lover to her side or his, "Their only

goal...," or so it's said. The trek's a trip...
along magnetic valences
of the Adirondacks, Great Plains, the Rockies,
the west Coast Range, the grand Pacific chasms—
always south by west, from south to southwest as

the origin of flight moves west to east,
toward convergence with the highland tropics
and a glinting in the eye....
Celestially aligned, the sun's angle
on the horizon and the moon and stars

as well, they fly erratic but relentless,
each to the other sooner or later a polar
field in the alto plano forests,
at once umbrella and comforter, of those
Transvolcanic cordilleras. There,

"After nearly 14 years traversing
continents, scaling mountains, walking
ancient trails, exploring seas, marrying,
divorcing, enduring wars, insurgencies,
the U.N. & other chaos" they pause, each

before the other, the laedie who speaks in season
and her beloved wayfarer, they pause
in a shock of recognition, in acceptance of
their improvisational lives, their years
traversing continents, they pause in cognizance—

she of his bright durance amid travails,
he of her lucid beauty amid travails—
and still does experience after all
fare well with them, as even from its wreckage
does the excellence of their love emerge.

The Bluegrass Musician's Wife

Emily Tipps

I.

Her bluegrass afternoons: bright from the sky
like abundant autumn, music

soft as pine ash, notes high
and shrill as birds escaping the blaze.

II.

A newly crawling child wends his swift way
through the house. There's a bag of knives

in his path, but a blink and it is gone,
was never there. Only his mother,

tall and singing as yellow poplar.
Her black eyes bloom, tulip-like.

The child knows already how to fruit:
bat his eyes at women, rose his cheeks.

She's in full leaf watching, in full love:
the squirrel fattened on her seed,

cradled in the creamy sapwood
of her arms—raucous, dangerous.

Heartwood smoldering yellow under ash skin,
her peaked crown threatens the Blue Ridge sky.

The husband's guitar sighs from a neighbor room,
but neither mother nor child will cry.

III.

Early on, the guitarist pulls plums
from the dreadnought and feeds them mashed

to the baby, who gurgles and coos in a quiet halo.
And when her son is old enough to chew,

the musician pulls an apple from the same sound
hole. The song of the apple, its brilliant skin,

competes with her son's cheeks, tires his fierce
jaw. The baby thus contented, the guitarist

summons for his wife a rare Yellow Ladyslipper.
Don't touch, he says, *this mild poison. Just listen.*

The American Valerian dizzies her to sleep—
reduced, burrowed in the damp crook of him.

IV.

Slow nights at the bar she folds her limbs
across its mahogany, drawls commiseration

with the patrons, makes career plans.
When the band arrives, she uproots.

Her feet move. Sometimes her voice slides out
fish-oiled and lithe. *That's right*, she says,

and *Yes! Lord*, pulling the taps. And the beer
like seafoam. She drops her leaves and dances,

ecstatic as trout breaking the surface
without clear reason. Between sets she kisses

the guitarist, tastes the satin melody on his tongue.
Whispers with foam on her breath: *Let's go home.*

V.

On their couch under the pale glow of his skin,
she watches his hands work the rosewood slow,

the tones shadowed, the voice like fast honey.
She listens and her sap moves. Her bark

thickens, furrows. Bluegrass is a constant dying—
gnarled hands rising rebellious from a deathbed,

then returning to rough linen like roots in
dry sweetgrass. Poplars blazing hard in fall.

ROTATIONS

Jenny Cookson

The dusk senses a convergence:
too light the northwest sky and

there they come from behind
the day. All a cold

reminder of distance,
but ordered as invitation and
inevitability—

how to merge the beauty
of margin, the aridity of speed,

the sanctity of vaporous halo?
It is so effortless when orbit is

eclipsed by proximity.
Those perfect ellipses

align with the appetite of
eons, and all we see

is the strange fire of a night sun
on the edge of the silent
horizon.

Part of a Greyhound Bus Trip

Jenny Cookson

The fields
    carpeted in silver mist
they move as satellite gales   smoke stacks
building upon themselves drop by
    crepuscular drop—

    then in the luster a screeching and
the birds
    are the earth not mist
    but wings awoken
and alien   split by the engine of
            ascent

        in the creasing
    of feathers   soft membrane
impedes new breath and I hear
a steel choking   pliable mouth
            contained in mine   taste
lungs on that rough tongue
        breath to cold hand
            realized
        in some definitive   conviction.

NECROPOLIS

Jenny Cookson

Stone skirts submerged in chalky blue
earrings a firm pall in embalmed flesh
disembodied fingers rest on a knee   a pearl
fan in the fingers   a monarch on the tip of
fan bone   attached to limb even as the trunk is lost.

And all   all fans, all bones   hefted from land to island in an act of preservation.

Descendants carry   a figure with holes in his joints
detachable helmets
a granite hand outstretched
to the water's edge and blow.

The worshipper of the wind   teeth filed to sharp points   welcomes these relics
as shore celebrates the movements of sand.

There is fidelity in limb, in hue, as there is not fidelity in the present:

Give them an island and they rise to the life of the land.

It comes forth

Wallis Wilde-Menozzi

Who doesn't know
the instant of conspiracy
when the red sun disc
peaks and fires over the sky?

Who doesn't know
on a sidewalk turning rose
a sense of power
cannot call up the sun?

The inside self
like a drop of clear water
lost on the sun and its rising
is not lost. It comes forth

witness to its own moves—
wet and pungent
mass of dark and nearly no beauty.
Breaking down... convincing....

Its wordless strength
leaves, returns and bobs
grows old, white-haired then
golden

and unexpectedly sobs
out yes
and no
and more quietly yes again.

THE HABITS OF RAILS

Moira Linehan

Birding 101, he begins and I'm ready
to be attentive though thinking just now of my class,
women working on poems, the one I've assigned
for this Tuesday—an irregular refrain. Sudden
repetition, not where you'd expect it. He's saying,

Nothing sudden. No sudden pointing or raising
your binoculars. Should you see one, describe where
in terms of the face of a clock. Mid-May evening
at the edge of the Lynnfield Marsh. I've joined a group
looking for Virginia rails, bird I've never even
heard of, let alone seen. What am I looking for?

Surprise us, I tell my students. "Hen-shaped marsh bird,"
says the guide book when I get back home, "flight brief
and reluctant, secretive habits and mysterious
voices, bodies laterally compressed—hence 'thin
as a rail.'" These house-high grasses and reeds, ideal
for cover. We're following abandoned rail tracks

into the marsh. "Usually calls are the best clues
to their presence but by patiently watching
at the edges. . ." When we come to an opening,
the leader plays a tape of its call. Listening there
on a railroad tie, I'd swear a train's chugging toward us,
but no rail's flushed out. "Why do I write all this?"

and Yeats answered himself, "That I may learn at last
to keep to my own in every situation in life."
In the thick of things one woman calls, *Marsh wren, three*
o'clock, and a choreography of binoculars
trains on the spot. I fix where they're facing, but again
I'm too late. *Good eye, Elizabeth.* The leader knows her

by name. An hour and a half gone by. One Wilson's
warbler, tell-tale sign, its black cap. Now I'm trying
to find ten o'clock. I feel like a heavy bird.
Our leader reminds us it's the rail we're after,
moves us along. I want my students doing the same
assignment, finding out how the irregular

can delight. Someone spies *a marsh wren, eleven-fifty,*
but at the edge of my right eye—movement
on the other side of the tracks. There before me,
my binoculars bring it in close—a yellow bird,
its yellow could not have been more primary,
scarlet markings, as if someone's fingernails, dipped

in paint, had been drawn down its chest. I don't call out.
I keep to myself. I'm supposed to be looking for rails.
I know it's not the assignment, a student says
from time to time—and now I can say with her—*but*
one evening at twilight in a marsh in Lynnfield
the yellowest joy went shuddering right through me.

PIMPERNEL

Patricia Corbus

In the rain, alizarin spatters & runs down towers.
The breasts of the whore weep with regret & compassion,
& the gates, all 28 of them, open & close,
clanking in the red tail lights.
                                    Sirrah, then my face was my own,
all make-up washed away, nothing tweezed.
My eyes were wide-open catalpa blossoms
drinking rain, my mouth a green traffic light,
& men in tuxedos carried me arm over arm
from the Trocadero to the Stork Club.
                        I had never heard of Darcy, so lately dead,
hit by a flower-pot thrown by a monkey,
but I caught his desire for me, red-handed.
                        —Yet, in the long run, what could be better
than knowing one's own worth—
though by the time I recognized her, Truth,
                                    pushing a shopping cart,
had hot-footed her sweet face & tattooed butt out of town.

One Fabulous Bird

Patricia Corbus

It was like finding an eland
in Hansel and Gretel,
like turning the moon
into a moron with one small r.
She saw that some loved
the creator and loathed
creation, while some loved creation
and loathed the creator.
Some thought thoughts
were everything, some that
actions were everything.
Some saw truth looming
in the future, others looming

in the past. Some found that
forgiveness brings strength,
some that it wrings all resolve
from the soul. Some held
that evil must be wrestled
into its grave, others that evil
is fused to the good, or at least
pushes the swing that makes
good climb higher. Some act as
God's mastiff or his brass ax.
Others feel that truth lies
all around like dapplings of trees
over a canoe paddled down

a howling river, where owls
and ravens watch and drool,
and an occasional bright woodpecker
bangs his head against a tree
and finds a worm—and where
a bird sometimes soars so high
out of the vast, limitless forest,
that looking down, it sees nothing

but a pig iron goat, a sunken boat,
a fallen wing, a drunken flame,
a culture on a slide, a bit of fluff,
a flake of rust, gust of fever
—puff of dust.

To Keep Herself from Me

Dennis Hinrichsen

the use of plugs and potions;
talismans on a leather cord
around her neck

(the poor crying child—not yet a child—
adrift
in a universe of tears—*white blow*

among the white-blown stars).
While down here, in blind rooms
and attic crawl spaces,

on islands in the middle of a city,
the middle
of the day, tufts of grass

and wool
to dam the cervix,
sponges

soaked in oil and honey;
essence of alum, rock salt,
vinegar, soap;

a cut lemon on the nightstand;
intricacies of tongue
and hand…

And for my part, what?—oils of balsam
and cedar
to anoint the penis,

barriers of brightly-colored silk.
These things she ingested—
sap of pennyroyal

and Queen Anne's lace,
barrenwort,
birthwort;

stalks of rue—
the nights
(when she chose to speak

or did not speak)
quick with it.
Now each heart packed with coagulated milk,

concoctions of sugar and honey,
lard and honey—
let it leach out

and extend the muscle—
the burn of it gone,
a painless debridement;

the pale animal
writhing of our bodies
spent

like moonlight onto the shattered ivory of the sheets.

Poem in Three Voices

(Sappho, Catullus)

Dennis Hinrichsen

How many nights like a woman
in your woman's arms—how
many prone beneath moonlight—
the scent of lilacs over the
moist animal scent of ourselves?
Once there were days that shone
for us with rare brightness, O
tender girl picking flowers,
O sweet-voiced girl. Days
that shone with rare brightness.
Now this woman in your woman's
arms, a flower necklace at her throat;
her stature: precious, queenly.
How many nights her body
ghosted over mine in your slant
imaginings; how many nights
my own fragrant ghostings?
For me now, neither the honey
nor the bee, just this wasp
the color of charcoal, color of
smoke: how its madness
penetrates the very blue of the
glass. The windowsills—
a battlefield of domestic wreckage—
Achilles of the particled rain,
stung with dust; Brisêis in her
garments of bone-white silk,
happy that she's been stolen.
With whose eyes?
In mine she matches the gods,
that woman who sits there
facing you, but my tongue
breaks down saying these things
and then all at once a liquid fire
overwhelms my skin—dull,

wretched skin of the hands,
dull sheath of the body
turned inside out like a snakeskin
in moonlight. O the pessaries of
dough, red clay, grass, products
of the earth wedged against me:
day lily (crushed); columbine
(crushed); pale, fleshy hue
of the iris. This is what
the wasp says—*be all sting*—
its nest a harsh moon tucked
beneath the overhang,
soaked heavy with venom—fireflies lifting their delicate, banded
underbellies from the darkening grass.
"I was in love with you, Attis,
once long ago." That's what
she says, but what a woman
says to a passionate lover should be
scribbled on wind, on running
water. Now this scribbling
of wind of running water,
this ritual eating of bark...
From a dream: I kept a bumblebee
named Molly, or Lucia, Lesbia,
I can't recall—*my veil, my wave,*
my wife—

Amaranth Purple in the Cup

-for Katie Lehman

Sarah Bowman

Had we walked a long way and fallen down
to sleep we would have dreamed different dreams.

Of rough trades. Of old orders.
A spiral. A swan. Smoke.

A secret.
And another.
And another.

Withdraw the gift.
I turned to some cold, calm god
silent, pitiful in preference.
It's alright to say.

The girl, the woman, the older woman,
the veils and swaths and boxes of chalk
perhaps gather in groups or singly wait
by some altar apart.

THE MAGIC ANGLE

Sarah Bowman

of entry

two face a barbed hook, a fastened line, a net
chain-stitched, one drifting, one trawling

of deviation

the idle heart waits
beside
  cordoned green leaves
  yellow resin escaping
  a cotton seed white and flat
  the scale ridge it falls from
  a sticky bud stout and gummed
  a bract a spike
  splitting up its notched base
  a chute of pure sand
  a scrape that needs attending
  salve
  oil from warm hands
  a clean cut swath
  a chant

of incidence

open, irregular, an ashy blue vein
brittle and finely toothed
a cluster crown gone bare
a mange trunk
tapered lines climbing
through patched ice and fog
the mist where two meet
where a distant pack edges out
wide shadows
the shaded crag and shaded ground
crumbling beautifully

of refraction

the long lines assign distances
miserable silences, miserable selves
some dirt, some rock, some tree
some miserly forest
drunken, inconstant, mean

nothing supports a vine
no stone-gray branch,
no trench or false floor,
a staged scene
broken down and cankered

of reflection

here I find a secret to unravel and renew:
this is the place where sky makes of itself a sky

of inclination

of lives moving their own direction
of perfect frames out of which we come

a vastness that makes us
a danger to ourselves

or

the well formed thing we emulate
and say nothing of and try not to
despise and miss in ourselves

of direction

if a stone whirled round in a sling gets loose
the loss goes farther
I falter
a thin shadow, a northward tending arc,
a loss
less fierce and better

of nexus utriusque mundi

the cardinal points of a compass lead
to tree trunks steamed, an earthen wall,
a pinkish-moth pinned to where life is driven

of deceit

a divergent heart
    and mind

mostly tired
comes to this last tree
and stalls

all else falls false and tin
and concedes to silence

FIRE LIZARD

Lon Young

"For it lives in the midst of flames without pain and without being consumed, and not only is it not burned, but it puts the fire out."

–Isidore of Seville

It is late autumn; the leaves have fallen.
The salamander cools his back
against the undersides of flames.
I have seen his steam rising
from the wet earth,
rising from a damp thatch of leaves.

In fourth grade, Jesse Braxton
drew a wad of rotten leaves from a coffee can
and let me look inside.
It was empty,
just silver rings of light. Then,
Jesse's hand of leaves spasmed open
as if he'd been burned.
On the ground a sleek clot of jelly
slunk into the shadows.

Tonight there is a moon, but it's in clouds.
The salamander
clambers from an old log's hollow, out
from the sludge of cambium and peat moss,
and makes his slow way
to the pond
and to the pond's dark silt
where fire and ice sleep all winter.

FROM MESSENGERS ARE BIRDS AND SPEAK EACH LETTER YOU AND I SAY

Jenny Morse

January 21st
Tangerines in the water the day you
asked to spell my name backwards.
There are black crows on the four
oak branches leaning arthritically
against the shingles as if to explain
the first pretense of your flight.

January 29th
Green meteors fell from the iris
of a bird's beak
black   flash   sulfur   and you
conjured behind the gray steaming out
of the cherry. How came you to my earth
when I gave the shadow nothing in trade?

The crow's wing dreamt of you last Tuesday:
no more was said.

February 5th
Yours is a simple winging.
One click   the twist
     of spine and a thick desire

to rise up.

Duck beneath the overgrowth.
You can see fig and envy.

I sent these crows to you
but they sit here
       with honest faces and
       winking holly eyes.

February 8th
Why is it that sweat drops like icicles
or one feather beads a hennaed flavor?
Did you wonder the breeze into bearing?
I'm convinced of your existence on most days
when watermelon seeds
sing themselves
kamikaze into the bucket
at your feet.
Does fruit upset you?
A dilemma of petal or pollen? How strange
you are from me at this distance and how
the quick twitch of wings does frame you.

Schwermer in Paris

Jiri Wyatt

"In relation to them [the animals], all people are Nazis; for the animals it is an eternal Treblinka."
—Isaac Bashevis Singer, "The Letter Writer"

"Don't explain. Look."
—Jean-Luc Godard

I had not been in Paris for a very long time, thirty years, thirty one years, to be exact. I first arrived in Paris to work for the producer Joseph E. Levine in 1962 and left just under a year later, when he fired me. Somehow, what with one thing and another, I had not returned since. Back then, in the early 60s, Paris retained something of the air of the between-the-wars city of Hemingway, Picasso, Stravinsky, the Paris of legend and fantasy, and had not yet become the Paris of the student revolt of 1968. It was still the city of black-and-white movies (although the one I was assigned to was being made in brilliant Technicolor), of oo-la-la, bistros with checkered table cloths, Edith Piaf, and above all the city of cigarettes. Even if you went up the Eiffel Tower—and you had to do that surreptitiously, it was a thing only American tourists did, and as an American working in Paris you didn't want to be associated with American tourists—anyway, even atop the Eiffel Tower you could smell that marvelous black tobacco and the dense, sweet smoke that rose languidly from everyone's lips: the great age of smoking, heedless, luxurious. You just couldn't do anything without a cigarette and everything to do with cigarettes was a pleasure of the senses—women's hands lightly clasping the plump white rolls of packed tobacco or the jazzy tap-tap-tap you made patting down your cigarette before, in a gesture of studied need, placing it in your mouth or the scratch, snap and fizz of the red-tipped wooden match as it flared into flame. . . It would have been unthinkable to eat without smoking, to drink without smoking, and without cigarettes no babies could possibly have been conceived in the Paris of that time. The only person left who smoked like that now was Schwermer.

Schwermer was going to be in Paris for two weeks, staying in some palace lent to him by a friend where Cardinal Richelieu had lived, in the Place des Vosges. Typical Schwermer, a man with thinning hair and no discernible source of income who nevertheless seemed always to have his elegantly slippered feet up on some priceless antique with a book in one hand and a goblet of wine in the other. I hadn't seen him for some time either. He called me late at night Paris time, in a terrible state. He was in love. He was considering getting married. Was he the marrying type, did I think? Well, I told him, you've *been* married, why ask me? I added for emphasis that he should know that, as far as I was concerned, whatever his official legal status, he was *still* married. Whatever the state of Schwermer's love life, there was really only one woman he loved, and that was his first wife, Janice. No, no, he said, I had to see Marcella to believe her. Marcella, I said. Even her name is heaven, he said. What should he do? He was beside himself with indecision. He had had to get out of London so he could gather his wits.

"You have to come help me. You can't leave me here fretting alone."

"How can I help you? This is the first I've heard of the woman."

"You will adore her, although I don't know that I will ever introduce you to her, can I trust you? You should see this place, it is amazingly beautiful. There is a genuine Rubens in the living room and a huge film library. You will have a room overlooking the Place des Vosges, what could be better? At worst we will drink claret and watch old movies. Please, oblige me. I tell you I am completely at a loss, I have not eaten or slept for months. You know me, I'm not very good at decisions."

"So don't marry her."

"How can I not marry her? She says she'll leave me."

"You're not the marrying type."

"Why do you say that? I can too be the marrying type. If it had been up to me I would still be married. These years later I still don't understand what upset Janice. Who can understand that woman? You really think I'm not the marrying type?"

"You're not the marrying type."

But finally I thought: What the hell? Then, looking out on heaven at thirty thousand feet from my window at the rear of the Air France cabin, I wondered why I had stayed away for so long.

‡ ‡ ‡

I found Schwermer in the middle of a Brigitte Bardot movie, *Le Mepris*.

"You don't know how thankful I am that you've come," he said, stopping the tape. "There's a whole shelf of Bardot movies, do you know this one, I think it's her best. How was your flight? You look amazingly fit—although not as fit as I do. George," he said sharply to his spaniel, who was sniffing my shoes, "go away."

"I'm glad you brought George," I said.

"George knows a lot about women," Schwermer said. "But he is keeping his opinions to himself. I suspect he is jealous of Marcella. George, you know I love you, I will always love you."

George looked gloomily at his master and wandered off to his bed, where he gave out a loud sigh and curled up to sleep. I apparently was extremely tedious from the dog point of view.

"May I get you something? Will you have a coffee? Some wine?"

"I'll take a cigarette," I said. Schwermer handed me a fat cigarette in mustard-yellow paper. "Mmm," I said. "So. Anything new since I last spoke to you? Have you broken up? Is Marcella having a baby?"

"Don't be cruel. No, I have been considering my advantages," he said.

"Yes?"

"I thought I should be methodical, maybe that would help, you know, make a list of my advantages and disadvantages. I think I remember from his letters that that was something Henry James used to do once every year."

"What do we know of James' sexual preferences? Anyway, James never married."

"Yes, all right. But consider: First, I am the model of health for the middle aged man. I have my hair and my teeth, I am not fussy about food or drink, I sleep soundly, I have already been married, which is a great advantage, and most important of all, I have given up younger women."

"What do you mean you have given up younger women? This is more serious than I thought. Isn't Marcella a younger woman?"

"Well, I would say she has crossed forty."

"You have given up younger women and you don't know Marcella's age? What does George say? Is a woman of forty no longer a younger woman?"

"George doesn't think a woman's age matters. He's very persuasive, you know, George, but I have at last decided even he can be wrong. George still needs adulation, it sometimes clouds his judgment. It's true you can get adulation from younger women, well, for a while, but then you have to teach them everything, they don't know how to cook or worse they don't want to cook or they imagine they should follow a career, there's a terrible idea, isn't it bad enough men think they have always to be doing something—and of course in the end they all want to get married and buy a station wagon. I have discovered they all have lifetime memberships to the gym, you know, at twenty-two they have bought a lifetime membership to the gym and they only drink bottled water. I get exhausted just looking at them. I used to think younger women were best in bed, but even there I've turned out to be wrong."

"Why hasn't Marcella told you her age? I don't take that as a good sign."
"You know you can make too much of candor."
"You can?"
The t.v. screen was frozen on Bardot's face. It was a movie I knew well. It was the movie that brought me to Paris.

‡ ‡ ‡

Shortly after coming back from a summer in Mississippi, where I had first looked through the lens of a movie camera—it was a little Bell and Howell hand-held—Allard Lowenstein called me. "I have something you have to do," he said. "This is made for you, and it is very important, and—don't say anything, I know you don't want to think this way—but take it from me, it will make your career. It will open doors you never imagined. Take it from me."

This was Allard Lowenstein, whose every syllable implied he could pick up the phone and immediately reach the President of the United States. And I believed, then, that he could. For once it turned out that that was more or less true. It wasn't that many years later before he forced Johnson to throw in the towel and effectively ended the Vietnam War. So. This was Allard Lowenstein and I blushed at the other end of the phone. I was at a loose end and wondering what to do, what to do that would be appropriate to the Age. It was a dizzying time, you could hear the epochs reel, or so it seemed, and no one looked at you askance for overblown sentiments like that one. We were, quite simply, going to change the world, which is an idea that once it's in your system is very hard to kick. Lowenstein was a kind of cross between Thoreau and Lenin, a historical force, half lucid selflessness and half ferocity. I was never part of Al's circle in Mississippi, either in the early days or later in the summer of 1964, but still he was the one who set me up with a camera and told me to get what was happening on film. It wasn't something I had ever thought of doing, I'd imagined being a reporter, maybe. I had never imagined doing films, but soon I had become "a documentary film maker."

After I came back up North in 1962 I did nothing. I wasn't sure what to do next. I had been offered a job working for CBS News but for any number of reasons I wasn't at all ready for a job like that. It was perfect, a profound relief, to get a call from Lowenstein. He wanted me to go to Paris as an assistant to Joseph E. Levine. I don't know what his connection with Levine was, if there was a connection, but he told me Levine was looking for someone who knew something about movies and could speak French and wasn't too expensive and—"Now don't bridle yet," Lowenstein said—and someone who would do his bidding. Joseph E. Levine. "Levine doesn't sound too savory, yes," Lowenstein said. "But we need to have good relations with Hollywood. The Movement needs Hollywood. That's the role for you. Remember that no one took the Holocaust seriously until Hitchcock filmed the camps for Churchill. We are going to need the movies. Besides," Lowenstein added, "you'll get to work with Godard."

"Wow. Godard?"

"Look, do this thing, it's an important thing. I've told them about you and they're enthusiastic. A brilliant talent, guts and judgment—that's what I told Levine. It would be important to me for you to do this. It will be important for you to do this. It will important for *history* to do this. Go over and see."

Lowenstein paid for my ticket and then, as now, thinking, What the hell? I boarded an Air France jet for Paris. I met Levine at his hotel. He had one of those vast suites out of the movies—of course. There was a very pretty woman to greet me, and two ornate doors leading into Levine's rooms. As I entered, a man of medium height and build stepped rapidly from behind one of those enormous, royal, leaf-crusted, gilt-edged desks and met me halfway into the room, pumping my hand. "Hey, Joe Levine. Listen, Jerry, I want you to know this is great. I won't forget this thing you're doing, because the project is an important project and it's being fucked up, royally fucked up by this asshole, you understand me? You are my boy, Jerry. Get this on the right track. Go. Do it"—and he waved me out the door and turned briskly back to his desk. I was about to do as I was bid—puzzled, irritated, numbed all at the same time—when Levine remembered and called out, "Miriam will get you everything you need. She knows everything. She knows everyone. Whatever you need, ask."

And just like that I was back out in the waiting room. Jerry. I hated it when people called me Jerry. But I suppose it was right that he couldn't get used to my name since I couldn't get used to his. My idea was ***JOSEPH E. LEVINE*** —a huge screen, cinemascope, waves of background music, trumpets. "Joe" was impossible. Joe Schmo. Joe was the name of the bookie, the newsboy, the guy selling beer at the ballpark, the highest Joe got, the acme of Joe-ish elevation, was your foot doctor, and maybe that was going too high, that was a mountain too high, an air too refined for lumpen, lead-toed, tongue-tied, ham-fisted, chinless Joe. Joe Conrad. Joe and Mary.

"Why does he call himself 'Joe'?" I asked Miriam.

"He doesn't like to be pretentious."

Miriam somehow managed to work for Levine without losing sense, proportion, or sanity. She was beautiful, funny, and very well organized. Her mother was from Cleveland and her father from Lyons. She slipped easily from one identity, and language, to the other. I would have been fired a lot sooner had it not been for Miriam. The asshole Levine had hired me to straighten out was Jean-Luc Godard.

‡ ‡ ‡

Le Mepris (Contempt). 1962/3 103m. Technicolor Carlo Ponti, Joseph E. Levine, producers dir. Jean-Luc Godard. ph. Raoul Coutard. m. Georges Delerue. eds. Agnes Guillemot, Lila Laksmanan. ** Brigitte Bardot, Michel Piccoli, Jack Palance, Fritz Lang, Georgia Moll.

In the distance, below a stunning, almost baby-blue sky, a Mediterranean sky the color of which is everything human life cannot express and yet that expresses everything ineffable and ominous in human life, below this sky we see a woman walking slowly down a kind of abandoned industrial mews, apparently reading a book. She walks alongside a railroad track holding the book in both hands and reading. On the rails alongside her is mounted the camera and the seated cameraman, facing the woman and being pushed slowly towards us, the cameraman fiddling and turning levers. He is filming the woman as she walks. There is a portentous, melancholy, bittersweet, effusive music. She walks methodically, in a slow, rhythmic, swaying movement, as if she were an anthropology lesson about Woman. Woman walking. Woman reading. The camera follows her. Woman and camera come slowly closer to us. Finally they are atop of us and the camera, like two enormous metal eyes within a large metal rectangle, swings round and occupies the whole screen. It points directly at us.

Cut to Brigitte Bardot's backside, nude. She is lying on a rumpled bed, on her front; she does not have a stitch of clothing on. Her flesh is entirely smooth, not a wrinkle or crease. Her skin is of an extraordinary hue, poorly conveyed by the term "lightly bronzed." She is not pale, but neither is she tanned. If you could have seen the

Sirens and survived, you could say her skin was the color of theirs. This is the color of the skin on the rear end that killed black-and-white movies. Next to her is her husband, who is fully clothed, including a grey hat. She wants to know if he loves her nose. Her shoulders? Are her breasts her best part? He loves all of her. She asks these questions— what does he think of her elbows?—in the same monotone in which he answers them. The husband, Paul, writes. He is on his way to see about rewriting a script for some American producer. He has on a short-rimmed grey hat.

The American producer, Mr. Jeremiah Prokosch, is funding a movie, directed by the great Fritz Lang, of the Odyssey. No one seems to think this is an insane idea. Prokosch is unhappy with the film, which is abstract and violates the script he says he bought. He wants the movie rewritten and offers the rewrite job to Paul. He wants an updated *Odyssey,* an *Odyssey* for Modern Man (there's a philosophical streak in Prokosch). Unalloyed he doesn't think the story will sell. He wants "new scenes—not just sex—but more, more." Prokosch is played by Jack Palance. Palance wears a shiny grey suit, fully buttoned, in the Mediterranean sun (they seem to be in Rome). He struts and bullies. Our first sight of him is as he exits from a kind of low, whitewashed warehouse onto a loading platform. He flings his arms wide and proclaims, "This is my lost kingdom." He smiles, which is a formidable, scary thing that Palance can do, his cheekbones bulging, his teeth sharpening. He is imperious and dangerous. He tells Paul that of course he, Paul, will take the job that he, Prokosch, is offering him. Why? Because, he tells Paul, Paul needs the money. How does he know Paul needs the money? He has heard, he says, that Paul has a very beautiful wife. Prokosch says this without ever looking at Paul. Paul is wearing a hat in imitation, he later tells Brigitte, of Dean Martin in *Some Came Running*. He wears the hat all the time, even in the bath, and looks slightly ridiculous.

Cut. Once more the portentous, mellifluous music of the opening, the astonishing blue sky, and Neptune, a white statue posed as if to fling a spear. The eyes of the statue are painted blue, darker than the sky but mimicking the sky. We see the statue from below, the camera swings round the statue slowly, then in close-up. Behind the statue the blue sky, and the portentous music.

‡ ‡ ‡

Schwermer laughed. "I *am* expected to laugh, yes? This *was* supposed to be funny?"

"Well, I don't know...he doesn't have much of a sense of humor, Godard. Or I've never thought he did. No, I think he had in mind A Big Idea: behold the two realms, of the humans and of the gods. They were going to call it 'Betrayal,' actually, did you know that?"

"Really?"

"That was the original title but the more pissed off with Levine Godard got the less he liked the title."

"I don't suppose Levine had ever read *The Odyssey*."

"Levine didn't care so long as there was a lot of Bardot undressed. He didn't even seem to mind too much that Godard was mocking him on film. By the time I got hired Godard was well into his mock-satirical mood. It had all gone too far by the time I came aboard and there wasn't any hope I could do anything about it. Can you imagine? Who was I? I had never made a movie, I had never been in Paris, or Rome. How was I supposed to get Godard to make his film more commercial, which was my assignment? Thank God for Miriam."

Schwermer sat silent and dabbed some ashes in a large ashtray. Then he said:

"And Bardot?"

"I used to tell people that I never got to meet Marilyn Monroe but that when I worked in Paris I saw quite a lot of Brigitte Bardot."

Schwermer laughed.

"But did you...like her? Did you...uh..."

"To begin I was—I mean this was Brigitte Bardot—I was afraid of her. But finally Levine wanted me to do something on the movie and I couldn't avoid her any longer. The problem was that Bardot hated to work outside Paris. She was willing to work in Paris and in St. Tropez—but anything else she hated and made everyone's life a misery. She wasn't awed by Godard and scared of Levine, like me. She wasn't for a moment going to go to Capri, she said, which was one of my few contributions to the movie. I found that amazing villa. We needed somewhere spectacular for Prokosch's retreat house and I found that villa in Capri. That was our first conversation, about filming there. I told her I'd persuaded Levine to use the villa and I'd get fired if she didn't go film on location. We took a helicopter to look at it, even though she hates flying too, and of course the place is even more amazing in real life than on film. Out on that promontory jutting out into the most amazing blue water. Who could resist it? I think I promised her a look at some dolphins. She was always an animal fanatic. I can still remember the helicopter landing on that roof. Amazing! She loved it immediately. She said it would be great sunbathing. That was my one triumph. I got a lot of mileage out of the fact that I persuaded Bardot to film in Capri. From then on she decided I needed protection and gave me a place in her court. She guaranteed I had a great time, and I did have a great time, a fabulous time."

"But she had left Vadim and was sleeping with Trintignant."

"She hadn't actually left Vadim, I think. I don't remember. It wasn't as if her being with this person or that in any way restrained her sexual life. Or not then anyway. I understand she's become quite domesticated."

"Really?"

"So they say. And very right wing."

"You must have been much prettier then."

"Nonsense. You can see I have improved with age."

"I bet she hasn't."

"You know what? On screen she looks both better and worse than I remember. She liked to walk across the set nude, which was curiously almost natural and rather lovely to look at. She told me what she really wanted to do was dance, ballet, but then people began taking her picture."

"Let's invite her over."

"What? Here?"

"If *she* doesn't know what I should do about Marcella who will?"

‡ ‡ ‡

I tried Baby—people called her "BB" which came out as Bebe, "baby" in French, but fooling around I started calling her "Baby," in English, and it became our little joke; she liked nicknames and private codes—I tried Baby at La Madrague, her house in St. Tropez, but she wasn't there. I finally located her in Paris.

"JIRKO, JIRKO, JIRKO."

"Baby, how are you?"

"Baby, no one calls me that anymore, not since you left me for Avenue B or what was it? You are the only man who ever preferred a street to me. Where are you? Oh Jirko, Jirko, I can't believe it's you."

I told her I was staying with a friend for a few days at a palace in the Place des Vosges.

"A palace? Who would have believed a boy like you could live in a palace? I will be right over. Don't move an inch."

George made a dash for her the moment she stepped through the door, despite his advancing years and his arthritis.

"You must come live with me, you beauty," Brigitte said, kissing George's head. "Is this your's, Jir—"

She stopped and stared at Schwermer.

"Schwermer!" she yelled. "You too!"

"What? You two know each other?"

Brigitte giggled.

"You sneaky…! When were you going to tell me?"

"Well, I somehow couldn't fit the information in once you were off and running," Schwermer said.

"Since when do you know each other? Where did you meet? Tell me. You sneaky son-of-a-bitch."

"*Du calme,* Jirko. First let me have a look at the two of you," Brigitte said. "Let's see what the years have done. You can look too, I give you permission. Being looked-at is my area of expertise, and not anything else anymore now that I am an old woman. I was at my most beautiful when you knew me, Jirko, that guy," nudging her famous nose at Schwermer, "came a little too late for the best of me."

She lifted her arms and twirled around.

"Well, what do you think?"

She was dressed in jeans and high boots, a style she always liked, and that in her youth knocked every male within a ten-mile radius for a loop. The boots were bright red. She still stood like a ballerina, with that bit of frolic in her posture. The figure had held up well enough. Her hands, though, had thickened and crinkled, and had that pudgy, sausagey look. She had let her mane of hair return to its original brown, except at the front, where she had streaked it blonde, and she wore her hair up in a bun. Stray hair fell around her face and neck. Charming and dignified. She wore no jewelry around her neck, nothing in her ears. Except for eye shadow and mascara, she wore no make-up. Her eye-shadow was dark tan, too dark, patted dull but still shiny; her pupils, once crystal clear and sharp, were blurred and the whites of her eyes, once pure and utterly clear, were the color of café-au-lait and had little explosions of veins and blood in them. The stately neck was creased and lined, as though someone had tried to hang her, and the skin of her face resembled more W.H. Auden's famously craggy visage than the stunning, flawless, smooth and firm flesh that I had known. She had done no repair work. The sun she had worshipped, and that perhaps had worshipped her, had scribbled lines everywhere and cut into her skin, with deep crow's feet at the corners of her eyes and gashes in her lips that the lipstick couldn't disguise. Gravity, that she had often defied, had pulled at the flesh of her cheeks and chin. And the sea air had pummeled her nose, leaving tiny craters in its once eggshell-smooth surface. The fullness of her lips, the pout that launched a thousand ships, was gone, and now there remained simply a mouth, like any other. Her gums had receded and her smile revealed coffee-stained buck-teeth.

I went over and hugged her, and then kissed her three times. "Schwermer was just telling me he has given up younger women. He's thinking of getting married. What do you think?"

"Marriage is good at every age," she said. "Younger women, older women, this is a very boring subject. Who lives here, Schwermer?"

"An Italian count."

Brigitte wandered into the rooms. She stopped in front of the Rubens. "Is that real? My God, what flesh. I should have been alive for him to paint me. You boys are making me sentimental, which is not in my character. Gone is gone, *n'est ce pas, mes vieux* ? Let's talk about the present. Who is this you want to marry, Schwermer?"

"Ooh, she is a gorgeous, luscious Italian."

"You need to be careful of Italian women, once they are married they begin to eat more pasta than is good for you, and she will want to have babies. I prefer kittens and ducklings. I was a very bad mother. Schwermer, have you ever heard of diapers?"

"Why do I have to be like you? I could be a father. But Marcella has a boy already, a young boy, nine years old."

"Money?" Brigitte asked. "You know I'm an old *bourgeoise.* There are only two important things in marriage. Love—don't exchange looks, please—I say love, and money." She began to sing, "Romance without finance is a nuisance.... You know that song? Charlie Parker."

"So Baby," I said, "I hear you've gone into dignified seclusion, no one ever sees you, you are no longer notorious."

"How could there be 'BB' without notoriety? No, let's be serious, I am a private person. You know that perfectly well. I was always a private person but I happened to be in the movies."

"Right," I said.

"I see no one any longer, it's true. I read. In my dotage I have become a great reader."

"What do you read?"

"I read about horses."

"Horses."

"Swift, Dostoevsky, D. H. Lawrence. Does this palazzo have any books?" We went into the library. There was no Swift but there was Dostoevsky. Brigitte pulled down *The Brothers Karamazov*. She knelt on the seat of a chair and leaned her elbows on the back, holding the book open—like a little girl. She looked suddenly like her old self. George, who had not left her side since she had come in the door, curled up contentedly under the legs of her chair.

> Our historical pastime is the direct satisfaction of inflicting pain. There are lines in Nekrasov describing how a peasant lashes a horse on the eyes, 'on its meek eyes,' everyone must have seen it. It's peculiarly Russian. He describes how a feeble little nag foundered under too heavy a load and cannot move. The peasant beats it, beats it savagely, beats it at last not knowing [here Brigitte let out a sob] what he is doing in the intoxication of cruelty, thrashes it mercilessly over and over again. 'However weak you are, you must pull, if you die for it.' The nag strains, and then he begins lashing the poor defenseless creature on its weeping, on its 'meek eyes.' The frantic beast tugs and draws the load, trembling all over, gasping for breath, moving sideways, with a sort of unnatural spasmodic action—it's awful in Nekrasov. But that's only a horse, and God has given horses to be beaten.

Her eyes had welled with tears, and watery brown lines ran down both sides of her face. "Well, I don't believe that. God did not make horses to be beaten. It's too awful, I can't bear it. When I think of what we do, we, you and I, to the poor animals, I hate us. We are despicable, we are murderers."

Schwermer and I said nothing. Brigitte climbed down from her knees and slumped in the chair. George came out from under it and curled up at her feet.

"That's cruelty, though, and it's universal, what's there to do?" Schwermer said. "Animals are cruel, children are cruel. We're not very nice and they're not very nice."

"They don't beat us." she said.

"They eat us, though," said Schwermer. "They don't hesitate either. They open their mouths and close their mouths." He snapped his fingers. "You're a gonner."

"They eat us if they have to. They don't torture us, they don't terrorize us, they don't drip acid into our eyes to see if when 'BB' puts on her mascara she will cry."

"That's only because they don't think," Schwermer said.

"George," I said, "are you going to take that lying down?"

"What does it matter if they think? Anyway they do think, you don't think George thinks? He just doesn't think like you do." She grinned. "Or maybe he does. You were never much of a thinker, Schwermer."

"Now you're angry with me."

"'BB' is sixty, in a matter of days, too old for anger with old friends. Shall I have a party? How long are you here? If you stay I will have a party. But I had planned nothing, no, it will be bad enough without providing a special occasion for photographs, the scandal sheets will be full of pictures of me as an old woman anyway. As if I should be ashamed of myself for not having died when I was twenty. I am not afraid of what my body does, but look what they do, portray me as some kind of traitor to eternal beauty. Well, I can no longer be angry, not even with them. What idiot believes what he sees in the movies? But I don't complain any longer, what good does it do? I am going to die of old age after all, it seems, and it troubles everyone."

"The Hindus—or is it the Sufis?—because of reincarnation," Schwermer said, "what they see when they look at George is some poor bugger of a relative who royally screwed up his chance at Nirvana and was reborn a dog for his next try. I like that. Animals are just people trying to be good so they can visit the delicatessen in the sky and finally wolf down all the heavenly bagels they want. That's George's ambition. George, what's your real name?"

"If you looked at George and really believed he had a soul you would not make feeble jokes."

"You believe he has a soul? Incidentally, what do you think of that phrase, 'wolf down?'" I asked.

"I hate these crafty arguments. What is a soul? I know one thing, and that is that *you* and Schwermer do *not* have souls."

"Is that the point, whether animals have a soul?" I said.

"That's not the point," Brigitte said. "I don't know if he has a soul. I don't know if I have a soul, God forgive me. It doesn't stop me from praying. Am I praying for my soul? I have lived my life as a woman, a woman with a body and feelings like everyone else. Now I am to think of myself as a soul? I don't know how to do that, and I don't imagine George knows how to do that. But so what? Is it fine to torture George because he does not have a soul? If I step on George's foot"—she leaned over and picked up George's paw—"yes, sweetheart," she said to the dog—"if I step on his lovely little foot, will he be hurt? Will he cry out in pain? Yes, he feels pain, he feels pleasure, he is sad, he is gay. When I prick him, does he bleed?"

"Now wait a minute," said Schwermer.

"Aah, now you will be insulted, I have brought in the Jews. Isn't he a Jewish dog?"

"He's not circumcised but you're right, his values are very traditional. He likes food and women. In defense of the non-Jewish dogs, however, never mind the sheep and goats, what does it matter, Jewish or not?"

"Slaughtering animals prepares us for slaughtering people," Brigitte said.

"You really think so?" I asked. "It's a matter of proportion, isn't it? And maybe of genes. I worked on a movie about evolution once with Jane Goodall. One day we followed some chimps on a hunt. They hunted small monkeys, little creatures smaller and lighter than the chimps, they were very nimble and could climb higher, up on these little thin branches. The chimps worked carefully like a hunting party and finally killed one of the monkeys. You should have seen the glory and triumph. Tremendous noise and excitement, and great care in dispensing the meat. They didn't *have* to eat this little monkey, they survived on nuts and whatever. But they relished eating meat."

"Just because chimpanzees did this or did that, what does that mean? That we have to slaughter animals, without any care or pity, terrorize them and slaughter them, because we were once hanging in the trees?"

"Have you ever tried to kill someone, Baby?"

"Why? Have you?"

"Did I ever mention Allard Lowenstein to you? Does that name ring a bell?" She shook her head. "He was the guy who got me the job with Joe Levine."

"Ah, it's *him* we can thank!"

"You can't thank him any more, he's dead. He was killed, shot, by someone close to him, a friend of mine."

"Poor Jirko."

"As it happened, I almost walked in on the shooting, I was supposed to meet Lowenstein at his office and arrived late."

"But this terrible thing, you don't mean to say you find it natural, you're not going to say that?"

"The man who killed him—his name is Dennis Sweeney—he wanted to kill him. This was someone I admired, I mean Dennis. It was the first time I seriously thought, you know, actually thought, anyone can kill, I too must be able to kill."

"Well, this is not news," Schwermer said.

"I mean *actually* to feel you yourself could just suddenly flare up and kill someone. Not abstractly, all men are created evil, or whatever, but for a moment I felt, actually felt, I could be savage. It was in me, it was possible."

"Yes, well, of course we can all kill," Schwermer said, "but we don't. George would kill if he had to, but the thought never crosses his mind, not as much as does it mine, I can tell you that. There's no question some person, any person, is more likely to kill poor George than he is to kill even a rat. But now George does have some limitations that do not apply to any human. He doesn't understand the concept 'tomorrow,' for example. For him there is only now. He understands now beautifully, and maybe, to stretch his capabilities, his stomach remembers from day to day about feeding time. But he can't look ahead, and so he can't fear death. He doesn't see his own death coming and so he can't be terrorized by the thought of his own death."

"He can smell death," Brigitte said. "When you are making love to one of your older women, Schwermer, what are you using, your head or your nose?"

"Well, I'm using . . ."

Brigitte giggled. "All right. Next you are going to exhibit yourself to add sauce to the argument. Listen, George can smell death, like any animal, and George knows good from bad, as do my horses. They eat horses here, you know, in great numbers, so horrible and thoughtless. My horses can anticipate death. I know. I have lived with horses. George too. Can't George be frightened? Of course he can. What happens in the stockyards do you think? Don't tell me the animals are mindlessly enjoying the present moment. They are scared to death—like people in the gas chambers. You know the model for the gas chambers was the Chicago slaughter houses, you know that, don't you? First you slaughter cows and horses, then you slaughter Jews. If the one is natural and the prerogative of humans, then the other is natural too. What I don't understand is how, after the gas chambers, Jews can be so barbaric and cruel to animals, all that ritual slaughter. The Moslems too, more ritual slaughter. As far as I am concerned the Jews and the Moslems have a lot more in common than they are willing to admit. The same terrible cruelty."

"What? Because they both eat animals? This is now the criterion for everything?"

"It should be. Yes, it should be. Here, give me one of those wonderful looking cigarettes." She took a long, gleeful puff. "Oh my God I will have to smoke again! You know, boys, I have suffered cruelty more than most people. Yes I have. I have had to look at my body sag and rot with horrible, painstaking attention, more than anyone. *My* body, not that mess of yours, Schwermer. Every part of me has been magnified and shoved in my face all my life. I know mortality, believe me, and"—her eyes once more welled with tears—"it is very frightening and awful. Sometimes I think God is a cruel jokester." She stopped. "When you look around at people, you can be forgiven for thinking like Gulliver that they are ugly and smelly and vicious. We are responsible for the beautiful little Earth we sail on. How should we be judged if not by how we treat the rest of creation?"

"I hope it is not God who is going to make this judgment because I have begun to wonder if God is Jewish," Schwermer said. "He may very well not be Jewish. I don't think a Jewish God would choose the Jews. Besides, God has no Jewish attributes—he has no sense of humor whatsoever (well, except, as you say, a sadistic one), he has very boring taste in food, and he is usually petty and grumpy and he certainly has no concern for those who love him. I think all these religious Jews might well be praying to, I don't know, a gentile!"

Brigitte smiled. "I knew you would cheer me up," she said. "On Thursday, my friends, I am going to dig the first shovelful of earth for a new animal retreat on the outskirts of the city. It's going to cost a great deal of money and will be a great refuge. Come to the ceremony, you two, I will pick you up and return you to home in style, a huge limo with a full bar. What do you say?"

‡ ‡ ‡

About halfway through the filming Al Lowenstein called me. "How's it going?" he wanted to know. I told him his scheme for making me the Movement's link to Hollywood was dead in the water. "I expect to get fired day to day, or hour to hour. The man's an egotistical maniac. Whatever made you think I would get along with him. Fortunately I don't see him too often. He has a great assistant, thank God, beautiful too. She's the only reason I am still on the payroll."

Lowenstein changed the subject. "How's Paris?"

"Paris is good. Rome is good. Capri is stunning. St. Tropez is good. Coutard, the cameraman, is a right-wing extremist but I'm learning mainly from him. Maybe it helps he's French, the extremism doesn't seem the same in another language."

The truth was my fling in the French film industry had gone to my head. I could now talk like someone out of the pages of *Cahiers du Cinema*, I had changed my whole outlook on what happens when you point the camera. The camera, I explained to Lowenstein, is our modern god, or God. The camera eye makes reality. There is no reality outside the bright screen. And so forth. I explained to him what a brilliant allegory Godard was making about modern man, that is, *Le Mepris*. I explained to him that the film didn't explain, it just looked at these alternative settings, Rome or the modern West; Capri or the world of nature before modern civilization. Modern Man lived like a shipwrecked Crusoe on an island of cement and glass, without nature or the gods.

"Ok, ok," Lowenstein said. "Hang in there. You need me, call me."

French *amour libre* had gone to my head too.

"How do you mean?" asked Schwermer.

"Well, I went to Paris a huge romantic. I was still in the black-and-white movie stage, you know, sex has to do with love and so on, I thought things were sexier if they were suggested, and I wanted romance, old-fashioned romance that sends you to suicide if it doesn't work out."

"That's very American of you."

"Why? You think I was being prudish?"

"Puritanical. Why is it you Americans have never come to terms with the disarming fact that we have bodies, you're always washing and deodorizing. Love in the head, a clean-cut Hollywood movie." He offered me a cigarette. "Women without body hair, women without odor. What good is a woman who doesn't smell? I think that's Marcella's best feature, I tell you she walks into the room and I swoon!"

"Marcella's best feature, you told me yesterday, is her aristocratic father. You've always wanted to marry an Italian aristocrat, admit it, and live in a crumbling house in the middle of an olive grove."

"That would be fine if her father had any money. She's been living off her work as a translator for years, how I can't imagine. I'm afraid there's no money there."

"Well, maybe you'd at least get a title. As for body hair, what I remember is Brigitte shaved her armpits, and the one thing we know about her for sure is she's not an American. She definitely shaved her legs, and I don't mean just when she was being filmed. Miriam, Levine's assistant, now *she* didn't shave her armpits and she didn't shave her legs either. Her hair was darker than Baby's too, her body hair. Baby was pale all over, paler from all that sunbathing. They were a very provocative pair, the two of them, not like Brigitte onscreen, not morose but quite the opposite, mocking in a light-hearted way. They would sidle up to each other and look at you and giggle, as if they were so giddily aware of being stunning to look at, not in the usual way of a pretty woman but in excess, just being plain ravishing, so that they knew other people, men and women, couldn't resist looking at them and being drawn to them. And they *really* knew how to look just unbelievably seductive and provocative, rubbing up against each other and whatnot. The two of them brought that out in each other, it was a kind of performance they just instinctively fell into, and to them as you stood there with your mouth dropped open you became laughable and silly. They became nymphs and you had to play satyr. Ooh, we're so scared of that big thing of yours, you wicked boy! Well, *they* scared me, but I honestly didn't see what was so sexy about it, either."

"What a distressing story!"

"It *was* distressing."

"You sound like one of the pale goyim in London, if it isn't stingy it can't be right. The conspiracy against pleasure is a criminal feature of the regime of the pale races, don't make any mistake. Which is why London is such a gloomy city full of grey buildings and horrible food and ugly carpets and ill-fitting clothes. Dr. Freud explained very exhaustively that sex is about pleasure, pleasure not procreation or anything else worthy and high-minded. "

"Even Baby in her sybaritic prime would slash her wrists when a love affair went sour. Even for her sexual pleasure wasn't just sunny and mindless. Freud or no Freud, meaningless pleasure is no pleasure—don't you think? Not to mention the pleasure of being wicked. If you can steal candy without any fear why steal candy? What would be the fun?"

"I rest my case. You are next going to tell me there's no love without sin."

"That was God's plan, wasn't it? The joy of sex requires a bit of shame."

"Very clever. Now you sound like me."

"All right, Schwermer, I want to know how long you have known her. I am owed a very detailed explanation."

"You will be disappointed. One night about ten years ago I was walking on the beach in St. Tropez, where I happened to be staying at a beach-house of a friend of Janice's father"—

"Naturally," I said.

"—and I saw this woman, fully dressed, stumbling in the waves, and I said, 'That can't be Brigitte Bardot' but it was."

"She had overdosed?"

"Yes. You can imagine how odd it felt to drive her to the hospital and wait to see if she was going to be all right. I didn't know whom to call or what I should do. I just waited in the hospital and then actually took her home. I think I smoked three packs of cigarettes waiting for her. It was an absurd situation, but what was there to do? When we got to La Madrague she said she was frightened to be alone, would I mind staying? She had been left by her lover, she told me the next day, and was too old to live alone. It wasn't fair, why should she be denied love and be left by herself at the end of life? She went on and on about how unfair it was, how everyone left her, how everyone wanted to take pleasure in denying her love. It was dreadful. I stayed for three days. Her sister came and took her to Paris. That was all."

"That was all."

"We have not met again until she walked in the door today. Once a year we would exchange holiday cards. Hers have got increasingly Catholic. She was in genuine distress for those few days I was with her, everything seemed black to her, men, of course, ageing, dying, not dying. She was way down in the well of depression."

"I guess she's come close to killing herself several times."

"That's why I forgive her her new husband, who otherwise just sounds like another anti-Semitic shit."

‡ ‡ ‡

The following morning around eleven the concierge called up on the house intercom to announce a guest.

"Are you expecting someone?" Schwermer asked.

It was Marcella. She carried a small day-bag and flew to Schwermer's arms. "*Caro*," she said, and gave him a long, close kiss. "Will you forgive me? I couldn't keep away. I'm only over for a day or two, I will soon leave you to your heavy thinking—I have to get back for Tonno's school."

She was a short, dark woman with a head of very thick black hair, cropped close. She wore a black T-shirt, black linen pants, and flat sandals. She had a full figure and, as Schwermer had said, there was an alluring scent to her, although it was clear I received its aroma accidentally: it was all concentrated on Schwermer, who seemed not altogether sure what to do with his unexpected visitor. She clung to his side, paid no heed to George (nor he to her), and after taking my hand absently in a limp clasp, turned directly back to Schwermer.

"I am stiff and sore with traveling," she said, laying herself full length on the rug. She slipped a pillow from the sofa onto the ground. "Come talk to me," she said to Schwermer, pulling him down next to her. "And how about a nice rub, right here," she added, taking Schwermer's hand.

I said I had a letter to finish and went upstairs.

Schwermer and Marcella—the owner of the palace turned out to be Marcella's uncle—cooked dinner, having earlier in the day wandered out, arm in arm, to do the grocery shopping. They returned laden with specialties. The cooking was a slow affair, and took a lot of intimate laughter and body contact and dirtied every counter in the kitchen. The lovers had decided on lamb stew done in Greek fashion. Schwermer said lamb stew never tasted right if you had not used kosher lamb, and he had of course already investigated the kosher butchers in the Marais, and found one from Lvov, a discovery that especially pleased him. He also bought chopped chicken liver, and Halvah (someone in the shop was from Aleppo). Marcella, still in her black T-shirt, had put on black running shorts—short shorts that, from the rear, showed a sliver of sunkissed Italian butt-flesh—and went around barefoot, fiercely chopping up herbs with a *mezza luna* and tearing open figs. Schwermer roasted the potatoes, rubbed with kosher salt and rosemary. I went out and located a shop that sold Retsina. It was a feast. We ate at the formal table in the ornate dining room. Marcella drew her legs up under her as she sat to eat. It was a long table, big enough for at least twelve; Schwermer and Marcella sat on one side, and I on the other.

Marcella was irritated at finding *Le Mepris* in the video machine. "What was so great about her? She couldn't act, I don't think she had such a phenomenal body, either."

"You should never put two women together in the same room," Schwermer said, "even if one of them is on tape."

"She's an old friend," I said.

Marcella said nothing.

"We both knew her a long time ago," Schwermer added, though not quite with his usual insouciance.

Marcella continued to eat silently, a dark cloud over her head.

Schwermer reached for his cigarettes.

"I wish you wouldn't smoke while I am eating," Marcella said.

"This is what things have come to," Schwermer said. "It used to be everything tasted better with cigarettes. You couldn't enjoy a meal if you weren't smoking at the same time. Now if you approach a sidewalk café while smoking they call the police." Nevertheless, he pulled his chair a bit closer. He must have touched her leg under the table, for Marcella pulled away theatrically. He stubbed out his cigarette, a great sacrifice for it was a beautiful Turkish one in black paper that he had bought in some out-of-the-way tabac. Immediately Marcella changed, the aroma drawing Schwermer close once again. He inched his chair towards her, and whatever was happening under the table was not repulsed this time.

I carried the dishes back to the kitchen, by now utterly filthy. The counters, bad enough to begin with, were covered with soiled plates and yet more spillage. Discarded gobs of meat and fat lay on the floor along with Schwermer's mustard-yellow cigarette stubs. A jar of rosemary had spilled and still lay on its side. The sink was full of coffee grounds. It looked as if someone had broken in and simply thrown things around. "Don't bother yourself," Marcella said. "The cleaning girl will set things right."

"What shall we do tonight?" Schwermer asked.

Marcella glanced at him, vaguely ironic, from under her lashes.

"Ye-es," Schwermer said. "But George needs his constitutional." Their two chairs were touching, and Schwermer leaned closer still. At the sound of his name George lifted his head from the rug, but didn't stir.

"Let's go to the Select," Schwermer said.

"Oh, no, darling, that will be very boring and old-fashioned. If you have to be literary take me to Harry's Bar."

"The cakes are no good there," Schwermer said. "Jiri has to have his millefeuille."

"We can get one of those right downstairs," Marcella said.

"Let's go to the Select," Schwermer said.

"Once around the Marais should be enough for George," I said. I wasn't very excited about going across the city only to be stranded by the love-birds. We were an unruly group anyway, even on the Parisian sidewalks. Schwermer paid no attention to George, who did not like having no attention paid him and either dragged along or criss-crossed in front of us. Marcella walked with an arm around Schwermer, her hand stuffed in his back pocket. Lacking a free hand for a cigarette, Schwermer finally gave up and, with a shrug, passed George's leash on to me. Marcella was pleased. We had our pastries and sweet wine at Mariage Freres and headed home.

The next day was the same. The day after that was Thursday, when we were to go along for Baby's groundbreaking.

"I can't come, I haven't been invited," said Marcella, who didn't seem the type to mind whether she had been invited or not.

"It's not an exclusive engagement," Schwermer said. "Brigitte won't mind, I assure you."

"Call her and ask her to invite me."

"Don't be silly, that's not in the least necessary."

"I won't go unless I am invited."

Le Mepris (Cont'd)

Prokosch, Paul, Fritz Lang, and Prokosch's assistant Francesca, the woman photographed as she walks and reads in the opening shots, are in the viewing theater to check out the takes of Lang's movie so far. We hear the celestial, portentous theme music and see the statues of the gods against the expanse of pure blue sky at Capri. Prokosch hates what he sees in the viewing room. This is not the script he was sold. He begins throwing things, tossing film reels like a discus thrower. Lang says this is exactly the script he was sold. But it is not what Prokosch wants. He tells Francesca to bend over, brandishes his check book, and writes a check on her back. He gestures to her to offer the check to Paul. Paul hesitates and accepts. He looks sheepish and ridiculous.

Lang is good humored about Paul's assignment. He quotes Holderlin to Francesca in explanation of his film. "Fearlessly man stands alone before God.... His candor protects him until God's absence comes to his aid." He tells her Holderlin first wrote "God's presence" but then changed his mind and wrote "God's absence."

Cut. Brigitte Bardot arrives, on foot, outside the studio. Paul meets her, kisses her perfunctorily. She runs her finger along the shiny bright red hood of a sportscar, in which the camera then discovers Prokosch. "Let's have a drink at my house," he says, opening the door for Brigitte. "You won't be comfortable in this little back seat," Prokosch tells Paul. "Take a taxi, or I will come back for you..." "Let's both take a taxi, Paul," Brigitte says. "Go in the car. I will follow immediately," Paul says.

Brigitte never forgives Paul. Later they argue about whether she will come along with Paul to Prokosch's villa in Capri. Why should she go? She doesn't want to go.

> Nevertheless she goes. On Capri she allows Prokosch to kiss her so Paul can see.
>
> Cut. On the grounds of the Capri villa Paul explains to Lang that Penelope resented Ulysses' having urged her to be nice to her suitors. He loses her love by appearing not to care enough. The only way to win her love back is of course to kill the suitors. Lang replies, "Death is no solution."
>
> . . . .
>
> Brigitte and Prokosch go off in his car to return to Rome. She tells him she is leaving Paul, she is sick of men, and is going to work as a typist. Cut. Brigitte and Prokosch are slumped over, bloodied, dead in a crash with a truck.
>
> Cut. Lang sits in a director's chair on the roof of the villa in Capri. We hear the film's effusive, portentous music. Ulysses has his first glimpse of home. Below him, the shimmering sea; behind him, the pellucid, depthless sky.

"I see what you mean," Schwermer said. "but that's just a touch too clever, don't you think? The camera as our modern God? The boobies may be fooled but I suspect even they know that the images have all been manipulated, there's a script and a crew and designers and camera angles . . . If the point is that the camera watches like the gods watch then the point is very limited."

"I don't agree. Of course we all 'know' there's a script, etc. But we don't know while we're watching. When I watch a movie I still get sucked in immediately. I can only remember with an effort that there's a crew and twenty people are looking on as the lovers kiss, or whatever. To be fair to him that's why Godard wanted to eliminate editing and even eliminate scripts. Of course he never managed to make a movie quite to fit his theories, or not one that wasn't unbearable to watch."

"I also find the connections far-fetched. Brigitte is just playing Brigitte. Who knows what she's thinking? She sulks right from the start. I assume that's what Joseph E. Levine wanted, a beautiful sulk, preferably without any clothes on. What does she want from the poor guy? Does he love her elbows—how perfect. You have to be very careful about praising women, if you don't praise them with enough enthusiasm they storm out of the room and if you happen not to have praised their elbows because for Christ's sake who wants always to be praising elbows, well, you can be sure they won't speak to you for a week."

‡ ‡ ‡

When even Miriam's ingenuity couldn't keep me from harm any longer and I was fired, Coutard, Godard's cinematographer, took me to lunch at Bofinger off the Place de la Bastille. It was the sort of place he liked.

"It's very important to be fired by the right people, and Mr. Levine is not only the right person but the perfect person. So, my friend," he lifted his champagne glass, "congratulations. You will stay in Paris?"

"No, I'm going home," I said. Home meant first a reckoning with Al Lowenstein. I didn't look forward to seeing Al Lowenstein. I didn't want to explain, and I knew that despite everything he would see me as having failed, and I knew Al didn't like failure. A few weeks before I was fired Dennis Sweeney had swung through Paris. He had been in London, and was in Paris to meet with the North Vietnamese. Then he was going to Germany and Prague. I think he went to Hanoi too. He was preparing the way for a kind of international underground railroad. He wanted me to go to London just as, a few years later, he would ask me to go to Montreal. "We are going to need places for people to stay for a while, and for people to pass through safely, with papers and so on. We don't have anyone trustworthy in London, Jirko. You could just go over for a few months and set it up, and come back to Paris. What do you say?" I told him that wasn't possible. There was no way I could just skip out on Levine for a few months. Maybe when my stint here was over?

But when Levine fired me I decided to return to the U.S.

"Professionally, I can only speak professionally," Coutard said, "you *should* be in the U.S. You know me, I am disgusted with the politics of your 'Movement,' but professionally that is where the action is. Opportunity is a fickle woman, my friend, she does not like to be rejected. When she makes seductive overtures, you are obliged to submit; there won't be a second chance. So I approve, with all my heart I approve. Go back to New York or to Atlanta or Washington. Go tomorrow."

"You know," I said, "I've learned a huge amount from you."

"Please. Let me tell you, and I am not distorting or saying this for you, no, but let me tell you the young filmmakers who appreciate the documentary, and even more, the philosophy of documentary, they are not many. Sometimes they come to me and want to know what to study, or how to do this or that. I tell them. You should see how they look at me when I tell them the greatest art is photo-journalism, to know the eye of modernity you must study photo-journalism. They look at me with pity, yes, I am not exaggerating, they look at me with pity. Poor Coutard. Poor mad Coutard. And I never see them again. But it is true, nevertheless. We have forgotten how to look. What else is cubism except the conclusion that we have to start all over again if we are to see anything? Instead everyone has opinions. Hollywood is strictly opinions. Television is strictly opinions. But to see what is there, not to put the self in front of the camera, no ego, no opinions, but to see what is there—Yes, well, they look at you as if you are mad. Godard, you know, believes that if you simply let the camera look people will see the evils of power, capitalism, and all that. Film as revolution." He laughed. "He has forgotten his Darwin. We are here by accident, we are what we are, we are going nowhere. To look is to see us as we are. Not pretty, but we are not pretty. You, my friend, well, you are a child of the Holocaust, you know how pretty we truly are."

I listened intently, memorizing everything Coutard said. He gave me a going-away present. "When I started in journalism, this was my first camera." It was a beautiful old Leica in a worn leather case. "No, no, I insist. Because it will remind you. Your friends will want you to make propaganda. You know they will. They will have excellent arguments. History demands it!" Coutard laughed. "So, my friend, it is so you will remember. I will be happy to think of it, you see, the present is for me."

I took the camera feeling distinctly like a fraud. It was meant for someone else. For years I never went anywhere without it, however, and each Christmas I would send Coutard a card with the year's best photo. He only wrote me about one of those photos, which was a picture taken over the shoulder of a man in the street in Montreal reading *La Presse*. The paper has a large photo of Baby, in Canada on the occasion of her campaign about seal hunting. She looks angry and a little old. In the background is a young woman in a short skirt walking on the other side of the street. The photo was in black and white. "Ah, classic," Coutard wrote.

‡ ‡ ‡

Brigitte arrived in a long white limousine an hour early. She had called ahead to say she had an important stop to make on the way, something special she wanted to show us. Schwermer whispered into the phone about Marcella and Baby obliged and formally invited her—but now, at the last moment, Marcella decided not to go. "I'm not feeling well, you go without me," she said, in a wounded tone, pouting. Schwermer hesitated. Brigitte came upstairs. "I should have recalled you cannot be anywhere on time, Schwermer," she said. "But come along now, don't disappoint me. I am counting on you." Marcella did not look at Baby and flashed her black eyes at Schwermer but finally dragged herself to her bedroom, and gave us the liberty to flee.

"You are not going to marry *that* woman?" Brigitte said to Schwermer. "Thank goodness she is unwell and has had the good sense to leave us in peace."

"Where are you taking us?"

"After our little talk I have been reading again about ritual slaughter," she said. "I want you to see. We are going to visit one of these holy places, where they do *shechita,* have I pronounced that properly? We are meeting an Orthodox friend who has arranged it."

Baby's Orthodox friend, Samuel, wore a pin on his black coat, "Jews Against Slaughter." "Because it is religion," he explained, "the state does not poke its nose into what happens, not that anyone cares about conditions in *any* slaughterhouses, but in the religious ones no health official ever bothers. God forbid there should be protests in the Jewish community! Or even worse, because that's what things have come to, in the Arab community!"

"You're going to wear that pin into the slaughterhouse?"

Samuel laughed and removed his pin. "Of course they don't know about me."

An hour's drive later we arrived at the slaughterhouse, a long one-storey brick building somewhere on the outskirts of the city, next to a railroad track. The cattle arrived by train and were herded into an indoor corral at one end of the building. "There are a number of these serving Paris," Samuel said. "From the different Orthodox to the Hassidim and so forth, each denomination more or less has its favorite."

Brigitte stayed in the car. "Oh no, I couldn't bear it."

The stench and the noise once you entered was overpowering. We were given rubber boots and white coats, or coats that must once have been white. At one end of the building, where the process commenced, cattle were milling around, being poked with prods of about two feet in length to maintain a steady flow into a narrow passage made of two rows of metal railings, quite close to each other, something like what the police use for crowd control. This passage led, through an opening in the wall, to the next room. When prodded the cows would jump and squeal. The room was filled with the smell of fear and singed skin.

"What is that they're poking them with?"

"Those are electric prods. They get a little shock and behave themselves," our guide answered. He was a young man, maybe thirty years old, who wore a blood-soiled white apron over his black garb and had a scraggly beard of reddish hair. He was intelligent and business-like. "It is difficult to keep order, you see. To get a day's work done the cattle have to move efficiently, which is against their nature."

"Maybe they are frightened," Samuel said.

"They are not very smart, you know," our guide answered. "They are easily confused. With a stupid animal you can only maintain order by force, there is no other way. Reading them poetry will not be effective."

The cows were hopping, squealing, and shitting, bumping into each other and trying to turn this way and that. Nevertheless, in a steady flow, one at a time, they entered the fenced alleyway and went quickly through the opening into the next room. Once they entered this room a worker threw a chain around one of their hind legs, the cow kicking and squirming in alarm. The chain, which was attached to a pulley system running along the ceiling, was tugged tight and the cow lifted off the ground by its hind leg. The cow's skin rubbed off as the chain pulled tight, and each steer—they were steers only, that we saw—hung writhing and twisting by a bleeding leg, the bone exposed and skin torn away. Sometimes the weight of the cow and its kicking caused the bone to break. The cows growled and moaned. They hung by their hind legs, upside down, throwing themselves around on the end of their chains, and were moved along into the killing room. They had given us the boots for this room, which was a slippery pool of blood. As each cow swung writhing into the room the *shochet* sliced her throat from ear to ear in a swift motion, difficult to accomplish because the cows, hanging upside down, were in evident panic; usually a second cut followed the first and the *shochet* tore out the animal's throat which now hung grossly from her gored neck. Blood rushed from these cuts and tears and drenched the ground. Even so the cows were still kicking. Some stood up once they were lowered to the ground again further down—ritual law said no cow could be eaten if it had stood in another's blood—and began to stagger around.

"Don't be misled into thinking they are conscious. They are not conscious. These are just automatic muscle reactions. For all intents they die the moment the first cut is made."

"They don't feel anything?"

"Their blood pressure drops so suddenly they simply lose consciousness immediately. Perhaps there is a microsecond of suffering. But you know, let's be frank, an animal's life, raised for slaughter, is full of moments of pain.

The microsecond of suffering at slaughter is not the most painful moment for the animal."

Still the cows kept trying to stand or managed to get to their feet and wobbled for a few gruesome moments before finally collapsing. The flesh hung drooping out from each neck. Our guide pointed to the spray nozzles, eerily like the nozzles in the ceilings of the gas chambers, found every few feet along the base of the walls in the killing room. These would later shoot out water to flush away the blood and cleanse the building.

We didn't stay to see the skinning and cutting up of the carcasses. We stumbled from the building silently. When Brigitte saw us she said nothing as well. We must have looked ghastly.

We dropped Samuel off before heading for Brigitte's ceremony.

"Why are you leaving me, you know how nervous these events make me."

"Truly I would come if I could. I am so sorry, I just cannot. Next time."

Brigitte seemed jittery and anxious. She took a cigarette from Schwermer and huddled by herself against the side of the car. "Everyone leaves me," she grumbled.

We made a solemn trio in the expensive interior of Baby's limousine. The slaughterhouse had even silenced Schwermer.

"We are almost there," Brigitte said at last. "Thank God. I am sick of sitting in this tomb."

A fair-sized crowd had gathered up ahead—Baby's opening looked to be a success. There were a number of police cars, television crews, and a surprising number of paparazzi. Only when we were much closer did what had drawn so many of the press become clear. This was not an appreciative crowd but a demonstration. Men in yarmulkes and black suits, wearing outsized yellow stars, carried placards saying "Stop Anti-Semitism," "Our Ritual, Our Life," "Bardot the Butcher," "Brigitte Bardeau" (Brigitte the Joke), "Shechita Our Right," "G-d Gave us Meat," and "Bardot is Ugly." There was a large banner reading "Jewish-Moslem Alliance for Religious Ritual."

"What's this about, Baby?"

"There was a slaughterhouse here," she said. "Pigs!" she yelled.

People rushed at our car, the police locking arms to keep them at bay.

"When we bought it it was a slaughterhouse, yes a Jewish slaughterhouse, they were doing horrible things like you saw this morning. Now it will be beautiful, a place of peace and refuge and look what these idiots do. I hate them. Humanity!" She opened her door and stepped out. "Murderers!" she yelled. "Racist! Whore!" the crowd roared back. Brigitte plunged forward, screaming. There was a roped off area in front of the building, barely visible through the crowd, where the ceremony was supposed to occur. The police cleared a path for her. "Baby," I yelled. "I can't go." She stopped and turned back to me. "I'm not going," I repeated.

"You are going to leave me now, *now*?!"

Schwermer looked troubled. His cigarette was shaking. "We can't leave her now."

"I'm not crossing a picket line, especially a Jewish one. I can't go. I'll see you back at the Place des Vosges."

"We can't just leave her alone," he said. "We can't leave her to this crowd."

Brigitte was by then lost in the mass of police and black suits. I'd seen her this way many times before, swallowed by the crowd. I caught a final glimpse of her forcing her way ahead. She did not look back. Schwermer went after her and I went to find a metro to the Marais.

‡ ‡ ‡

Marcella was waiting.

"Where is he?"

I told her about the demonstration.

"He is with *her*?"

"He was worried about her, it looked ugly."

Marcella puffed on her cigarette, one of Schwermer's black ones. She was drinking brandy.

"I could use a brandy," I said.

We sat under the Rubens with our drinks and black cigarettes.

"Why is he with *her*? I need him here."

"He's being generous, you know, really, it's not that he wouldn't rather be with you."

"You think he would rather be with me? I am beginning to wonder."

I thought: Oh Christ. "I am absolutely certain. Really. It's his best quality that he feels for others. He's very generous that way."

"Others, but not me. Do you think he will marry me? You know him. Will he marry me? We have been together almost two years. Does he expect me to stay with him like we are forever?"

"He loves you," I said, thinking, Oh Christ.

"He loves me? Sweet. Maybe he *does* love me. He loves to fuck me. But will he marry me? Can he be just a little bit settled? *You* didn't stay with… with *her*," she said.

"Well..."

"If he really cared, tell me the truth, do you think he would be with her? It's the same when Janice calls. Immediately he's engrossed in her. I don't spend every other day talking to *my* first husband. No, I don't think he will marry me. I deserve a bit of quiet and certainty."

"I'm sure he's crazy about you," I said. "I can tell you for a fact he's crazy about you. He wants to marry you, I'm sure he does," I said, thinking, Oh Christ.

‡ ‡ ‡

I left Paris a few days after the slaughterhouse fiasco. Schwermer and I pretended nothing had happened; we were uncomfortable, could barely look at each other, and were both super-nice. Marcella did not return to London as she said she would, delaying her departure on a daily basis. It was better to leave.

I picked up a few papers in the airport to get me through the flight to New York. In the news summary of the International Herald Tribune I read that Dennis Sweeney was coming up for some sort of parole. The headline read: "Notorious Killer Moves Toward Freedom." Dennis was to be let out of his psychiatric hospital on a daily basis to work as a carpenter near Middletown, New York. Apparently he was engaged to be married to his shrink, too. I had the sudden feeling that I would have to go see him again. The subhead in the Trib said: "The murder of the charismatic former Congressman by a deranged disciple epitomized the end of an era of political idealism." It was strange that Dennis had achieved this dubious and iconic status. Mainly a terrible thing had happened to him, and more or less everyone who had once thought of him as a hero had immediately washed their hands of him. There was some archetype involved that comforted people, in the same way that it was comforting to think of Hitler as crazy. The Holocaust was just one of those things. Crazy. It was all the fault of a crazy man.

I have some pictures of Dennis, taken with Coutard's Leica, in Al Lowenstein's office. The two of them are sitting on opposite sides of Lowenstein's desk, looking solemnly inspiring. I had just returned from being fired by Levine and was first meeting up with Lowenstein. It was an uncomfortable meeting, neither of them very happy to see me. But we did go back to Mississippi together that summer and in the years that followed I periodically produced work for Lowenstein. Dennis and I for a time frequently crossed paths—my last photo of him is in front of the office of the American Deserters Committee in Montreal in 1968. But by the middle seventies Dennis dropped out of sight; no one knew where to find him.

As for Al, I got my last call from him in March of 1980, another and final call out of the blue. It was six in the morning. He didn't say, excuse me, did I wake you? He operated as if it was obvious the time of day doesn't matter when Greatness calls. He wanted me to do a project, of course, he was on to the next big thing. I would be in on the ground floor, he needed a starter documentary, it was the sort of thing only I could do. The time had come, he said, and he was going to do it. He was talking about Gay Rights, his next cause.

We arranged to meet when I would next be in New York which, as it happened, was March 14, 1980. I was late for our meeting. I hate being late and was angry at myself, in a foul mood—but this time the accidental irritations of life turned out to be one of those turns of fate that in another era would end with your entering a monastery or speaking in tongues. Lowenstein, the arch-liberal, had his office up in Rockefeller Plaza. People were still ice-skating, it was cloudy and brisk. In that great art deco lobby, waiting for the elevator, I thought, well, you begin blindly with good will and in the end remain blinded but you no longer know by what. I had no idea how understated a world-weary observation that was going to prove.

Because when I got to Al's office, late and irritable, it was as if the place had been hit by a bomb. People were rushing all over, people were sitting on the floor, dazed, a building security guard was yelling hysterically into one of the office phones. The door to Al's office was open. I could see him at his desk. He was twisted in his chair, covered in blood, all covered in blood. Only then did I notice Dennis sitting smoking at the secretary's desk.

"Dennis," I said, "what happened?"

"Hello," he said. "I am so happy it's you. Did they send you? I had to kill him, Jiri. He was persecuting me, he said he wouldn't stop it, I told him I couldn't take it any longer, I gave him a last chance. When he killed my father, I knew I had to end it. You don't know what happened to Al, he became part of the world Jewish conspiracy, the I.G. Farben Jews, they were using me and I don't know how many others, they were telling me to do things, voices. For years I tried to escape them, Al, he was persecuting me. I am so happy to see you. You look good."

He smiled the charming old smile, he spoke in the calm persuasive voice I knew well. Every few words, though, he would shake his head, as if he wanted to clear water from his ears. There was a gun on the desk.

"I still hear Al, Al's voice—do you think he might not be dead?" he asked, suddenly worried.

"Dennis," I said. "He's dead. That's why I'm here."

I took one of Dennis' Pall Malls. I was shaking and trying desperately to seem as ordinary and composed as he did. I had never known anyone so well who had so obviously gone altogether mad. I was scared: if he had shot Al—it was impossible to say if he was dead or alive—what was to stop him from shooting me? But Dennis was obviously happy to see me. He looked gaunt, but he had his old, engaging smile. When he smiled at me, I still felt I wasn't as committed, I wasn't as dedicated, I wasn't as good a person as Dennis. Sitting in Al Lowenstein's office, in a rush of people—and soon of medics and police—Dennis still had flashes of his old charisma. Maybe, I now thought, the old charisma was a flash of madness. But more I found I was thinking of the light, automatically I thought of the light. It was long since Coutard had given me his lovely old Leica, back when Dennis and Al and I and Baby too were starting out, sweet and clear. Back then I had not yet got used to having a camera always around, but for the years since I had never left the house without the Leica, I literally never went anywhere without it hanging around my neck. But not that day. What happened that day? This is how the story ends, I thought, the late-winter light pouring through the big Rockefeller Plaza windows. This is the end, and today of all days I don't have a camera.

COMPASS

John Kinsella

1.
And so...depoliticized
                    shilly-shally
trendsetter off-centre, off looming water in-city,
cracking encampments
as aspirator or pater hedges semi-mountain uproar
a law unto chemical mosquitoes
unto sentinel banksias
unto silhouette
open public comment, to shudder passing
or bypass three-trailered
roadtrains: triple tropes: helter the towerlike chasm
from park to shutdownfire;
calling back-damaged calling back
collaborative
semble last impression,
superscript
      ment to borate bearings;

                                        come down back, come back down
                              anti ana extra,
any prefix & ~ or `, not café or cafe: just
      "secular suns", just asterisms,
who we are
and who we are in reading;

      reflecting diagonal, south look north by south, look vice
all verses in the canvas deckchair crouching under
York gum clotting red-brown sap—dried, fractures;
affected minor keys, walk up through cutaway to crashing ocean
(creasing ocean), white mist as high-up rusted hooks
exuded by granite, headcap to Antarctic, slush of zephyrs, fancy
being stuck in memoirs of Chelsea hospital's archives,
records lancing rotten planks from gathered bilgewater,
waiting to show your harvest organs:

"In the chapel are deposited the standards of Tippoo Saib, the whole of the eagles, 13 in number, that were wrested from Napoleon's legions...",
such transmitters of personal poems.

Fridge magnets: numbers (repeats)
no letters. Uzbek singers were professional, of one of, of two schools
of one of or two of.

2. or did he?

Isosceles hubbed in the name of God
stretched equally
untotalised; sighs
of statuary, lies
of landfall and global positioning left on someone else's desk;

hear yourself think weft in lyrical honours; sliprail bias, shrewdly ditching
ecos
and "rebels' day";

Mnesarchus and Pythais
were there on the cliff looking out towards me at the back of their heads,
and I return there often
in *my* head;

square on hypotenuses: blue metal in low-profile
type
ticks on road surface, like damaged brake calipers,
like dynamic soul locus,
like the lightly-taken middle syllable.

3.

Different route 'cause the Greenough
flooded veritable surge from Walkaway down
six-metre surge cutting Brand Highway at bridge 23ks out Geraldton
fore Geraldton
so cross from Three Springs
to Morawa and then on to Mullewa to Geradlton police
say road safe way it crosses Greenough River

upstream at mouth
broken through: need impound
regulatory info

4.

One stop wordshopped by degrees
school shoe compass crushed
north out of blue diamond contract
coins and loincloth saintliness.

5.

A girl with a pinny is Quaker or Shaker
or Christ's daughter where new model
printers and DVDs make music
and theory shorter by the Yard
or Metre.

6th.

And so…in laurels and domesticity,
survivalists gathered round the wagon wheel
of transitive closure, their argument for productivity
blossoming ordinal cardinal rivalry; successor predecessor
stuck in the mud with their book of set theory
quantifying sprouted potatoes (heat, humidity), reading:
"an ordinal $\propto$ is a cardinal number if $|\propto| \neq |\beta|$ for all $\beta<\propto$."
Not sure, childhood experience ladles
chores, manic at chickenpox parties.
By now, smelling rotten starch and fibre,
tendrils appear at cracks in canopies,
set aside: collars, chains, hames and winkers.

7.

<either>

fate whole changeless whole fate changeless named mortals
as colour my world O sphere (O *doxa*) seeming *eidenai*,

and so spread about bedecked *stephanai*
they made it through, distinctive passport decorations: plausible
fingerprints, *hoion* in the masterchip, as diligent *oboli*
changeless fate whole on nortal waiting places.

8.

And so, master…

"We love the venerable house…"

or array, of finding an artist that'll be *your*
thing, your *thing, your thing,* your thing…
                                        as floods will have it,
the Avon is due to break its banks yesterday…
                                        to hyphenate a breath
less difficult as cooling day uptakes river
and plausible margin, washed "farm nutrients"
to rage an algal augmentation rank wants "a chat";
                                        big bat
shape of bat thousands sprung out of caverns,
                                        a large rat
in the ceiling, data stream clogging drains;

God-built.

9.

Lacking notochords, they festooned sea eclogues
and jilted lovers in Oxford; training always north-east
a seeing saw them off repellent as lip gloss.

Or up to Andes, compressing mountains lackadaisically, at least
a foothold into silage, into rambunctious dilly dallying
about axes—an axis tired with sameness, an axis deceased

in phobias: to ease the case of ECGs busting
out of ward rooms, the blithe "take this valium
to know it only", "how do you know not sampling

O golden emblems?" And so in methane, and so in ream
of ram of carbon dioxide, and so in temperate climates.
Here I felt pangs of grist and floodgates, laminate gleam.

Toren van Babel

Robert Estep

All things that were set high
are now, it seems, to be lowered.
Caught between the horizon
and as far as one can touch,
all projects will be trussed and tarped,
left to shake their scaffolds
in the breeze. The word will
come shortly, by horseback or dove,
and those who look sharp
will be stamped with loyalty's red pox.
The apprentices are bewildered,
and lacking the deceit of experience
their lamblike milling lightens
those around them, to loiter and laugh
at the Master, soaring in his makeshift
tower, charts weighed down by coins,
compasses, and dust-bleached sleeve.
To go forward into the past,
or stand still in the commanded future,
to whistle or pray, to hold one's water
in decorous shuffle or urinate from
battlements into shadow.
The squat man in the open-air
nest looks only from his blueprints
to the curve of the watery world
and back again, listens to no one,
scorns all dither, is struck mute
by the fawn of diplomacy,
the bow-wow from below.
Pieter is a ///\\\ no sooner scrawled
then graffitied over in its turn,
such final snowfall drawn for reprimand
from local taxes, as if to pay for love.
Still no word, and the Master calls down
for sand and clay, a little wine
to ease his genius through vertigo

and heartburn. A greyhound
starts alive from the blue of its keeper's cloak,
a cat vanishes into its mistress's house,
the window latch chimes on beveled glass,
a passenger pigeon coasts upon a current
and drops exhausted from the
dusk-stained uneventful sky.

Antigone In Petrograd

Robert Estep

Tonight Antigone works her will
upon the newsprint,
harped by poison,
stung by reprimand,
a tally of lost souls between the red lines
of the sad charter.
Time for one last look around,
this Abdication's Eve.
The shrinking of the world has come
by rotten stages, a cookery so odd
the Arctic looks half-eaten into blue,
the map's upper edge some twelve
feet up the wall,
the dolphins' key and sidebar,
eye-level to a staggering infant.
The hotel menu has been posted
by a kitchen royalist,
though appetites are measured
in republican servings and no one
can remember the glamorless new names.
A misplaced Duchess, raped
in the observatory, moans
against a jut of chalky tower,
the sky a fizz of winter light,
gray clouds smothering the opposite coastline
with such Slavic lack of ambiguity
that even the urgent rapist felt his lungs
grow damp, his legs watery
upon the middle-landing where he paused
to catch his breath, to puzzle
at the allegorical wreckage he'd made of her.
Not being the one the crowd was roaming after,
he was apprehended like a starling
in a bull's wide net,
and asked politely to select among
the mercies he might throw himself upon.

The victim suffers through her own interview
    with a lamb's mien and Lavinia's
        hangdog mane, although her vocabulary
is neither dumbed nor wistful
    and the stenographer's compassion
        burps in tired veins and almost (it seems)
the weather might succumb to color.
    Here, at this very juncture of justice
        and antigonal blindness, a funny uncle,
Creon with a Bolshevik's red star,
    should stray from character and rave
        against the slut-gay light spilling
from the Winter Palace's high window
    its hourglass of golden sand
        upon the snow below,
packed tight by Cossack boots,
    the canvas hooves of Mongol ponies
        pining for the prairie.
Antigone is weary of these anthems
    meant for men alone,
        remembering the scorched-earth backlash
of rejected gods.
    Her heels echo to a tablature
        of drumshot clicks and sudden stops,
a harrowing of the lowest rooms
    that leaves the thuggish curators
        gatemouthed and panting, pawing
behind a fez-topped monkey
    whose only parade is this way or exit.
        Three devils stoop to enter, rain
shimmering down their trouser legs,
    and the regulars look up with marvel
        at these strangers who've left the engine running.
Statements are taken, witnessed, notarized,
    and then they're gone again.
        The rain rages down upon the streets
that rubber and twist, one broken hole
    and guttering shine and then another,
        cobbled two-lanes that ribbon and shoot

to where the river bumps its barges
    like annoyance made majestic,
        a break in the weather
but not tonight.
    She moves like nightmare through the
        groggy crowd, surfacing from their swim
in the wine cellars of Theatre Street.
    Their crushing is blocked
        upon her uncle's calendar
like a promise of dominos,
    feast days of solid red
        to mark the turning year,
a year in which his niece (herself)
    will cease to worry him,
        give up reactionary politics,
demean herself to some pretty profession,
    allow herself to be seduced
        by someone sufficiently fraternal,
whose Party card she'll never see,
    nor the coded cables from the Ministry.
        The crowd gropes itself and surges
and someone shouts that Christ's been
    sighted, walking purposeful upon the
        bitter Neva, white-suited as a snowman
on the river's monked black shudder.
    A hundred yards within the Pale of
        Petrograd, her brother's corpse
continues its open air disunion,
    dragged from a shallow grave
        by the same sad plotters who earlier took
her shovels and bribes, the homemade marker
    of a double-winged cross.
        What good will this latest Jesus be
to her, consumed with the delivery
    into silence and shelter
        of a bag of bones she once loved, loves still?
The crowd catches her in its smelly tide
    and she is borne along towards the river,
        the mob's excitement infectious

as bad manners, the red and white
provocateurs the rudest of the lot.
Torches line the quay,
bristling in the wet air
like a dozing dragon's spine,
the eddy of the crowd
a muddy foam against white stone.
The floating Son of Man turns out to be
just that, a tramp from the vodka swamps,
polar-beared in a Brigadier's burgled furs,
a refuse barge to bear him down
the river, his lost disciples
a pair of tough-talking urchins,
penguined close behind.
Unimpressed, the mob moves on,
their marching hymn a brood
of piety and idiot's delight.
Antigone remains, predicting,
against all proof,
the ultimate triumph of white terror
over red, her brother's
violent tendencies and reckless pride,
to one day be the stuff of
commissions and memorials,
no cluster of victor's roses
without its share
of thorns.

Consolation Baptist Church

Donald Platt

Console me, O Lord,
for I have been driving again the back roads of your promised land,
past Temple, Georgia

and Mt. Zion, where the red clay has been soaked and washed
in the blood
of the slaughtered Lamb and still shows its fresh stain. Out of this ground

come your congregations,
Church of God of Prophecy, Just Endtime Revival Ministries, Full Gospel Choir,
Joy of the Lord

Deliverance Tabernacle, and Pleasant Grove Baptist. Out of our red clay
come sweet-smelling
pines with bark scaly as the backs of alligators, and the Speedy Spot

convenience store
where you can pump your own gas and buy Mayfield milk
at the same low price

per gallon. The people of my land have tied yellow bows
with yellow ribbon
around the rusted mailboxes at the ends of their short, dirt drives to celebrate

the defeat of Saddam Hussein
by their sons and daughters in Iraq's deserts. This morning I passed a sign
that said, "Let's Kick

Some Sand, Nigger Ass" next to "Doughnuts and Fried Pies."
Sweet Jesus,
why is hate the daily bread we eat? Why do half

the farmhouses
fly the stars-and-bars over fields where cows graze the dew-drenched
starry grass?

When I opened my car door in the Piggly Wiggly parking lot
to buy
spring water last night, a white man in tan overalls

with a three-day growth
of straw-stubble beard shook my hand and said, "Let me witness
to you, good brother!"

Lord, forgive me. I told him I was a Catholic, which in these parts
is one rung above
being black. He flinched. I walked away. Holy Mary,

virgin mother of God,
let me witness to the roadsides of west Georgia, where day lilies bloom
with their pure orange flames

among the litter of beer cans, paper bags full of cold
congealed French fries,
and crumpled crotch shots of centerfolds from *Hustler* or *Stroke*

thrown out the open windows
of pickup trucks at 2 a.m., eighty miles per hour. Flowers and litter
are equally anointed

by morning's heavy dew, that star sperm. Let me count again
the freight cars
of the Norfolk Southern slowly crossing Hog Liver Rd. with their steel wheels

grinding and ringing
against the rails, while I wait in my car for the train to pass, couplings
clanging on the downgrade,

and see the graffiti on their sides, swirls and broken arcs
of spraypainted
rainbow letters elaborate as the Book of Kells, FAT BOY,

JASPAR,
and FUCK ALL HONKIES. Let me not forget the beautiful, expressionless
face of the black

woman at the DQ's drive-thru as she handed me my soft-serve
vanilla cone,
our hands brushing against each other briefly like the wings of shy birds

as we passed
money back and forth. I will always remember the riddle and its answer
scrawled in permanent black marker

on the gas station's smut-glutted urinal wall—WHY IS AN APPLE
LIKE A NIGGER?
GOD MEANT FOR THEM BOTH TO HANG FROM TREES.

Father, how
can you forgive us? In one of the stained-glass windows of Consolation
Baptist Church,

where I have come at noon to get out of the heat,
Thomas puts
his fingers into Christ's raw flayed side. There is no other

way. *Put*
your hands into each of my wounds, the harsh light streaming
through the window

commands. *Touch me. Bear witness to these nail holes.* Outside
the white-washed church,
a small sign announces that Pastor Peter Hollowell will preach

this Sunday
and that his sermon's theme will be "Keep the word of the Lord
alway in thy mouth

for it is sweet as the honeycomb." Shall words console us?
I try them
on my tongue. *Miasma. Wrath. Gardenia. Finch's wing. Heat lightning.*

The silence doesn't
answer me. The turquoise-tiled baptismal pool beyond the altar is empty
and dry, flooded

only with musty dark. God, pastor, good shepherd,
                    cradle me
in your arms like a child, dip me down into the future's shadowy pool

                    so I may rise up
shining, so that my human flesh may evaporate with the dew
                    and I become

one of the congregation of roadside morning glories that last
                    only a few days,
that twine and climb the barbed-wire fence and make it flower.

Blue Starred

To J., who will ask what took me so long out in the yard

Diane Furtney

A few blocks away, downtown,
a train crossing the river holds down,

again and again, a complex chord on
some huge accordion.

The notes waver off toward
mostly empty air. There are no clouds.

Consolidated, blue stillness moves
straight to the moon. Above

the maple branches it's so clear
the upper atmosphere has disappeared.

Which might be a fluke of the climbing
half moon, or of this winding

breeze, cool and slotting like a key,
it feels like, through the lattice of this body,

then blowing into the spaces
of other mesh-works nearby: the interstices

that make up the slatted fence,
the trumpetcreeper vine, the cat that in silence

is stepping onto the gravel drive, the insect
instars asleep in the nets

of the ground. Five billion years
before this night, a blue star, rare,

supermassive, nearby and boiling,
probably on this spiral arm but possibly roiling

out from the nearest curve of the Perseus,
blew up. In this direction, the concuss

of its shock wave
surrounded and concaved

a standing cloud of primordial hydrogen.
The cloud condensed

to an oblong, stirred throughout
with blue-star bits. Then the grout

of angular drag and slow glue of gravity
flattened it to a disk that eddied

into rounding points: comets
and bolides and running planets

around an igniting sun,
each of their separate evolutions

always another version of the carbon-
oxygen-nitrogen proportions

only a giant blue
in nova condition can produce

—reassembled of late into the soft and hard
arrangements in this cube of a yard,

its blood and wood. And one glowing day,
my love, when the sun is blowing away

and a similar if warmer breeze
has begun to rotate its long, slender keys,

we and other blue-star particles
will loosen in our Tinkertoy mesh and travel

into wider space again
—stay close to me, I'll stay close if I can—

arcing out in ionized light,
freebooting amidst bits of this white

moon, enroute to our heirs, the next
and heavier-metal mix

of planets and star and eventual awarenesses
in their temporary solitudes: the endlessness

of being caught in shapes
and being freed. Including now the shape

of a sound carried back on the breeze
from under the Norway maple tree's

squared leaves, where last night's cricket (or
is it another?) calls again (more

urgently?), out from some ease or some crisis
in the blue and white grass.

Note: The sun, now a middle-aged, fattening star, will have doubled its size in its red-giant phase in about a billion years. The inner planets may become temporary moons of Saturn or Neptune but eventually the gas giants will also vaporize and be puffed into interstellar space.

Two Lovers in an Abandoned Nuclear Missile Silo While, Unknown to Them, Biochemical Terrorist Activity Destroys America Above

Ryan G. Van Cleave

Pink lipstick tattooing his neck, his lungs prickled
by radon-thick air, he leads her into the black water
tank which once held 30,000 gallons of undrinkable
fluid but now is an empty cement drum that echoes
his steaming breath. *Totally boss*, he says of the rainbow
graffiti, her naked body curved atop a tongue of gray
asbestos pipe insulation, their discarded clothes
glowing like ghost skins in the halo of their lantern.
As explosions in Scranton go unheard—smashing
her parents like dropped dinner plates—he asks
her to model the spaceman-white Rocket Fuel
Handler suit they saw in a beam-crushed closet,
to wet her hair in pooled rainwater, to lean against
the blast doors and give him a typhoon blowjob
while he watches to see if her nipples can poke
through the chestplate of a fire-proof radiation suit.
An iron staircase in antennae silo A collapses
from the tremors which rock the building, the world,
but these lovers cling to one another, thinking not
of how the Titan II was the largest ICBM the US
ever developed and how it brimmed with precious
liquid death, but rather that if they let their bodies
erupt in a soul-splitting fusion of molecules,
they might become their own revolutionary idea,
a moment both past and future, a verb tense
that exists on an ocean of breath which eases
into a slow, single, insistent heartbeat that needs
nothing but itself to survive.

The Art of Conquest

—for Leonard Nathan

Ryan G. Van Cleave

First, we'll take all your chairs.
They aren't yours anymore.

Later, we'll fill your wells
with pine tar and pack
your cannon-throats
with cement.

For too many years,
your republic has stood
for persimmons and
the death mask of Byron.

That is now at an end.

We'll put a stop
to your high-school
biology teachings.

We'll sweep clean
the mouth of every
        child.

It's true.
Your dead
will pile up,
fragrant,
blooming,
on the fire escape
of the palace.

We'll fill
the dump
with your terrycloth
robes.

We'll teach you
how to fume quietly
in a succession
of specific
angry gestures.

The nasturtiums
and national parks
will be plowed over;
after, we'll set
the hills ablaze
with night-blooming
jasmine and mayflies.

We'll pass out
kerosene lamps
and oil for your
grandmother's loom.

We'll employ
every itinerant tinker
to make padlocks
and boot grommets.

The republic is gone.
The palatial terrace
 is empty.

When the blood dries,
we'll make orange
our century's color.
Red is too grim.
Black is too true.

You will thank us
when we're through.

BLINDNESS

Ciaran Berry

Whether arrived at in the womb or through old age,
or because hatred in a hoop skirt and whalebone corset
has been welcomed as honored guest into your home,

the result, it seemed, was much the same: a darkness
emphatic as when the clock's short arm breaks back
an hour to let the shadows loose over the lawn, to make

welcome the fall's first frost. In double science after lunch,
one boy argued it would happen if you touched yourself
too much or spent too long before the goggle box—

revenge of the body on itself by way of an unraveling
within the tissues, humors, rods and cones, so that
the soul's supposed door could no longer open to usher

in the objects of desire, to carry word and image upside
down into the flesh. Those fledgling years the sightless
were a nation unto themselves, their flag crow-black,

their head-of-state the shopkeeper, whose eyes were like
two hardboiled eggs without the shells stirring below
the jars of clove rock and jawbreakers arranged in rows

across the shelves; whose identical twin was taciturn,
pure strange, forever, it appeared, *staring* into space.
They knew far more, I guessed, than we could know

about the grave, about the afterlife, and how the world
could be so cruel, why in the third act, the seventh scene,
of the play we were reading that year in school,

the King's daughter must conspire with her husband the Duke,
who will use just his fingernails to gouge out the Earl's eyes,
leaving behind these two bloody sockets a loyal servant

will dress, as best they can, with "flax and whites of eggs."
Our teacher, whose vision was perfect, swore the walk
to Dover's chalk cliffs, its "crows and choughs," was metaphor

for something or other of how the future would describe
its arc, whispering softly into our ears, then leading us away.
Later, he told us of the cloistered monk who kept a poker

in the fire until it glowed a bright orange and he applied it
gently to both eyes, so that the dark he craved would be
seamless, so that he could not lose his way to what he saw.

Foundlings

Ciaran Berry

I: "Wild" Peter

You come to us out of the woods, out of history's long corridor,
naked, mud-flecked, but pure, wholly yourself, your yellowed teeth
bared in a crooked smile as you approach that lone haymaker's
stunned gaze. And what I want to say is turn back now, while

there's still time, while that man who's dropped his scythe and stands
completely still in that half-stubble field can put all this down
to the second beer his wife packed with his sandwiches, to some trick
of the light in the late afternoon, or of the mind after so many hours

alone. Go now before he reaches deep into the pockets of his coat
for the red apples he will hold—one in each palm—as, part pied piper
and part first sinner, he lures you towards Hamëln. Foundling,
our world will dress you in a purple suit and make you the plaything

of kings, a curiosity who loves his gin and bites the heads from house
sparrows and wrens. Better to disappear again into the leaf-dark
you stepped from, into the rumor of your kin, said to stalk the pine
groves on all fours and suckle the pert teats of sleeping bears.

II: Victor

In Caucasus, whenever one of the sacred slaves wandered alone
into the woods, apparently inspired, the high priests had him
bound in golden chains and fattened on the best fruit and fowl
in the kingdom. After a year, a spear was driven through his side,

the future told by how the body fell. And so tomorrow, the doctors
will come once more into your cell with their pencils and paper
to try to trace a line between instinct and learning, to probe
with questions in a language you neither speak nor understand.

In the meantime, you press your nose between the bars of the window
and welcome a familiar cold that tastes of loam and pine needles,
the sky low hanging, turning slowly pinker. Soon it will snow,
an unspoiled down will fall into the walled gardens of the Bicêtre,

obscuring the pathways and the outstretched palms of the statues,
swelling the waters of the pond you stare into sometimes, transfixed—
a startled Narcissus, unsure whose face it is that hovers on that
calm surface and why the hand he reaches up never meets yours.

III: Kaspar

That day you staggered like a drunk into the village square, you
carried your entire story with you. It was in that picture of a dead city
tucked into the red band round your hat, and in the rosary beads
and scribbled prayers that swelled your pants pockets—the loss

of place, the religious fervor of that vague figure you called *man,*
who came by sometimes to beat you, or to bring leftovers. You wore
so many scars, and, as you fell further into the glare, you must
have looked just like one of the mole people I've seen stepping

from tunnels, filthy and bruised, daylight searing the white balls
of their eyes, making them blink and cry up here where no one
welcomes them as seers. Not even the shoemaker, who stood before
his shop smoking a corncob pipe when you showed up without

the words to ask him where you were. Who could have guessed
that, years later, you'd find your way into his plosive tongue only
to plague us with the old questions: "Who made the trees?" you'd ask.
"Who puts out the stars?" "Where is my soul and can I look at it?"

BREVITY

Deb Olin Unferth

Setting
It could be so much worse.

Adventure
They held machine guns. In the distance, jungle.

Romance
I will not go back to him, she says.

Spy
Even the cover-up has been covered up.

Western
This town is criminal. This town is made of mud.

Biography
He went on like that for fifty-six years.

Travel
They stop, look, start again.

Serial
How long can we keep this buggy running?

Pilgrimage
It's hard to climb a mountain of any sort.

Crime
He's too valuable to kill, too dangerous to leave alive.

Revision
Some changes need to be made around here.

Backstory
He had a brother who lived for only seven days.

Setting
No one around here has teeth.

Deleted Material

1. Numbers
Eins zwei drei vier fünf
2. Pet
Pet pet
Petpetpetpetpetpetpet

Characters
They went staggering off one way or another—in buses, mostly, but also in cars and airplanes, on bicycles.

Hero
I recommend him very much. He does everything. I taught him a few words.

Heroine
She is not rightly equipped for this awful business. Has no hat, no flash-light. Needs compass.

Plot
The tulip lady brings us another cup of tea.

Oulipo

1. Ins zwi dri vir fünf
2. Pt pt
Ptptptptptptpt

Plot
Listen for instructions.

Setting
Rectangles, antennas, hot-water tanks.

Exposition
All lives are difficult.

Postmodern
You are reading.

Satire
You are reading in a clown suit.

Sci-Fi
You are reading in a spaceship.

Speculative
You did not exist in a spaceship.

Revision
We've been through this before.

Conflict
The wind is tearing outside.

Author
You can still see her sometimes in the village. She's got crutches, face bandages.

Detail
The scorpion clutched the bedframe.

Antihero
What could you expect of him? He never made it. He turned around and went back.

Subplots

1. At the tone the time will be.
2. Please do not lean over the edge.
3. Attach no bikes.

Narrator
He can't guarantee anything.

Reader
She lies on her bed. Knows all that could be.

Unreliable Narrator
The fingerprints have been identified as his.

Climax
An event of longing and triumph.

Resolution
Oh, who cares what will become of them? They will die, that is all.

Dénouement
No payments for a year.

Ending
The end.

Ransom

Trevor Dodge

I am holding your attention hostage.
Here is my list of demands.
Pay careful attention because I will not repeat myself.
I'm a consumer in your consumer nation.
I've been trained to want things, and not only things like physical things but things like abstract things.
I am supposed to covet these things.
Have you ever noticed how close the words "cover" and "covet" are?
Luckily, I've owned a fat, leather-tooled dictionary since I was six years old, so I know the difference between the two.
Where's your dictionary?
Get it out now.
I'm not joking around here.
We're going to do this like they do in that Mel Gibson film, by the way.
You're going to come to a point where you refuse to pay me.
You're going to come to a point where you yell at the top of your voice.
Notice I didn't say "lungs," I said "voice."
You were expecting me to say "voice," weren't you?
If you don't know the difference between your lungs and your voice, you are truly fucked here.
But I'm getting ahead of myself, so let me articulate what I want first.
I want you to pretend that you're holding a letter from someone you love.
I want you to think something nice about that someone.
Like a kiss.
Like a pinky ring.
Like a mole on a big toe without any hair growing out of it.
I want you to want to finish reading the letter you're holding, so please try to concentrate.
This is important.
I want you to tell that someone something for me.
I want you to tell that someone you won't be taking their phone calls.
I want you to tell that someone you will only communicate with them through notes on a napkin the next time the two of you have lunch.
I want you to tell that someone you can no longer be a hostage.
So that's the first thing.
I know you're disappointed that this is continuing, but if there was only the

one thing, this wouldn't be called a "list of demands," would it?
Stop it.
Stop it right now.
I want you to know that this won't last forever.
Everything else, on the other hand, will.
I want you to consider what drove Verlaine to publish Rimbaud's poems.
The ones R's mother and sister begged him not to publish.
Think long and hard about that.
I want you to consider what drove Poe to trash his own novel, calling it his "silly little book," refusing to pay it any attention or tuck it in at night.
Spend as much time as you like on that one.
I want you to consider why Alisha Klass tattooed Seymore Butts' name above her ass before she ever met him.
Now consider how that name became a dolphin.
If you're not already looking up Klass on myspace, don't bother.
I want you to tell that someone something else for me.
I want you to tell that someone there is no such thing as freedom of conscience.
Make sure you put as much stress on the first syllable in "conscience" as you possibly can.
Come on, don't be like that now.
We're just about to get to the good part.
I want you to tell that someone there is neither a thing called "freedom" nor "conscience" that is worth fighting for.
Scratch that.
I want you to tell that someone there is neither a thing called "freedom" nor "conscience" that is worth *dying* for.
Because having a conscience is predicated on having a choice.
Because having a choice is predicated on being free.
And it comes down to the simple fact that you and I are not free.
And I don't mean "free" the way the New York Times and the Fox News Channel mean it.
And I *certainly* don't mean "free" the way that someone you thought about earlier means it.
I mean "free" the way Sorrentino means it when he says that plots are absurd.
I mean "free" the way Burroughs means it when he implores us to raid the prisonhouse of language.
I mean "free" the way Adorno means it when he argues art is a social antithesis to the very society which produced it.

It just kills me having to spell this out for you, by the way.
Let me back up a second.
What did you think I meant by “free” in the first place?
Perhaps we’re getting ahead of ourselves here.
Perhaps we’re trying way too hard to get to the end of this.
I can hear you sighing.
Fine.
Just fine.
Go on now.
Go ahead.
Before I change my mind again.

A WITHOUT Q WITH/OUT SELF

Carol Novack

A: It was at no point whatsoever at which I realized there was nothing else to do and that was that. Well, maybe it was that or that was that or this. I couldn't be sure until I'd gone through the process. When I was four or five at the beach near my house, peering into the beach bags of bathers, finding banana skins and eggshells. I seem to remember an ovular moment.

A: The first thing to think of after that was this. So with that in mind, I would naturally have to be the centerpiece of the allegory. Then I thought I could possibly relate the tiresome ontological metaphors, the isms and ologies and ohms and ohmygods, you know Being and Non-Being and it's all the same and everything but not but no thing and illusions and all that and this in an innovative way, meaning by means of an interview with me, my Self, and that by so doing, I would be original.

Then of course there are so many possible audiences, a veritable cornucopia of ears. If you are performing in front of a Rumanian audience, you don't want to play Indian pop tunes, do you? Well, that's the point precisely now, isn't it?

A: That may be so, frequent fragility, I admit, and it could be vitamin deficiency during pregnancy, too many martinis, I'll say Mother's fault to be kind to you. But it was hard to find anyone else available off the bat and with time, people disappear, or in time they become lost. Oh oh there was this one and that one, and theoretically, I weep. Either way, scheduling is always a problem; then there's the mortgage, much to lose, little to gain, though in truth of course property is a laden donkey, but on the other hand, there's crème brûlée. So to cut corners became critical and then of course money and also fame, objects of desire. The audience always takes bets: this one will be a winner, 10 to one; that one will place second, and so on. With the right agent, consider Self as syndicated in scarlet or lavender, black, teal, indigo, non-fat or 100% fat with anti-toxins. Sold! Voila! It's a matter of flexibility. Mother told me I could become. But with money and fame would I strut about the globe blowing kisses from yachts and exhibiting my latest endangered species fur? I would be stealing the allegory of myself. Horrors!

A: Oh now you're talking ideology and semantics. Your insistent literalism and exactitude is exasperating. You take all of this and that much too seriously and think the only people worthy of being interviewed can be found on amazon.com with five star reviews or viewed on talk or news shows. That tells me a lot about you. Frankly, your imagination has close walls.

A: I am most adamantly not a dog, chasing my tail. Simply let's say childhood was okay as childhoods go, probably better than yours but maybe not. I've heard of worse. Nobody locked me in a cellar, shoveled dirt into my mouth or poked objects into my delicate overtures. Nobody told me I couldn't eat ham if I didn't first eat my peas. So I am very lucky to have gotten away with a tolerable childhood. Not the best but not the worst, no not by a long shot, even better than worst though lesser than best, if you get my drift, you understand, the occasional nagging and smothering, to be expected, and my head hurt when she brushed my hair.

Asleep during childhood, we can scarcely remember details, but emotional tones, themes, as in subtle transformations of the child in her own eyes, in kindergarten, first grade, summer camp, and so on, by means of humiliating experiences. Example one: two older boys tugging at her underpants, tearing them off. Example two: she forgets purposefully. So there are memories, tales and rumors, but you can never believe any of them completely. Take what you want and discard the rest I say. End of temporary reverie and on to the next.

A: Well, it's a mark of maturity to realize that one's most attentive audience is Self. But also one's least attentive. And then one must ask what is Self, most often referred to as one's self or my self, and that is where the amniotic fluid gets murky. We ourselves have wondered that so many times. But contentment?

Okay, I understand a diversion, though we are so tempted to try, say this or say Eastern methodology or phenomenology, to empty Self of self or resist self without resisting Self or become either a cathedral or gargoyle. So the question is: will you dance with me? But can one tell the dancer from the dance or know that one is not say, a butterfly? Unless one falls into a bucket full of collective shit, no question mark. So the bottom line is let us return to Exhibit "A.," the dear forgotten womb, nostalgia of beginnings, terrifying tabula rasa.

A: Now it's your time to listen, so listen. I have this to say. Picture a donkey with a cargo of bananas and hens. She is stumbling on stones through the night, smells a bewildering frenzy of unidentified flowers, somewhere under the shared sky of dim, far flung stars. She hears the voices of creatures she can neither smell nor see and trembles, feeling vulnerable to their genetic destinies. Inevitably, the donkey, exhausted, sits down by the roadside if she is allowed. Her nose longs for only one scent, her eyes for only one vision, and her ears for only one sound.

A: The first aroma: the one that assaulted and tempted all of her senses as she emerged from womb, warm, sloppy scent of milk in the breast or could be roses tossed by an appreciative audience, as in congratulations, happy birthday, cherished miracle! The first vision: through fog, breast and light. And the first voice: well, one might ask if it's the mother or midwife or father in the labor room. Or is it the infant's own voice? Or the hollow black hungry sound of the cosmos? Or is the sound-vision of the cosmos merely a mirror reflecting our reckless, dull mirrors? Not to mention the taste of custom-made milk and the feel of attending mother breast and hands, sound of hands clapping.

A: My dear pathetic Self, you are so distraught with my distractions you've forgotten your questions. My audience is you, my Self, or not mine, as I can't own Self. Self is not as it would be or I would wish it to be, would wish I to be, heroic and coherent, glorious and true. It is frequently breathless and comes in a cacophony of colors, nuances of light, sweet and bitter aromas and tastes. Naturally, Self is subject to the effects of negligent parenting, Bombay Sapphire, nasty people, broken clocks and hurricanes; sometimes goes on vacations, threatens suicide, and believes it loves another Self, and then it sometimes propagates its self. That is who is interviewing me or we. And that is what we have to say to the audience. Are you my audience? Are you listening?

A: Tell me where you are and who you are. Please do. I have a tale to tell, no time to waste, no time.

***CUT*.**

BLUE ANGELISM

Eckhard Gerdes

Peer evaluation time again. I had to observe colleagues' classes. I drew a nasty assignment this year: *Blue Angelism*, a practical how-to class.

Poor Heinrich Mann must be disquieted to see what's become of his novel. Woe to any society whose cautionary tales become prescriptive.

The class was only open to the most beautiful and the youngest. Frau Schadenfreude selected her students carefully from among the hundred applicants she had every semester. They had to be trustworthy: they were entering into a binding mutual code of silence. Once taught the code of the Blue Angel, they were not permitted to discuss it, especially with men. We men, though, especially those in the public eye, from teachers and politicians to performers, know the game. It was designed to strip from a man his dignity, his reason, his humor, his financial resources, and his soul.

"Hello, Man."

"Hello, Beautiful." From the commission of the first adjective, she knew she had him. True, she was the most beautiful fly ever tied. Perhaps the best men wouldn't even touch, afraid of messing up the only aesthetically perfect fly. Most of us snap. Caught. You can whip around your tale all you like. At the time you are doing it, you are in ecstasy, unaware that a multi-pronged, barbed golden hook has just gone down your gullet.

Don't worry—it's been designed to pull out more than your guts. Your heart, your wind, your dreams have all been pulled out as well and also forged into weapons against you. This, to you, is what love must feel like.

Then you are on stage—pulled up there by your love—and then she turns on the house lights. You are up there being looked at by beautiful 21-year-olds, and the second you begin to believe you are cool enough to belong there, she signals to them to begin laughing at you. Then she disappears.

Wedded Words

Kass Fleisher

words nanosized dancing on the head of a spin she can't but inhale them shit they creep into the corners of her eyes piss she tries to rub them out but they're already halfway to the amygdala which is fuck pores jammed with prepositions in particular she can no longer make cunt she can't even see them anymore what is seeing something about cocksucker comprehension calm preening tension they continue to but she can't motherfucker all around all within they have steeped marinated soaked there is no her them there is only TITS If, while dancing, you get dizzy, spin the other way and your head will clear Keep your steps small Keep your knees bent Keep your heels low they are your brakes What is it 'bout girls that makes them so pretty What is it 'bout garlic that makes it so sticky Our baseball is broken Rain is also of the process, blown white in the wind All My Allergies—hey, that's funny Originally she was recruited for marriage but they declared her 4F Alpha conch/beta waves/charlie delta/special forces get me the fuck you rearechelonmotherfucker out of here I mean it if without living is you [changed in the author's orange notebook from you to fuck off] Hannah saw words on faces I mean it I'm tellin I'm tellin on you Naturally, these fictions run ran run the risk of tumbling down the formalist Webdings and ending up at the bottom without readers without Leonard—except the heroic students of Roland Barthes or Umberto Eco, Wingdings ⌫ whose lucubrations were much more interesting than their antiestablishment dysenterianism [*sic*] Looking at her there on the couch with Carolyn, all I can think to say is *hörigkeit* [insert normal text] audial overuse syndrome excessive strain upon the drum pathological female submission An absolute victory in the Supreme Court today The positive horror of fried Twinkies™ An investigation to discover how troops responded to being fired upon Where is it going What does it mean How will it end What was it Joyce said—what was it Joyce said—what was it Joyce said—please, please, *what did he say again??*

[See title.]

[Oh. OK.]

[So. Do you feel better now?]

Unpacking My Stuff

Kim Chinquee

This guy was a mover. He seemed okay, did a good job with my stuff. He was blonde and thin and extra careful emptying the boxes. He had blue eyes and was going to school to be a pilot. He told me this after I bought all of them sandwiches from Subway. I'd felt sorry for them all, unboxing my belongings, carrying my dressers. I don't remember the other guys. His name was Chris.

He gave me his number, so I asked him over after I put my things in cabinets.

I got a sitter. He picked me up and we went for beer and pizza. We went to his place afterwards and all I remember was the basement: pool tables and dart games. I was still in the Air Force and he said the word bloody over and over, saying it should be familiar to me, just coming from England and all. He asked me about the farm I grew up on and said he could fix me up. He said he liked to fish, and then he pushed my head down to his dick, and I thought about fishing and farming. His penis wasn't small, but it wasn't big either. I could do anything. He settled for a blow job.

I got home thinking of what a big pile of junk I was. I paid the sitter and then watched my son sleeping in his Batman quilt.

Later on, I got a part time gig at a bar, something apart from the Air Force, where I played a shot girl; I needed extra money to pay for my divorce. Chris came in one night in his parka and tried getting close with me in my bikini—that was the theme for the night. It was North Dakota. He asked how I was. I didn't say much, but he took one of the shots. He handed me a fifty, saying it was good. I took it, going for more.

Base Recreation

Kim Chinquee

After hours of marching and the classroom, we walked to Base Recreation, our limbs still stiff, and we ordered tacos and beer, sliding quarters in the jukebox. We were still in uniform, only one stripe sewed onto each sleeve; I sat with him and his friends, talking in spirals.

After that, while they played foosball, I sat looking out at a statue of a soldier. I heard the tunes, the bangings of a game, the dinging of a pinball, voices hard and low, and the statue held a rifle.

When they were done, they sat with me and he said, "How's my doll?"

He kissed me like a soldier.

We walked back to his dorm, congregating, studying things like coagulation, blood types, the ph of fluids. I lay on his cot with him while we quizzed. He played songs like "Proud to be an American." I didn't know much and we all sang.

I got ready for my dorm, kissing him, then saying goodbye to his friends. I walked to my room, finding my roommate asleep and I dreamt about my old boyfriend, the first and only one I'd slept with, who'd left long ago for college, riding bulls in Kansas. I had nightmares of him being trampled. I kept his picture in my room.

I got up in the morning and then I saw him, this airmen ranked as me—we were all stiff in formation. We got inspected then we marched: column right and hut two three four, twothreefour, forward march. We took the test and he aced it. We went out like before. We celebrated, studied. We got up and marched again, studied and slept, studied and slept, doing everything, performing. We studied and slept, studied and slept, marched to columns, testing.

PRAYER FOR A SIGN OF THE CROSS

Paul Maliszewski

Once, in Dallas, he went shopping with his mother and father and brother. He and his brother split off from their parents and were walking to the place that sold freshly squeezed lemonade when they passed a woman. It was late August. He was twelve. There was nothing noteworthy or even slightly odd about the woman. She just looked like a shopper. She wore a cotton dress—he remembers it being white, but doesn't completely trust his memory—and sandals. Around her neck, she wore a necklace of wooden beads.

What was strange though was that as he and his brother walked by the woman, he made the sign of the cross. Now, his family was not particularly religious. It's important to note that. They did go to church, but only out of habit. That is, they went because they had gone the week before. Nevertheless, when they made their signs of the cross, it was not some mere gesture. They did so with every good intention, but also, of course, because the service called for it.

His gesture in the mall was quick and then it was over. The woman probably didn't notice. He hadn't even had time to think, I am going to cross myself now. In fact, he no sooner saw the woman then his right hand moved from his forehead down to his chest across to his left shoulder and then back to his right.

He asked his brother, Did you see that?

See what? his brother said.

That woman. We just walked by her.

His brother looked back, over his shoulder, and shrugged. I didn't notice anyone, he said.

Years later when he thinks about this moment—and he will, at unexpected times, while checking to see that he locked the car door, for example, or standing in line at the company cafeteria, or walking to the post office on another day in another August—he will conclude that something, perhaps something about the woman, compelled him to make the sign of the cross. Something, he will think, came over me. Something must have compelled me. He will think the word "compelled," but he'll forever be at a loss to explain why he was compelled so, or just who it was that compelled him.

THE LIBRARY AT ALEXANDRIA

James Doyle

(Note: By the 3rd Century BC, the Alexandrian Library
had assembled the greatest collection of manuscripts
in antiquity, an estimated 500,000 books or scrolls.
Fire later destroyed the complete collection.)

Before the flames, Alexandria
was fat, insoluble, ancient.

It let its library loose
to stalk the desert. One

oasis after another turned
parable between thick covers.

The Mediterranean sailed in
from the north with poets

and scientists. The aisles
of books wheeled a slow

turn, came to a full stop
on fire. Finding the right

word in Greek, Aramaic,
hieroglyphs. An entire

religion later, illuminated
letters rose through the dry

palimpsest. Monks discovered
hour after hour between

the ticking of chants. Sand
castles, salt flats, sly

sea winds tuning the rocks
moss green. Alexandria lean,

modern in the monastery cells.
Ruins literate along stone

shelves. Tombs have broken open,
corpses disappeared. Books

and books and books. The dead
tuck us in like children,

read us the promised stories
for a good night's sleep.

Woman In the Red Mask

James Doyle

> "There will never be an end
> To this droning of the surf."
> —Wallace Stevens

The jugglers break the solid block
of day into pieces that fit their hands.

Suddenly a kaleidoscope, foam and spray
tumbling through the air, proven wrists

faster, more agile than the tides. Sun
on the water, moon on the water. What

a circus! And now the woman in the red
mask. She holds out her arms. And just

look at those grains of air pouring
through her fingers! The beach is running

towards her. What wouldn't want to be one
of the lavish party, cells by the millions

that make her up? Everything is putting on
a red mask, dancing at the shoreline

as if the ocean would never stop. So far
above that balance is taken on faith,

a tightrope walker threads invisible day
to invisible night. The operatic diva,

buried to her head in sand, rides a cresting
breath into the highest C. The ground

shakes itself awake, the sky unravels its last
backdrop, the surf blares woodwind and trombone.

Shadows like characters arriving at plot back
and forth against the bare wall of the eye.

SLOUGH

Susanne Kort

But in the sweep, the arc enclosing itself,
it turns out that afternoon is the Herculean—
its weft & weir & that it happens every single
goddam day & lasts so long
Mornings one sails through
what with coffee & the broken down, plants to water, ants to kill—
it's only after lunch
when life here turns Augean:
the fuschia silence, the drunken trees, the gaseous neighbors,
the school next door disgorging tidalwaves
of inexplicables, the afterwards vacuum, the terrifying sun, the cobblestones
dwindling to the end of us—incidental it's true—; the thousands of years
until supper condescends

THE WISEST OF VIRGINS

(Honeymoon, 1912- to L. Woolf)

Susanne Kort

The worst of it would be after you'd touched them
& so forth, against all you stood for or meant
to become but somehow it would happen: fatidic
Ceylon: the elemental stink

of parts; it was always essential for V. to have her privacy
once we'd arrived at the thing, gone through our litanies, the impossibilities of ever
metamorphing into Us. We went & did it nonetheless; she would then disappear
after dinner, nothing demure about it, an en tout cas

preparing of herself (what did gentlewomen do?)—We'd be in Avignon, Marseilles,
fresh off the train, reading & writing decently, during the day, it all building up
to this crisis of bedding down, according to time-honoured custom,
& trying our best to come off

with honour. That a person so chiseled & lean (Thoby's lumiferous idiom)
could ever turn so slimy like the rest of them, so fetid & slippery—
one felt quite ill when it was done,
& put it down neatly, I thought, at the time: Work in Progress: e.g. poor

pale body, long weedish limbs like turnips: forking, importunate:
Oh with her it was blasphemous thus to be fucking & the following morning
fiendishly napkin'd & sipping our tea

52 Tavistock Square, WC 1

V.W. to V. S-W

Susanne Kort

I am rather tired, a little tired, from having thought so much
about the unthinkables, the apses with lapses, the small cathedrals
one tends to wander in on the way home from anywhere:

the idea is to arrive, however one can, on time as he says, again, again, again,
but there are detours that insist
& make you late for the thing you can never remember: some stellar event

or just that the doors must be locked & the dogs & so forth
or Nelly informed or dear Leonard kissed, you must really persist
though in comparison he's won: Talmudic lucidity, attention paid

to heaps of mourning eggs & other forms
of albumen, getting them into me, lying one down in her proper shuttered room,
pushing them all away, far away, as if that were the way to

(shush!) Sanity. No one dares say it in front of me
except my darling grenadier, her legs like beechtrees, on top of our fires,
the Sissinghurst fuzz on her & her

bemusing pedigree: then Come away with me, to Samarkand, throw down
your lovely threadbare gauntlet;
no one you know will pick it up, they will talk & talk

& sip their muggy tea & gnaw & suck at their nasty biscuits, while we
shall frolic & commune: moonlit sand, tides aflood, desires let cataclysmically
loose
Somwhere I hear it's chiming half past ten

I'm scuttling round the bend yes as fast as I can
past the ghastly spikes that close us in
Oh what will he say

Oh I know I'll never flee
You must attempt to love me as I am: Take me:
but in context

FORECAST

Kristy Odelius

The wife is in the grip of being.
Anne Carson

*

All around me orchestra
was spinning out algebra.

I said *closed—*
but eyelids hum,
recurring there.

A fan unfolding
you, sketching
clean birds
on my gold-brown thighs.

I alleged,
I am my love.

*

I alleged pleasure,
breakwater,
a violet storm.

Bare knees on a girl's rum sheets
burned a steel distance in me.

Two-tongue. Sea-eyed.
Sweet fuck thinking
my pink dresses
away to real seas.

I won't, but bear harder.

*

Curled in
a star's mouth,
black.

Warm as sick cats,
and bright.

When I say *now*
bite straight down.

*

Sponge-flowers
drift in
lullaby chambers,

a view of lime seeds.

Cut a window in my palm
sometimes to feel you.

I heard—*a lucky girl.*

Wrung like a hand waking to rainwater.

*

Morning flew down the beach,
loose cash, the wing
we stash keeps a ruby fog.

Each root lodged in
your beautiful used-to—
dawn, my green glass,
what I can't do with you.

A PETA GEORGICS FOR GIULIO ROMANO'S *LADY AT HER TOILET*

Stephen Gibson

When you see your coat come out of the forest
bind it with ligatures
onto poles—do with it
as you would with prisoners in war.

Like yourself sitting before your mirrors,
cut the mother sow in half
on the killing floor,
then hang both hers from the rafters.

Nothing pleases the skin more
than moisturizers,
or the hair, pomades—their hosannas
begin with bone and fat boiling in water.

These simple creatures
feel nothing after or before—
a veal calf's tongue licks invisible fingers
while she is draining onto straw.

NEGATIVE CAPABILITY AT A ROMAN SUBWAY STOP (JULY 2004)

Stephen Gibson

Because of a bomb scare on the subway
where polizia brought dogs onto the cars
and walked with them along the platform,
leading them by short leashes to sniff bags,
men's pants, women's legs, I arrived late
at Keats' museum next to the Spanish Steps.

The museum was closed. I climbed its steps
anyway, up three floors, hoping some way
someone would let me in. I was late
because something in one of the subway cars
aroused suspicions—someone's shopping bags,
an unattended package—or on the platform

someone's forgotten backpack. Black uniforms
suddenly appeared, coming down the steps
with dogs leading the way, circling bags,
shoes, legs. I admit I wanted to move away
when a dog approached me. The subway cars
weren't going anywhere. People would be late

wherever they were headed—as I was late—
telling myself the bulletproof vests, uniforms,
holstered weapons, people inside subway cars
staring out, other people stopped on steps
and told to show their passports—the way
I was—was all necessary. The shopping bags

around me made me fearful—the bags,
the people next to them shopping on a late
July afternoon, the other people moving away
when I handed over my passport on that platform,
the people in the cars watching those on the steps
and those watching those in the subway cars.

I felt afraid. And then angry—that the cars
weren't moving, that someone else's bags
made me fearful, that being stopped on those steps
to show my passport made me guilty. Too late
the world returned to normal: on the platform,
people talked again and grudgingly made way

for others getting out of the cars, late for whatever,
their shopping bags on the platform jockeying
with me all the way to the Spanish Steps.

DIVINE

—To Tab Hunter

Johnny Horton

Just like you had no conscience, no self-
fulfilling doomsday prophecies, no falsetto

twitter outside the adolescence birdhouse,
you Shirley Templed across the island

without a shirt on. Just like a cowboy
in pajamas, Tony Perkins made a habit

out of bedsheets, turned up in the shower
at peculiar moments. You often said

whimsical nothings. Nine times out of ten,
said nothing. How Cinamascope, your life,

when every Natalie Wood could stand in
for love, when every horse bought for you

a kingdom. And you! Living in a stable
with Peter Lorre and Daphy Duck? Oh,

in those days the Soviets shot their dogs
into orbit. Everything was easy. Thereafter

Democrats took office, and magazines quit
publishing your photos. Just like the boy

next door quit shaving. And we stood around
transfixed by his sister's burning

brassiere. Of course, the dark years came
like rayon. But just like a chisel-chin

Messiah, you came back in *Polyester*.
Like a Baptist, you taught us to love Divine.

COLD WAR PHONETICS

Johnny Horton

Able went into aeronautics with his besr friend
Baker. No good time
Charlies, those two monkeys, wearing hang
Dog faces. Flying wasn't
Easy. They didn't want to, but it beat digging
Fox holes, or singing
George Marshall's praises. NASA wasn't sure
How to launch them, but they could
Itemize their plans, and there'd be eggheads dancing
Jigs around Houston, smoking
King-size Cubans, laughing at how they traded
Love for stability,
Micromanaged Dick and Jane at summer camp—
Nantucket, where kids played
Oboes, or else invented rumors concerning salt
Peter. Nobody wanted to tell
Queen Elizabeth. No Chief of Stealth was all like,
"Roger that, we beat your ass,
Sugar". Of course, they had too many teenagers
Tearing around like James Dean,
Uncles you couldn't trust. They had to be careful.
Victory was elusive.
William Shakespeare said it best. They'd need
X-Rays, not to mention
Yokels shooting stop signs, guys in lab coats testing
Zebra mussels for contagion.

Special One Time Limited Offer

Johnny Horton

Don't say a word until you hear about Mozart's recreation
room, the billiard hall disaster, the wreck racking
balls, all decked out like a hot house flower. Let me tell you
about the nun with a bun in the oven, the red-handed
priest on the cliché junket. Let me tell you about the handle
bar mustache in a life raft with the Buddha, a Rabbi,
and Natalie Wood. They could all be yours—if you act now—
but don't say a word; not until you've heard about the special
offer; not until you've heard about the French boy
raised by wolves. You could have the gourd Simon Peter used
for a tackle box. You could take it on the Barnum & Bailey
circuit. And—if you act now—you could have a one time only
roadside attraction on the western lip of Kansas, complete
with prairie dogs, rattlesnakes, and a stack of photos
proving that you took the poison. Act now and keep them.
Keep them in the family album. Keep them where the kids
can find them when they come with awkward questions.
All this could be yours—all this, and much more—if you act
before the Equinox. Act before the Transit of Venus and win
an Anglo-Saxon chieftain learning Latin from a Diva, a lamb
drunk on lion's milk. You think you're being bilked, but wait.
I haven't told you about the birds, black-capped chickadees
eating suet upside down, a northern flicker picking termites
out of grout. You can take them all. You can take the cake.
You can take everything in a rain-proof bag. Just unroll it
in the park. It comes with chardonnay, a basket full of cheese,
and if you order now it comes with a backdrop by Monet.
But that's not all. Keep your wallet in your pants. Don't adjust
your set. Don't say a word. Everything is yours for a song.

IMAGINE THE HOSPITAL

Rachel Richardson

full of mothers
all gone
bad like the morning glory
the neighbor dug out, promising
them the good, cultivated strand,
the one that knows its path,
that only climbs the trellis.
Not this deviant plant, thick vines
unstoppable, swarming
under the house, gone wild,
pushing through the crack
in the kitchen floor, writhing.
What mother wouldn't go mad?
What mother could handle
the oven, the flush of gas
igniting, could press her palms
into the scalding pan,
feed a family from that?
Who could raise up
a son to leave her, and what
could one do with daughters?
Each must have known
the fire she fed—
all down the block
the same sweet example,
and Vida's own mother
teaching her to sew.

Scene

Rachel Richardson

// Cut to the moment before Vida's mother crosses the threshold
into the house where she has crossed the threshold
ten thousand times / and cut to her feet
crossing the raised slope in the wood where the water
gets in and the muscular coil of her toes inside
her pantyhose inside her leather low-heeled shoes and beneath that
the microscopic filth of a room the water ransacks
and a house that turns each spring to poison
the family breathing spores the water's
slime decaying sloughed bodies left behind
the snakes the gators / cut to
the netted fabric climbing her leg and
clinging a shade darker than
her skin but still like skin as if hers
were less substantial / cut to
the lead weight of her leg and it not
touching this floor never
again touching no / cut
to her grip on the doorknob her key
in the lock the open door the same house
the same empty
the swamp rising inside her its green
tightness its net / cut / cut /

and then this

the moment Vida's mother /

cut //

Hölderlin's Garden

Tim Kahl

He digs up the dirt with his nails, looking for his sweet Jesus
and is seized by the power of the gods allied in the Aether.

He spies on the gods, waiting for their orders, but they are only
hinted at in his sudden awakenings as he walks through the garden

muttering to the Neckar and the daisies and the light of the sky
that fashions the notion *mortal man is best when loving.*

He roams the depths of his reason, from one place to
the dream of the next, a witness to the seasons of his convictions;

then he returns to the shattered clockwork of his own thinking.
His speech falls to pieces away from the core. Zimmer, the carpenter,

and his wife are there to escort him out of his hysterics during
his soul's long confession. In his calm he is left alone in his tower,

the lost son of the Alps fearlessly crossing the flimsy bridge
that stretches across the abyss. The gods assemble on the peaks there,

calling to him and telling him that abandoned thoughts flow
through a mind for a reason. He was made infirm to keep

their mysteries a secret. He despises the night for betraying him,
leaving him there in the dark with his dreams sent down from

the Aether. The gods preside over the loved one whom he was not
permitted to love, the wife of a wealthy banker in Frankfurt,

whose lost kisses and blessed radiance persist in haunting him.
Alone he tends his love of hidden beauty. He nurtures his suspicion

of happiness. His secret world, his kingdom of love, known only
to the gods, cannot be found growing in his garden in Tübingen,

where he peers out over the Neckar and gathers in the heavens,
hint by hint by hint, inscrutable like a river's ceaseless whisper.

IVORYBILL

K.E. Duffin

There all along. In the airless terrarium
of childhood afternoons, outsized one,
silken grenadier, cartoon of oblivion,
your white bill a planed, gleaming coffin,

your mourner's suit with stripe of honorand
and flaps of white tuxedo. Forests were scanned
and scoured to declare your final hours gone,
vanished cousin of all the vanished dozens,

nesting in books, your only bleary sun
my bedroom lamp, or so I thought. One
beyond the gate of death, Desideratum.

There all along. In roofless swamp cathedrals,
quelling your filibuster of silence with calls.
Above your brinksmanship a real sun stalls.

Suicide Notes

James Proffitt

A calf and mare followed us along a fence line as we trudged
in a snow thick as the lack of words between us.
So who could have foreseen disaster like this—big, bold, brash?
This is our note, *the* note, the one that comes after us.
Our postscript, let's say, tidy and fitting and perfect as you
the day we stumbled into one another, a little tipsy, a little lonely.
That was the first of our many implosions, our fabled un-doings.
Here goes: *listen to big snow settling from our dim sky.*
It was never in us to be together, alive.
Dumb tragedy, blind luck's always our queer print.
Look around at our shrinking walls, the panels of our heads closing in.
There's a rush of contradiction and untenable contortions
and in every vacant cell: loss and losing and lost.
In every lost room: vacancy.

EXPEDITIONARY LOVE SONNET

Ian Harris

In the photograph, Gerlach opens calipers
over a map of the South Orkney Islands.
He has the face of someone who cares nothing
for his wife, and wears a navy collar aboard the *Belgica.*

As a child I read each of the antarctic accounts.
I was fascinated by supply lists, pared according to weight.
boot oil…13lbs, tobacco…9lbs, waxed tarpaulins (3 qnty)…60lbs,
sewing kits, decks of cards, bourbon for the passage of holidays,
pemmican, pocket mirrors, bandages, black tea. I am lucky

I suppose, to have you to sleep against. Happy, surely,
we have heirloom tomatoes, icebox plums, shoes that require no oil.
Instead of a sledge, and a continent to go out on. Far away,

Gerlach packed himself in an eider down sleeping bag,
listened to a hairline crack forming for several days.

Supercalifragilisticexpialidocious

Ian Harris

The social complexity of balcony
parties—if you've read Roland Barthes and
Claude Lévi-Strauss—is as strange and ancient
as the corals of iron inside steam ship museums.

At first, we are all alone
in our clothes. One is wearing corduroy, and
another a pinafore. There is a day-trader and someone
who has just come from touch football. We hold
rum drinks and gin drinks and, some of us, cold beer.
We say something, and they say something back.
"This is reality, real activity, the process of real life,"
Ricoeur writes.

At first, we are all alone.

But then we hear a woman say the chimneys,
from here, remind her of Mary Poppins,
and suddenly the party metastasizes. Oiled
metal of the cumbersome machine begins to sugar, and turn.
What we say is said about Dick Van Dyke and bumbershoots
and suffragettes and sidewalk chalk. What we feel
is felt about each other, momentarily—
joined into one long word that is merry
and meaningless, except to us, for the moment.

The Allerton Hotel, Chicago

Drew Blanchard

O tower of light, sad beauty...
—Pablo Neruda

The sun, in a tower of light,
breaks through clouds heavy with rain,
blanching the face of a bell hop
who squints and holds up a hand

as if he were saluting the sky
or waving to the woman who,
in less than a minute,
will jump from the fifteenth floor.

He is, of course, not waving,
but waiting, like the small crowd
that has amassed to see a life disappear.
Before my mother understood

why so many people had gathered
on a gray afternoon in front of a hotel,
the woman dropped into a collective scream,
then silence, then sirens. I will not tell you

the color of the dress
that gathered around her waist,
rippled and snapping like a flag,
or the sound of her bones

folding into themselves.
What I remember—I was eight—
is not the falling, but the rows
of men and women hushed by terror.

Wrecking the Orpheum

Drew Blanchard

Above the empty orchestra pit and the gold
ornamental arches, above the hand-carved
theater faces and the blue mosaic columns,
above the glimmering glass of chandeliers,
a century of dust rises to the ceiling before it falls.
With a crowbar, I pry splintering floorboards
from the stage. I salvage, to the dismay of my boss,
this lacquered wood for the long tenured
Theater Director—his final holding on.
As I lever the hundred-year-old nails, they bend and whine.
In high school I played Mercutio on this stage,
and backstage made love with Juliet. She did not fumble
with the passion as I did—pretending it was not
my first time. Years later, backstage of another theater,
in another city, I experienced my first slow
melt from the needle—the initial taste
as explosive as making love. Now, clean
for six months, home again with steady work,
I am back on stage. As I sweat in the dust I can
almost hear the tiny ring of the curtain bell,
my backstage nervous breath, the whisper
of the audience and the rustle of programs.
Tonight they'll auction off the theater seats,
doorknobs, pictures of Dvorák, bristly beard
and serious eyes, as he directs the symphony
in 1893. Tomorrow, the wrecking ball, the masonry
and stone will fall, all but the façade, a memoriam,
a gateway to the glass and steel of the new civic center.

On the Rue Mouffetard

Lorrie Goldensohn

deep in the habit of guarding where my feet go
my eyes only graze the lovely colors
the spires and buttresses of St. Medard
its limestone the tint of old teeth
its iron the blackness of extremity
its walls like the bone of my brow
sheltering a dense assemblage of scenes

look how I carry with me my people
just as this church sustains its own

can you hear them in the church playground
and in the graveyard when time
is erased or stretched
folding the cries of the light bodies on the swings
into the cries of the Jansenist women
convulsing over the Bishop's tomb

miracle miracle miracle the women cried
until in 1732
they were stopped as a public nuisance

before us on the receptive pavement
spit dazzles
and street hose and bladder
write their own black trails

here too in their gaiety

cigarette butts saleslips and candy wrappers
dog shit and metro tickets

while two blood oranges
roll from a produce truck
and a little fluff floats by
like human hair

at hand the bright things to buy
above the head behind the bonny brow
the compound weathers expanding out
and also tending in

CLEPSYDRA

Leo Jilk

my sailboat says; ultimately my origin
goes back to you, it says—it stood on your summit—Zukofsky/Catullus

An architect's book   a book of pictures
a poet's book   a book
of words tho
the experience
closes itself here, not.
Even
reading
we try   something
terribly peripheral,
as sanctuaries in words   (floor below grade / high clerestories)
find their place
loose,
neither   products nor   breath

the ideas of measures false
flashings on graffitoed tunnels.
Easy saying so.   In time
neither   past   nor present moving
we stand.

nevertheless the translation
preserves, as upper limit

some oblique equivalent
voice we know

FORESTCAPED SHORE

Leo Jilk

ocean I saw
the other side of I was
swinging from chains
side to side
spirals about sand
won't tell a difference
between faraway / innerness
exists / im-
posed
world I thought
was now unexplored is mine
of old, unreal.

Okay keep
dreaming
the wet train
home morning
its silence

AUTOBIOGRAPHY OF SILENCE

Henry Hart

One side of my brain was a diamond merchant who owned a New York tram company.
The other was a missionary who sold Bibles for soup on the Mongolian steppe.
I was never fully born from the silence between them.
For eighteen years, oaks yawned outside my bedroom, but never slept.
I deciphered apostrophes hanging from moonlit dogwoods,
the night's carbon paper typed with asterisks by Shakespearean monkeys.
Dr. Applebaum's medicine bottles on my windowsill didn't help.
Once when I washed arrowheads during a thunder storm,
lightning rattled the pipes, knocking me out for eight hours.
Because the school bus sounded like thunder, I hid in our bomb shelter.
My teachers pinned the heads of assassinated leaders on the bulletin board.
They all looked like photographs of criminals in the post office.
If someone called my name, I spoke quietly in tongues,
my face a Rorschach stain nobody could decipher.
I wanted to camouflage myself as a snowflake in a blizzard.
In church, I searched brass crosses for a wounded body that would talk to me.
At home, my bedroom windows were the perfect temperature to crystallize breath.
O to be smoke from an oracle, writing prophecies in air,
a leaf shivering with a riddle no one could answer!
The news on our black-and-white TV was Darwinian.
It gave me nightmares of a crow sewing my lips shut with fishing line,
tying my neck to a post in a cornfield.
When I woke I thought night was the only solution.
The sun carving hieroglyphs in frost had a different idea.
The wind muttered: Scrape the gold splinters from glass, see
what you can see and get to work.

The Song of Vashti

Jennifer Tonge

A coloratura, perhaps,
for the robe that trails
on the extravagant floor
as she leaves
the site of her disgrace.

Around that a simmering nest
of drums and oboes,
the tense-timed crash
of cymbals.
(The feast, the feast.)

But for her self,
make one clear note
that goes with her
into the palace wastes.

Let it linger in Esther's ear
as she forges her dominion.
Let her never forget
the one that she replaced.

Fragment

Jennifer Tonge

I thought that I could allude
to it, as to some myth: a girl
whirling
among reeds and the man
clasping her, safe
as painting on an urn.
Some thing removed.
Some thing disposed of,
distant. Some thing
receded beyond the horizon.
But this fury alights—

GODSPEED

Mike White

It's the play on worlds
turning gets you from here
to the outermost sphere
of Ptolemaic non sequitur

since in the blink of an
island in the South Seas
you're reminding the brown hula girl
in drunken Petrarchan

she's like a frickin goddess
in that grass skirt
and won't she bless you
won't she touch you where it hurts

Thread

Mike White

We are forever waving

clumsily upon some threshold,
itching for a change of scenery

and its postponement, waving
vigorously goodbye hello goodbye.

My uncle who worked all his life
at an airport told this story,

the long elegant scarf flapping
beneath the blur of propellers,

and later, a ring finger found.

NATURAL HISTORY

Recounting the Seasons: Poems, 1958-2005. John Engels. University of Notre Dame Press, 2005.

James Walton

In his Foreward to this generous selection from a poet's life's work, David Huddle proposes, for a starting point, "The Garden in Late Summer" from *Walking to Cootehill* (1993):

> the world flowers: foxglove,
> hollyhock, calendula wrenched
> sunward, cosmos by its own weight
> downsprawled, cumuli
> of marigolds, beaded lily stalks,
> curl and shrivel of peony leaves,
> lightburst of gloriosas,
> and from the beds of alyssum, pink
> and white, shastas, dahlias,
> all grand manner of rose.

The passage is framed (and subtly inflected) by a consciousness of seasonal change that the poem takes personally. "Who among us," it begins, "can truly say/ he outlives the thick matters/ of cold?" At the end it reverts to summer's arrival, "bedizened, decorous,/ old, male and uncertain, riding/ conclusion, unwilling to last." No poem, of course, can epitomize the half-century's unfolding of a poet's craft and vision, but "The Garden in Late Summer," as Huddle suggests, seems a good place to start.

To a street-talking reviewer, John Engels appears to know all species of plant and animal life as if he had named them. He knows things (not mere phenomena) in their particularity, recounting their progress from the diluvial mud through an emergence into air and light to a violent shattering or slow, certain disintegration. In "Nothing Relents" (*Signals From the Safety Coffin*, 1975) the poem's "spade breaks through/ into the muddy cisterns of the earth," reveals a mock-resurrection of corpses disgorged by the flood, "digs like a legged worm/ into the belly of the planet." The plenitude of material objects forms a (nearly) impermeable barrier against abstraction, "transcendence," or the void.

Resistance to abstraction doesn't preclude an allegorical link between fishing and poetry. In "An Angler's *vade mecum*" (*Signals*) the poet's seasoned dedication to both enables a smooth accommodation between the literal sense and the dark conceit:

> there is considerable art
> to this, but it is best
> to speak flatly
>
> of such matters

Failure at this austere art involves an obtrusion of the personal—"the poet (myself)," he tells us in the Preface, "as hero":

> the salmon has eluded me.
> My shadow has fallen
> on the stream.

The shadow of the poem itself finds a place in the fish story:

> I have
>
> a *papier* model
> of a salmon. I am
> pleased with it, it is
> most natural, as a sportsman
> and angler the exact
> reproduction of natural objects
> appeals very much
> to me.

The reality effect is revisited in "Carving the Salmon" (*Sinking Creek*, 1998), where *papier* is exchanged for wood and the work-in-progress begins to assume an illusory appearance of life: "But it will be/ a long while before I learn/ to fashion the blood." In "Advice Concerning the Salmon Fly" from the same volume Engels returns to the question of craft:

> it is imperative
> that your pleasure in the making
> be not diminished by what no doubt
> will be error and mishandling enough.
>
> Remember, always, that craft is improved
> by exercise and discipline, in fact
> the vision (I mean this fly, this little roar of light...)
> . . . .

> being part
> of art's virtue, itself
>
> improves.

The art that improves by itself leaves room for mystery: "all this" the poem reminds us, is "merest recipe,"

> for the same fly tied by another, and apparently
> in detail of form and material utterly
>
> the same, may occasion twice
> the killing, or none
> at all, and what's
> to account for that?

In neither "*vade mecum*" nor "Advice" is the allegory developed at the expense of a highly particularized literal surface. The "artist's rod" is never less an angler's than a poet's, his "masterpiece" a real fish ("forty-three pounds"). Sometimes a catch is just a catch. The fusion of the poem and its referent draws attention to their separateness—a split that might serve as a (simplified) model for a body of work whose marked awareness of itself as poetry operates with and against—lets itself be drawn in or down by—the strong pull of the earth. "Come back," and again, "come back" becomes a refrain sung by the earth or the earthbound subject to those who have escaped its grasp. The phrase, usually repeated, seems merely enigmatic when heard by a speaker whose world has been colored by the gore of a slaughtered hen ("*terribilis est locus iste*," *Signals*). Its meaning is clear enough as a silent plea to the dead Christ, launched by the painted figures of Magdalen and John into the "intractable/ white field of the sky" ("The Fragonard, the Pietà, the Starry Sky," *Vivaldi in Early Fall*, 1981); as the bereaved poet's command, years after the event, to a child that died in infancy ("The Silence," *Cardinals in the Ice Age*, 1987); and as the appeal of earth itself to the speaker's old, addled, dying father, airborne for the first time ("Winter Flight," *Cardinals*). In just one instance—but shared by two poems—the words seem to come from a non-empirical place. In the long "Interlachen" (*Weather-Fear*, 1983) they penetrate an atmosphere rank with mortality. In "Eve Considers the Possibility of Pardon" (*House and Garden*, 2001) they accompany the sound of "a name we never clearly have heard." In both they're heard in a (mere?) dream where they descend with a "fragile rain" and must pass through the "delicate membrane of the fallen sky."

For the poet-as-empiricist, or -naturalist, *naming* (a key word in Engels) is the first imposed responsibility, and its limitations the principal challenge to a transgressive imagination. It follows that the figure of the poet in *House and Garden* should be Adam, abetted in this secular context by an Eve who not only shares the duty of naming but crosses more readily (as above) the line to the unnamable: "Everything," she declares in "Eve in the Garden at First Light," "Everything is named/ that I could name." But "much/ was beyond me. Too much," and she recalls the revelations of the *first* first light, "on which I hawked and choked" until "sight cleared and there before me, there they lay

> before me, the great meadows and mountains of the world,
> the morning rising, and the waters
> bursting and flooding up from the deepest centers
> of the earth, gathering, currenting, rushing down
>
> to pool in the low voids which filled and overflowed
> as I stood still close to breathless watching, all the while
> light exploding upward from beyond what I had not yet known
> to name as light, whereby I saw, I saw, and saw...

Now, in the sunrise of the fallen present, she sees again:

> Under the branches, in the green shadows of pines,
> the golden duff of pine needles softly
> thickens and the morning that enters the grove to drift
> among the scaling boles seems the remains of light—something,
>
> a further morning, a sea of light
> with no opposing shore,
> withdrawing.

Adam, for his part, resists at first the notion that the text of the world comes to us from elsewhere. For him the power to name has served as compensation for the Fall: "We've lost the kingdom, but borne away/ this greatest of its treasures" ("Adam Thinking Back"). His (postmodernist?) hubris has made him think he can "look down/ on the resumptive body of the world,"

> to make of it to see or touch,
> by which necessity
> it will bear names, and be. ("Adam Looking Down")

But his more characteristic note is one of disenchantment with the power of *his* "text," of language itself, to convey what is seen, heard smelled, and tasted of the earth's inexhaustible richness and changefulness. "Adam in November" dryly states the predicament of a series of projected figures of the poet himself:

I tend
to speak though lacking clarity,
not knowing the names, not having in need
the language, given to interminable

revision of the text. And this is where
the true anger locates itself,
that I have no ability or hope
that I may speak to the ordinary

with much in the way of truth or generosity.
And it must seem I make my rituals
to be the sole judge of the truth,
instead of what they are, mere sanctimonies

of procedure...and so
the names refuse themselves, and always it ends
in so unsatisfactory an obliquity as this.

In "Pilgrimage" (*Seasons in Vermont*, 1982), the poet ritually visits a river bank within a familiar precinct, "wishing to see the plain truth of maples in autumn,/ but wholly incapable, finding instead/ how exhaustible are the names of color." If he waits till dark, when the moon rises from the fog,

the trees will shine forth again
as if it were full day, in the last seasonal burst
of the last color for which, on this night
of a killing frost, my breath
visible before me, I cannot
and do not wish to find a name.

In "Letter" (*Big Water*, 1995), he complains of a loss of control that verges on entropy, prefiguring the collapse of Adam's demiurgic illusion, thwarted by the mutability of subject and object alike:

—you'll have
to imagine for yourself what I mean—lately,
though my eye for them persists,

the resemblances have begun
to resist my saying. This letter

is disorderly, I'm afraid, but things
are changing for me, therefore
for the world which over all these years
has accustomed itself
to being seen by me
in my particular way
and discovers it a grievous business
to have to reset itself, so that often
I wake up these days
in a confusion of recollection.

Together with "West Topsham" (*Blood Mountain*, 1977), "Letter" might be called "Confessions of a Repentant Overreacher." The earlier poem, also a letter, seems to have been (dis)composed by an aging, infirm Tom o' Bedlam. (Among Engels' personae a sense of physical decay acts as corollary to their moral and aesthetic anxieties.) "West Topsham's" poor Tom is a lover lost on the way to a reunion with his beloved, a poet estranged from his audience: "I think my words/ will echo only in my own mind forever, to what purpose/ I do not know." Recovery of the needed connection calls for a return to the "literal surface"—"and for all/ the extravagance of what has gone before I now repent,/ and make an image." The attempt fails—"I draw back always,/ I cannot be understood"—but "West Topsham," like "Letter," seems to succeed as one of a poet's periodic efforts to purge his work of its "obliquity," to create the space for such a pure "image" of estrangement as he provides in "Unfocusing on Window, Tree and Light" (*Cardinals*):

In one of those odd and idle
gestures of reconciliation
I have accustomed myself to make
toward the world I have through God's disfavor
lost, hoping to justify it

in the fullness and perfection
of a single word, I have proposed to myself
the locust tree against the sky,
its thorny branches enclosing light,
to be a figure of loss.

For formal restraint amid difficulties (indicated but obliquely in the prefatory "Short History of My Voice") the reader might choose among two very different sets of lyrics. In one of them, from *Vivaldi in Early Fall*, Engels impersonates three heroes of arts other than poetry. Van Gogh, prophesying the "Weathers of His Death," envisions the final state as a "dream without color" and constructs for it an image that anticipates the "figure of loss" from "Unfocusing":

> the way
> the slim branches of the young trees,
> themselves nothing like light,
> with the wind among them turned and brightened.

In place of "dead silence," the composer in " Mahler Waiting" wishes for an apocalyptic crescendo, a music to untune the sky:

> the clashing
> of boulders, trees battering one
> another, floods, tornadoes, the fires
> bellowing outward
> from the deep heart of the world!

In the volume's title piece the aged Vivaldi turns Fall to a kind of Spring:

> the pines
> just beginning to sing
> on the hillside, the rivers
> coloring with the first rains
> (which are, as usual, precisely
> on time). And there is also
>
> this young girl

Toward the end he returns to the beginning "in full belief," and "the face of God"

> passes through my walls to show me
> how the motion of song sleeps
> at the center of the world, as indeed,
> among the Angels, innocent of time.

A second class of poems deserving praise for their formal economy (and more) consists in a series of laments, not elegies, spanning more than two decades, on the death of Philip Stephen Engels, August 21-October 24, 1965. The earliest poems in this cycle (from *The Homer Mitchell Place*, 1968) are in quatrains that act as a measure of restraint. But their rhymes turn sharply slant or vanish and their meter becomes faintly irregular as if broken by a grief and rage impatient of the formalities and of the "music" of verse, like the last lines of Blake's "Holy Thursday" (*Songs of Experience*):

> "And because I am happy & dance & sing,
> They think they have done me no injury,
> And are gone to praise God & his Priest & King
> Who make up a heaven of our misery."

Later, in a section called "Exorcisms" (*Signals*) Engels provides, as a counter-example, an immaculate "Sestina: My Dead in the First Snow," closely followed by the shattering of the frame in "Nothing Relents," where he is "torn by the alarums" of his voice

> to cry out into the dazzle of Thy
> high noon O God such anger
> festers in the tree the flood the stone such
>
> bile and storm surge in the root and beasts
> in the foul walls race the planet bursting swelled
> with ripeness fat with fatness open to the light and I
>
> like a blind grub twisting in light
> mandibles wide in spasm the cold
> talus falling back and in the chasm squirming

The concluding three-line envoy of the quieter "Sestina" is left open, echoing the poem's most insistent theme—"It will take a long time"—assurance that the poet's history of grief will remain free of any fatuous (and now hackneyed) gestures toward "closure." The note of loss will persist beyond the last of the Philip poems.

By Engels' own account the loss of the child banished, "abruptly and violently," the poet as hero from the center of his earliest work, changing its direction. Place—northern Indiana, Wisconsin, Maine, Ireland, Yugoslavia and, above all, Vermont—came to predominate over personality; and over place, a power that he does not name, "nature" seeming by now too domesticated a word for the manifold and mobile, light-giving, dark and devouring force, by turns seething or "cold" and "dead" at its center, that is presented in these poems with unsurpassed scope and precision. Engels' "nature," in Joycean parlance, is a concretely realized "audible-visible-gnosible-edible world." Yet throughout the eleven volumes represented here (together with a group of uncollected poems), the theme of loss merges with a sense of the insufficiency of language, personified at last in the figure of Adam. Poet as hero finds a successor in poet *manqué*. The misgiving is hardly a new thing among poets. The perception of writing itself as "supplement" has been taken in more senses than one. It can signify the mere artificial tracing of an order of things (however elusive) already complete in itself, or the making up for a deficiency, a lack, in that order. Either way, the street-talking reviewer, sadly unattuned to the original, no less than a substantial class of less disadvantaged readers, will return with gratitude and admiration to John Engels' supplement for "a long time."

THE PROTESTANT ETHIC AND THE SPIRIT OF POETRY

Leaving. Laton Carter. University of Chicago Press, 2004. *Classic Rough News.* Kenneth Fields. University of Chicago Press, 2005. *Capacity.* James McMichael. Farrar, Straus and Giroux, 2006.

Robert Archambeau

In his ponderous classic of sociology, *Economy and Society*, Max Weber tells us a thing or two about the Protestants whose ethic of self-denial has formed the basis of modern capitalism:

> The person who lives as a worldly ascetic is a rationalist, not only in the sense that he rationally systematizes his own conduct, but also in his rejection of everything that is ethically irrational, aesthetic, or dependent upon his own emotional reactions to the world and its institutions. The distinctive goal always remains the alert, methodical control of one's own pattern of life and behavior.

The economic payoff for those who embraced these traits was quite significant, often resulting in their rise to positions of surprising prominence given the origins of their creed in a rejection of worldliness. But as every student of sociology knows, the realm of non-popular culture is a kind of economic world turned upside down, where the ordinary rules don't always apply. In the little world of American poetry, for instance, you can't expect a whole lot of payoff for embodying such stereotypically Protestant qualities as restraint in expression, emotional reserve, a relentless self-examination of the private conscience, and an individualism tending toward isolation. While in the Weberian economic world such qualities lead to great payoffs in terms of economic capital, in the poetry world they actually impede the accumulation of cultural capital in the form of prizes, awards, and widespread critical acclaim. That, at any rate, is the conclusion to which a contemplation of the poetry of Laton Carter, Kenneth Fields, and James McMichael tends to lead us.

I'm not entirely sure about the religious backgrounds of Carter, Fields, and McMichael—the surnames are plausibly Protestant, although the title of Fields' forthcoming novel, *Father of Mercies*, gives one pause. Be that as it may, all three write poetry very much in what one might call a stereotypically Protestant manner of expression: tending to plain statement, gun-shy when it comes to heated emotion, obsessively self-analytic, wary of gaudy images, suspicious of the irrational, and, in some measure, tending toward individual isolation. Emotional reticence has been on the outs in poetry ever since Robert Lowell shocked his eminently WASP ancestors with *Life Studies*, and self-analytic individualism has been largely eclipsed since the rise of identity politics and its aesthetics of group affiliation. Plain statement has suffered a few blows, too, first at the hands of the deep image aesthetic, and again during the current triumph of a watered-down, hybridized language poetry that too-often amounts to little more than a smug version of nonsense verse.

Perhaps these shifts in taste have been behind the late emergence of Laton Carter, whose remarkable first book went unpublished for eleven years after an early draft served as his MFA thesis. That the acknowledgements page cites only two journals as venues where poems from the collection previously appeared is further testament to the hostility of the current editorial climate toward his particular poetic. Kenneth Fields and James McMichael have also received few enough of the accolades accorded to American poets, although McMichael's new elevation to the respectable status of a Farrar, Straus, Giroux poet indicates that his stock is on the rise. But compared to their Stanford classmates, the former poets laureate Robert Hass and Robert Pinsky, Fields and McMichael have both been relatively unrecognized talents. This speaks less of the relative merits of the poets, I think, than of the shape of the American poetic field, and the kinds of poetic virtues it is most prepared to reward.

That Fields and McMichael share certain low-key poetic virtues is by no means an accident: both were students of that anachronistically Augustan poet, Yvor Winters. Winters advocated a poetry of plain statement, emotional reserve, and relentless examination of the self. His abhorrence of the irrational was legendary, his defense of reason absolute. While poets like Hass and Pinsky learned from Winters and moved on, Fields and McMichael engaged with him more deeply. McMichael's doctoral dissertation is an application of Wintersian ideas to poets unexamined in Winters' critical work, and Fields was hand-picked by Winters to be his successor at Stanford —a post Fields holds to this day. Laton Carter is too young to have been a student of Winters, but he studied under McMichael at UC-Irvine, and seems to have been drawn to McMichael for his more Augustan qualities. All three poets are in some meaningful sense in the tradition of Winters, without being doctrinaire followers, and all three have to some degree been kept at the margins of a poetic field that has never quite been able to appreciate the kind of work they do. I don't imagine they'll be the main beneficiaries of whatever new taste emerges from the wreckage that has ensued from the collision of Iowa confessionalism and Buffalo language poetry. This, of course, only gives us all the more reason to take the time to appreciate them for their very real, and somewhat unusual, qualities.

Max Weber would certainly recognize Laton Carter's virtues as typical of the Protestant temperament. Consider the opening lines of "Counter," a poem in which an unemployed man makes a short shopping trip:

> He writes *6 a.m., 7 a.m.,* down to noon,
> and starts again with numbers,
> all with spaces in between for the half-hour.
>
> If, at six, he feeds the cats, follows the template he's
> tried to leave as open as possible,
> he can feel better about what he's doing.

One imagines Weber taking out his carefully sharpened pencil and writing, in a tight hand, some marginal notes about how the man in the poem "rationally systematizes his own conduct," and how this sort of deliberate self-control embodies the notion of an "alert, methodical control of one's own pattern of life and behavior." When, a few lines later, we see that the man feels "guilty, self-reproaching" and "returns two books he bought yesterday" we can imagine Weber noting the deep suspicion of impulse, and the rejection of immediate emotional reactions to the world.

Perhaps the same concern with carefulness and deliberateness that lies behind a poem like "Counter" informs Carter's poetics of clear, direct statement. His poems often have something like a clear thesis statement, and proceed in a mixed expository and narrative manner not unlike a well-written essay. He is not a poet trying to imitate the idiosyncratic cross-currents of the stream of consciousness, nor does he try to give you a sense of the mind as it tries out different avenues of thought. Instead of a drama of mental process, he wants to deliver well-tuned products of careful meditation. Here, for example, is the beginning of "Silence," a poem that proposes a general thesis, then illustrates and complicates that thesis:

> There is an unmeasured distance between two people that means,
> if they do not already know each other, they do not have to talk.
>
> The distance narrowed, the two points moving toward each other,
> causes decision: what necessary act of salutation or aloofness.
>
> Glass dividing this distance obviates the act.
> Behind a windshield of double-pane storm window,
>
> a person's separation allows for closer, less regulated study of the other.

We're at a far pole from the elliptical poetry of a John Ashbery here, and at a farther one still from the disjunctive poetics that have become so fashionable. We're operating in a mode more like that of the Augustans, with their essayistic verse. We're also operating far outside of the norms of the old-fashioned poetry workshop, with its emphasis on the showing of concrete detail. What could be more abstract than the description of two people walking in opposite directions than "two points moving toward each other"? It's wonderfully spare, distant, and minimalist— it's almost geometry.

I don't think it's a coincidence that so many of the people in Carter's poems seem to exist at a remove from those around them, seeking connections that never quite come into being. It seems of a piece with the rest of Carter's sensibility that this would be the case: scrupulous self-policing deliberateness is rarely the product of a warm and all-embracing community. Since I've already invited one German sociologist into this review, I'm tempted to invite another, Ferdinand Toennies, to explain the phenomenon. Toennies is the creator of the *gemeinschaft-gesselschaft* distinction, a dichotomy that distinguishes pre-modern from modern society. In pre-modern *gemeinschaft* societies, community is organic, interactions are face-to-face, and interactions are governed by traditions. Modern *gesselschaft* societies have none of this warmth. Capitalistic and industrial, such societies are highly administered, socially atomized, and emphasize interactions governed by rules or laws. In the world of *gemeinschaft* you are born into a definite social position and belong there; in the world of *gesselschaft*, you're on your own, one atom among others. Needless to say, *gesselschaft* is the world built by Weber's Protestant ethos, with all of its self-policing deliberateness. *Gesselschaft* also seems to be the natural habitat of Laton Carter's characters, who yearn for the warmth of human connection from a great distance. Here, for example, in lines from Carter's "Silence," we see the speaker watching an unsuspecting person's face through a window:

> The kinesics of the face, watched unmonitored from a distance,
> issues its own private speech. When the distance is at once collapsed,
>
> the face's eyes drawing a line to the watcher's eyes, the speech too collapses.

The irony is palpable: in Carter's world, we come closest to really knowing each other when we catch each other unawares and give away some element of ourselves other than our public personae. When we actually encounter each other face-to-face, we withdraw behind our social roles. It's chilly in Carter's neighborhood, and not neighborly at all.

Even the titles of Carter's poems indicate reserve and isolation: the volume includes poems with names like "Unspoken," "New Distances," "Separate," "Brief Hesitiation," and "Tentative" (the last of which contains the statement "A thought can be stepped back from, / watched from a close remove"—something very close to Carter's *ars poetica*). Although Carter shies away from traditional rhyme and meter, many of the poems in *Leaving* follow the general form of the sonnet, containing fourteen lines and turning either between an octave and a sestet or after three quatrains. This is surely a further expression of Carter's concern with the deliberate and the controlled. Word on the street (by which I mean the internet) is that his next book will consist entirely of sonnets. One hopes it won't be another eleven years in arriving.

Ken Fields is also drawn to the sonnet in its looser manifestations. Almost all of the 64 poems gathered in *Classic Rough News* are sonnets of sorts: fourteen-liners, loosely rhythmic, occasionally working with rhyme, and sometimes involving the *volta*, or rhetorical turn, of the traditional sonnet. They are inhabited by a cast of imagined characters reminiscent of those populating the psychological territory of John Berryman's *Dream Songs*. Where Berryman had his Henry and Mr. Bones, Fields has alter-egos named Billy, Billie, and Burton. As their names indicate, Billy and Billie are doubles of sorts: male and female versions of psychologically fragile violence-prone alcoholics tending toward multiple personalities. Burton, too, manifests in many guises: he resonates at some times with Robert Burton, author of *The Anatomy of Melancholy*, at other times with the explorer and erotic *litterateur* Richard Francis Burton, and once with the Richard Burton who played opposite Elizabeth Taylor in *Cleopatra*. In Fields' pages we meet Burton academic, Burton erotic, Burton alcoholic, Burton cinematic, but above all we meet Burton melancholic. Together with the various personalities of Billy and Billie and the poet *in propria persona*, it's quite a posse.

The core influence behind the book isn't Berryman, though: it's Yvor Winters. The Wintersian doctrine was Augustan not only in its embrace of clear, expository, discursive verse, but in its distrust of impulse. For Winters, our great challenge in life was to resist our instinctive desires and impulses, and it is this element of Winters' (very Weberian) ethos that we see most prominently in *Classic Rough News*. But where Winters liked to celebrate his hard-won victories over impulse, Fields' book tells a tale of failed resistance, of impulse distrusted but, more often as not, yielded to. The melancholy that pervaded the book is the melancholy of the junkie, the addict, the frequently failing policer of instinct and desire. Sometimes it is erotic impulse that Fields distrusts, as in "Eyewhite Nightlight," where the temptation represented by "That scrap of shredded paper in your wallet / The number scrawled in a stranger's hand" becomes one of "the tiny pale white flowerlets of our pain." More frequently, though, the distrusted impulse it is the lure of drugs or alcohol. In "Right Now," for example, Fields remembers the days when he was never without "a drink in his hand," when he

> held his breath while smoke
> Filled as much of him as he could stand
> Till, letting it out, he sought oblivion
> Of the trace of memory or anticipation,
> And his life fell into a death spiral.

Now, from a position of ever-tenuous recovery, he meets others who live as he once lived, and "talks to the ones who are not even sure / They want to learn how to stop killing themselves." The necessary resistance to the lure of oblivion was a great topic of Yvor Winters, who liked to make much of this theme in Keats' "Ode to a Nightingale," and it is a central theme of Fields' book as well. Like Keats and Winters, Fields has felt the full strength of the attraction he so distrusts. In "The Hinge," a poem near the end of the collection, Fields begins by revisiting all of his characters—addicts and alcoholics, his oblivion-loving Billies and Burtons—then goes on to explore the origins of his own obsession. Remembering a childhood moment when he underwent surgery, he recollects how, on his recovery,

> the nurse told me
> "I've seen a lot of little boys dragged in here
> For this business, but not a one of them
> Ever said he loved the ether."

None, that is, until Fields, whose dangerous impulses seem to run very deep indeed.

It isn't just the impulse toward oblivion that Fields distrusts. In his world even our nobler impulses turn out to be dangerous. "A Country Story," for example, retells an old family story from Fields' grandmother, in which a mother sends her German measles-stricken daughter away to quarantine. When the rest of the family seems to fall ill too, the mother's acts on a loving impulse and brings the quarantined daughter back so the family can die together. This impulse proves fatal, though: the family had not really fallen ill, and the formerly quarantined daughter brings the disease back with her, fatally infecting her sister.

Fields does not confine himself to the examination of dubious impulse, though. He writes of personal humiliation, he writes poems in which he laments his own constant self-examination and self-recrimination. He only really falls flat in the poems where he vents academic spleen, complaining about dimwitted administrators, petty colleagues, and various faddish theoretical tendencies (I'd be in a better position to complain about the pettiness of these poems if I hadn't written too many of the species myself). But the theme to which he constantly returns is that of the need to keep impulse in check, and his own failure to fulfill that need. Perhaps Fields puts the matter most concisely in "Being of Sound Mind," in which he says of his alter-ego Burton "For years he'd been a cultist of control / With none for himself." An ever-prodigal Wintersian, a backsliding Weberian protestant, a clear-eyed chronicler of a flawed self—with *Classic Rough News* Fields has given us his confession.

James McMichael has written his share of poems about dubious emotional impulses—they form the core of his early book *Against the Falling Evil*—but his new collection, *Capacity* is remarkable for its ability to keep the emotions at a distance. *Capacity* consists of seven poems, or perhaps I should say seven parts, since they do add up to a single, book-length whole. *Capacity* is a strangely disparate and restrained book, but no more so than his earlier long poems. Like the first of McMichael's truly ambitious long poems, "Itinerary" from 1978's *The Lover's Familiar*, *Capacity* takes on matters of historical importance (in "Itinerary" his matter was the expedition of Lewis and Clark; in the present volume he addresses the Irish potato famine at some length). Like *Four Good Things* (McMichael's book-length poem of 1980) *Capacity* contains many apparently disparate topics. I'm not sure which of the two books wins the prize for breadth. As Robert Hass put it in an early review, *Four Good Things* is a poem about "worry, death, taxes, planning, probability theory, insomnia, stamp collecting, cancer, domestic architecture, sex manuals, the Industrial Revolution, and real estate." *Capacity* begins with a book of photographs of the English countryside, goes on to describe the wave forces working in the North Atlantic, comments on the nature of Newtonian space, describes a scene of family drama, details the process of human fertilization and gestation, outlines chilling episodes from Irish history, and works its way back to the book of photographs via World War Two and the nature of the will to live. You be the judge. *Capacity* also has much in common with *Each in a Place Apart*, McMichael's 1994 effort, most notably in its deep distrust of our most primal impulses, especially our sexual urges, which leads to ill-advised actions in both books. Like all of McMichael's long poems, *Capacity* is discursive, a poem almost essayistic in its drive to lay its materials out in expository fashion.

One could make a pretty good case for the Protestant ethic of McMichael's verse just on the basis of what we've covered so far: a sober, essayistic poem distrustful of the primal drives is in some meaningful sense a Weberian poem. But there's more. *Capacity* is notable for the strangeness of both its syntax and its diction, both of which seem designed to distance us from the immediate emotional pull of the dramatic, sometimes even melodramatic, subject matter. While most poets who invert syntax do so to add to the music and emotional punch of a statement, McMichael seems to aim at an interestingly opposite effect. These lines, for example, come from a section of the poem dealing with the urgent needs of soon-to-be-separated lovers in wartime. A man thinks of his own mind as a garden, and:

> He practices his absence
>
> as the stilled reflecting surface of its pool.
> With features of her person in his
> stead there,
> to what is not its
>
> own anymore in wanting
> the self is sent
> back by the other.

Odd, isn't it? That second sentence would read more easily, and deliver its emotional weight more directly, had its clauses been ordered otherwise. But McMichael doesn't want that, he wants us to experience emotion from a greater distance.

McMichael employs all sorts of devices in pursuit of this emotional distancing, including the symmetrical A-B-B-A pattern of the chiasmus, which makes an appearance here, in lines describing the changing way of gardening in England in the nineteenth century:

> Need had been made less natural.
> Replaced was the old
> productive ideal that the useful
>
> good was desired.
>
> The desired good was
> useful in the new ideal.

I suppose we shouldn't be surprised. McMichael's enduring scholarly interest is Joyce, who made of the chiasmus the organizing principle behind *A Portrait of the Artist as a Young Man.*

You've probably already noticed the unusual nature of McMichael's diction, which even in these short passages seems remarkably abstract. He often uses terms from logic or the sciences, especially physics and biology, to describe events not normally discussed in such terms. Here, for example, is a passage on the Irish famine of the 1840s:

> Persons are
> separate in time when they are living.
> when certain maincrop tuberous parts go on being
>
> missed at the hearth, back as
>
> one again with time are persons now
> outside it for good.

With "tuberous parts" the language of biology steps in for the colloquial (and, in this context, emotionally loaded) word "potato." And the business about being inside or outside of time picks up on some very abstract physics-talk from earlier in the book. It is a very accurate, but tremendously emotionally restrained, depiction of the situation. McMichael is not one to gush, or to invite his readers to shiver with emotion, at least not in any immediate way.

Perhaps the most extreme instance of this curious distancing comes in a passage in which a man and a woman who share emotionally-charged secrets meet after a long absence. When they come together, the as-yet unspoken emotion strains at their fragile composure:

> His having come could pass for a family call.
>
> She can take it as that. So can he,
>
> if beyond the frugal
> greeting she tenders
> she does not speak.

When she finally does speak, after a two-page buildup, we don't hear the words, nor are we told about her tone. Instead, we get an almost clinical description of the process of speech:

> ...the next column of
>
> breath she issues still gives
> nothing away.

Not so

the column after. As it leaves,
the lappets that she draws around it
make it tremble so positions of the
tongue, teeth, lips and jaw can sound it

abroad

I suppose we could interpret the tremble in her voice as emotion, but then again it could simply be a matter of the formation of a vowel-sound. What is significant here is the way McMichael chooses to depict moments of intense emotion: with restraint, and through the least-emotionally charged perspective possible. You can't get much farther from the spontaneous overflow of powerful emotion than this. It is this anti-Romanticism, this Protestant ethic, that makes McMichael a rare and important figure in contemporary poetry.

The Protestant ethos in poetry, embodied variously in Carter's careful self-analysis, Fields' self-recrimination, or McMichael's masterful acts of distancing and emotional control, will leave some readers cold. The dominant poetic tastes of our time tend toward cleverness, emotionalism, or both, and those who have absorbed those tastes uncritically just won't know what to do with poems like these. We would do well to let this be their loss, not ours.

PASSAGING IS HIS ANCHORAGE

Red Strawberry Leaf: Selected Poems, 1994-2001. John Peck. Chicago: The University of Chicago Press, 2005.

Igor Webb

Reading John Peck's most recent selection of poems, *Red Strawberry Leaf* (2005), roused memories of my first real lesson in poetry, from Mrs. Feldschuh of Brooklyn Technical High School, who taught that encountering a poem is like entering worlds not your own. In the case of John Peck, whose uncompromising career has brought him to a place far from the centers of contemporary poetic practice, the sense of reading your way into other worlds is strong and palpable. Peck's work is situated on a high plateau resting on two, at first glance distant, foundations. One is theology. Peck is a religious poet. Behind each of his poems are the questions of Gaugin's famous Polynesian painting: Where do we come from? What are we? Where are we going? Peck looks for the answers to these questions in theology, an inescapably bookish and not infrequently arcane affair. *Red Strawberry Leaf,* for example, opens with three obscure epigraphs, one from Ecclesiastes, one attributed to the dying Thomas Aquinas, and one from the Flower Ornament Sutra. What binds these quotations is the premise of the Flower Ornament Sutra, which, if you are unfamiliar with it, reveals a cosmos of infinite interpenetration of things, suggested by the image of a world text in which each word consists of the phenomena that make up the world; the text is vast as the cosmos but every atom contains the text ("To see a world in a grain of sand."). *Red Strawberry Leaf* is the culmination, mature and assured, of a lifetime devoted to crafting a discipline and a form capable of conveying this dizzying notion ("World is one action," Peck writes in "Single Wing," "and where is the measure for it?")

In addition to theology, Peck's work also draws on the great oral literatures, especially the Greek. In oral cultures, language does things we have long ago shifted to other powers: it brings the rain, it stops the rain; it heals the sick, it wounds enemies. It speaks to the living in the presence of not exactly the dead as much as the legends of the tribe (a word that shows up often in Peck's poems). As the American Indian writer N. Scott Momaday has pointed out (Momaday, like Peck, is a Stanford writer and student of Yvor Winters), in the oral tradition stories are possessed by the person, have to be memorized and thus become part, literally, of the body. Print allows us to store words, to leave them and then when we need them to retrieve them once more. In the oral tradition there is no distinction between words and flesh: words are of the body and produced, as voice, by the body. Print culture obscures these qualities of words. Peck's precise vocabulary, which often sends his reader (and certainly *this* reader) to the dictionary, is one feature of his prophetic ministry, of his aiming to make sacred once more that which our contemporary world has obscured. Having lost the visceral *elan* of language, we can only be brought to awareness by being thrust back into unfamiliarity, to be made novices and divested of our dulled but voluble sophistication. Similarly, the world of the oral tradition, like the world of theology, is regulated by, and profoundly responsive to, natural rhythms and patterns, which are also obscured by contemporary technological culture. When you can turn up the heat to keep warm in the cold, or buy strawberries year round, your sense of cold and strawberries gets dulled; pattern is obscured; nature recedes—and with it, meaning. Or that meaning of which Peck's word-world is composed, and without which the sacralization of experience—the goal of Peck's poetic quest?—is unattainable.

Peck's journey—the dominant metaphor of his writing—occurs necessarily within our post-World War II history: but it occurs in the presence of history full stop and in the company of historians and other makers of poetry. In "Transmission Lines," a poem addressed to "E.G.B., visiting after ten years in 2001," the poet recalls Robert McNamara being attacked on the ferry to Martha's Vineyard, an incident which he recounts in a kind of simultaneity of narrative—

> And this time Laios was recognized at the crossroads,
> the father who in his panic had deep-sixed—
> so he thought—an abomination, his deadly child.
> Yet this time not even his own boy: a stranger, blank
> confronter: so many sons...

Peck is not happy about our time (are *you*?) but he accepts his role in it, with a curious mix of humility and grandness. He says to E.G.B.:

> And now, friend, your visitation.
> Your Pindar, your Mithraic converts to Paul,
> your Homer, hanging back with you at ten paces,
> are curious—a little—to see what I'll do.

Those looking on, and to whom Peck usually looks for example, are many and various, ranging from great figures of art and history to John Peck aged six. For the most part this looking is not about figuring out what's right or about whether one measures up or about what to do or even about *how* to do things—all core aspects of initiation—but about vision. I mean that Peck is not interested in himself or the Great as persons; his theology is not about getting into heaven but about Being. In a beautiful, complex, revealing poem in the second part of *Red Strawberry Leaf,* titled "Anangke," the young Peck, aged six, is taken by his mother up the belltower of Riverside Church, overlooking the Hudson near Columbia University in Manhattan. Anangke is the primal goddess of Necessity. She has no parent or maker but appears at the moment of creation, wrapped in the coils of her complement and mate, Kronos, the god of Time. Between them these two split matter into the order of the universe. They are what must be and what can be (fate and history). They reign way above the poor little gods we spend so much time worrying about; they ARE and cannot Not Be. The young Peck is stunned by the bells, experiencing but not understanding—of course—what's happening. The mature poet can clarify what the boy could not grasp—for example, what the boy "felt as fear" the man can "decode as wonder." Caught in the belltower in the resonance of overwhelming sound, Peck instructs his younger self, is not to be "above things, really, but entirely within them." What is the lesson of the poet's recollection of this moment in time? He tells his younger self: "And you have been the thing struck into sound"—which is a good answer to Gaugin's question, What are we?

As "Anangke" demonstrates—and Peck shows us over and over—there isn't anything to be done about Being. There is, rather, the question of one's readiness: each moment we are suffused with light, sound, vibrations that we do not see, we do not hear, we do not feel. The discipline of awareness can however be like a cell-phone: a mechanical tuning-in to a very restricted wave length. That's the danger of our time. Peck wants something else, as he tells us in "Rhyming with Davie's Sonnet in Mandelshtam's Hope for the Best":

> Bottom-dwellers, crawdads, we're not to fly
> too far…yet so we must come of age, not with
> fire but silt. For now sky rides in the earth,
> its dizzying reaches—quarriers of marble
> open a way, the worm's jaws are a-zing
> with nebulae and the cycles, up the scarp
> of a tiny peak within crawls my double, whirls
> misting him; through them, valleys, orchards in
> bloom, winking lakes with pike to be hooked and netted….

Peck accepts the price Anangke has exacted for his reverence for this vision. Uncompromising, a man living in our heedless time, he is fated to write on the margins of contemporary literary practice. At best, after all, a poet like Peck, writing in the prophetic or Bardic tradition, the declamatory tradition of Blake, Whitman, and Pound, is an isolated, unappreciated, misunderstood, and not infrequently maligned voice. People don't want to hear, have lost the disciplines needed to hear, what he has to say. Peck has some of Blake's and Pound's anger at the boobocracy, and probably not enough of Whitman's lustful *jouissance.* But joyful or not, Blake, Whitman, Pound…did not live with much in the bank, each was courted by madness, and whatever the number of their disciples, the room was not overly full at their deaths. Peck can count his blessings. He is admirably sane. He doesn't have to etch his books himself or publish them at home or write his own reviews. He has readers. That he doesn't have more readers, let the record show, is our fault.

POETS OF OUR SUFFERING

The Whispering Gallery. William Logan. London: Penguin Books, 2005. *Approximately Paradise.* Floyd Skloot. Dorset, VT: Tupelo Press, 2005.

James Matthew Wilson

William Logan's work has frequently elicited comparison with W.H. Auden and Robert Lowell, and for good reason. In Logan's insightful and salted vision of modern poetry, the two poets stand as the masters, though hardly the representatives, of their age. Auden is our knight errant of poetic form and unbuttoned Horace of public art, Lowell the Caliban of savagely vivid language and, of course, the self-referential persona that reinvents itself as it adapts poetic conventions to present needs. These are the two figures of the recent literary past whom Logan holds up as great and effectively takes as models for his own poetry.

Only Lowell, or rather, only the "confessional" aspect of Lowell (an adjective Logan alternately questions and modifies) strikes him as bequeathing a legacy to contemporary poetry; we are all familiar with the backyard epiphanies and lurid brief narratives that fill out the more coherent if less challenging pages of our literary magazines. It is this aspect that Logan most frequently rejects, in hopes of salvaging the savage and stentorian brilliance of Lowell's language, not only in the early metaphysical poems, but in *For the Union Dead* and the late sonnets as well. This language has haunted Logan's poems since very early in his career. In the burning and clenched poems of *Difficulty* (1983), for example, we hear: "The evening light slaps the orchard floor / where twisting sprinklers hurl their load / through gnarled lines of peaches." If the verbal tensions in this stilled, unpeopled scene intimate violence, the remainder of the poem confirms it with radiating images of the preying of a snake and the deliberate movements of soldiers in a minefield. Personal agony, but especially the torture of our public history, insinuate themselves into every line of Logan's early lyrics as well as those more recent. This gift for the pained expression, for stanzas of bent wire, is Logan's chief inheritance from Lowell.

But *Macbeth in Venice* (2003), Logan's sixth book of poems, allowed the public style of Auden to glimmer forth in unprecedented ways. Divided into four sections that function formally as long poems, *Macbeth* eschews the personal at every turn. Opaque though "The Shorter Aeneid" frequently is, it remains a poem about history, about exile and the displacements of World War II. The more playful "Punchinello in Chains" and "Macbeth in Venice," offer hints of Audenesque humor; they show their debts to the English poet even more so in their use of almost medieval tableaux to frame broken but moralized narratives. "Punchinello" reminds one of "Musée de Beaux Arts" mixed with Auden's sonnet sequences; "Macbeth" is an unmistakable abbreviated pastiche of *The Sea and the Mirror*. Most remarkably, the series of travel poems grouped under "Venetian Hours," which cry out for a character, for an embodiment of its voice, refuse the request. As in much of Logan's early work, their language, metered according to an undersea telegraph, and mailed and maimed like the statue "The Massacre of the Holy Innocents" describes, obeys the strictures of the concrete and the objective as it moves from disappointment to decay to terror. The poems in the volume as a whole move with Auden's zest from fixed forms to open rhymed stanzas, as well as to loose blank verse tercets that Logan has established as his more satisfactory equivalent to Auden's syllabics.

For this reason, *The Whispering Gallery* appears as something of a departure, although it may better be described as comprising the side of Logan's work born under the sign of Lowell. The poems in the volume return and return again to private moments of tension between the violence of endings and beginnings, past and future, as the last poem in the volume, "The Old Burying Ground" concludes:

> The promises the living swear
> betray their long decrease –
> the mourner's lie In Memory Of,
> the fraud of Rest in Peace,
>
> where buried on this sacred ground,
> in frozen, barren earth,
> lie the distant soiled past
> and frenzied rage of birth.

Desecration and anger, and worry over their fate and impact in the present guide Logan's new book in directions that are, initially, more accessible and engaging than the marmoreal mazes of *Macbeth*. Venice has served, and continues to serve, him as an image of opulence and decadence, of sweltering pocket empires whose achievements are slowly sinking into the sea. Similar paradoxes of place appear in "Welcome to Paradise" and other poems, where "paradise" in its Edenic and absolute sense crosses unfortunate paths with "paradise" as the banal name by which we describe the fruitful but rotting and polluted landscapes of Florida: "Passed by rusting cars bearing bored / children, the gator on the peeling billboard // looks down on the roadside attractions and recommends / they stay shuttered for the winter that never ends."

These are vivid and ominous poems, and generally are the more so for the presence of an identifiable character, which allows us to understand why such landscapes should educe such language. To a degree often lacking in Logan's earlier books, the sense of a narrative helpfully intrudes and gives the imagery a meaning that it could only promise or threaten in the past. That said, one is put off by some of the narrated tricks that read like punch-lines but are really unprovoked stabs. After a lengthy description of a self and a world, the speaker in "The Rotting Stars" suddenly confides, "I knew then that my mother was dead. / Yet she wasn't dead." This is as perplexing a pair of statements in context as out of it. There are other unearned shocks within.

The frequent successes and occasional failures of the poems that open the book almost seem practice pieces once one reaches the long "Penitence" that occupies the middle third of the volume. Here the figure of suspension between birth and death offers itself as a form for meditation, a theme to be refigured in twenty-six nineteen-line poems written in that same loose pentameter. Each section turns about the persistence of past sins and evils as well as the almost promised oblivion of death and the future; this concept Logan characteristically grounds in the concrete of landscape: "The lake turns a circle through Ptolemy's spheres, / nested one in another like Dante's *malebolgia*." Appropriately the historical turns of sin are primarily public and mortal events that Logan is careful not to absorb into a narcissistic "autodrama." As, for instance, "Jews," where, "Death dines with a reservation,"

> never too hungry, knowing his next meal will come:
> the ash, the dust of unwilling dust.
> Years after the war, the towns had lost their synagogues.
>
> No one living remembered where they had been.

No passage could better illustrate the two maxims that echo throughout. The first, "We are responsible / to the sins that gave birth to us." The second, the hideousness of present and past alike do not result in wisdom but exact further penalties on the defeated through forgetfulness and ignorance: "a century later, / knowing their fate as they could not, as others / will know our fates, though we cannot." These concerns Logan draws into the circumference of a central persona, thus drawing the poem as a whole closer to the tradition of Lowell's late sonnets of confession, intimacy and history.

The volume is less an achievement than *Macbeth* primarily because it is on this one, well-constructed but sometimes tediously worded, long poem that it must be judged. The earlier poems, often good in themselves get lost with the ambition of "Penitence." The last third of the volume is more varied, and indeed includes several pastiches of Auden that are amusing but remain merely pastiche. "Odalisque" and a handful of raw sexual poems are well executed, but seem more attempts to rework Lowell's "confessionalism" on Logan's terms than poems of lasting merit.

‡ ‡ ‡

Last winter, in a local cafe, I watched a man guide his very old mother, an evident Alzheimer's victim, to a table by the window steamed with the interior warmth. He went to order at the counter, but had almost immediately to return as she began to cry, lost in the crowded and unfamiliar room. After failing to calm her, he had to lead her back out, back to their car, back to their home, the invisible powers of a disease *as* confining and *more* frightening than any prison walls.

Such a moment epitomizes pathos rather than tragedy, and it takes great skill to respect the suffering of the sick and their families while also grasping and transforming it into a work of art. Floyd Skloot is the first poet I have run across in possession of such powers. Though far too many poets have tried to paste pathos on the page, hoping to overwhelm with raw power and impress with a rather egoistic display of profound feeling, Skloot impresses with an ear attuned to the counterpoint of sentence rhythm, rhyme and meter, and with the true artist's commitment to making the most private and personal suffering revealable to others through a selfless attention to the vivid scene and dispassionate narrative.

His poems depict artists past the height of their powers, who stand in almost symbolic relation to the literal victims of age and disease. Tragedy, Aristotle tells us, is the failure brought upon a man through a flaw in his otherwise great character. Skloot's chronicles of pathos depict the human individual (sometimes distinguished by accomplishment, sometimes simply by being family) who is robbed of his rightful powers through what is literally internal, but is external to the soul and therefore feels like an act of violence or confinement. Why, beginning with Yeats, did poets take for theme the "unjust" fastening of the soul to a failing body, including a failing brain? Such a question requires an explanation that transcends poetry. But Skloot's depictions are startling, because they cast the frustrations of one's sense of internal imprisonment and failing light in scenes that capture and elevate rather than betray their subjects. Of a senile hospital inmate he writes,

The old man only wants to walk
the hall. He cannot smile. He goes
from locked door to blazing windows
and back, fists clenched, able to talk

Of nothing but his need to get
out. Blind in light, he scowls and turns
back. The dark at the far end turns
out to be a door again, yet

his faith in escape never dies.

The spatial imprisonment compounds that of terminal disease, and Skloot's sense of physical suffering aids him in depicting other kinds of loss. The first poem depicts an actor who cannot play Lear, not because he cannot personify an individual who has suffered great misfortunes, but because he cannot bear a role where he would have to feign insanity – one's mind becomes more precious when one realizes it can be lost as easily as a watch. A dream vision of Gauguin draws the fear of illness and death into the great stakes of lost genius: "He died / at fifty-five, dreaming of food and wine / and I am fifty-five, dreaming of burial / by fruit trees that bear no fruit." "Yeshiva in the Pale, January, 1892" depicts Jews immolated in the middle of their worship by Tzarist soldiers who torch the "old wooden synagogue." A poem recounting Scarlatti's forced piano performance in competition with Handel and before a Cardinal captures the humiliation of all imposed trials. Many poems that other poets would clumsily cast as first-person lyrics, Skloot renders with the restraint of the third-person. When he does introduce himself as a character in the poems, as in the startling poems of "The Alzheimer's Suite," he remains careful to focus on the vivid cast of his mother. Such clear vision is the highest respect art can pay the suffering:

Sometimes she forgets
to swallow. Sometimes she holds a spoonful
of soup in the air and loses herself
in its spiraling steam. In a whirlpool
of confusion she may suddenly sink
in her seat and chew nothing but thin air.
She is fading away. Her eyes grow dark
as she looks at the old man sitting there
claiming to be her son. She slowly shakes
her head, lifts an empty cup and drinks.

There are many poems in this book and they are of uneven quality; even some of the best poems display a slight mismanagement of meter or rhyme where precision was called for. But these are gripping poems that surpass all others I have seen in an increasingly crowded genre.

MERWIN'S PROSE

Summer Doorways: A Memoir. W. S. Merwin. Shoemaker Hoard, 2005.

Christopher Merrill

A time apart: these are the watchwords of W. S. Merwin's memoir, *Summer Doorways*, which traces his first journey abroad, in 1948, when at the age of twenty-one he sailed for Europe. If in his nearly thirty volumes of poetry and prose he is honored for celebrating both the mythic underpinnings of daily life and the marvelous textures of places that seem to stand outside time, this is the work that proposes to tell us how that came to be—the doorway to a world, long vanished, of money and parties and travel, of shepherds and minstrels and traditional ways of life, where Merwin found his literary bearings.

His story begins one July morning on a Norwegian freighter, registered in Liberia, which seems to slip out of the New York harbor "enveloped in silence." Merwin and his wife, Dorothy, and two teenaged boys in their charge, are making the Atlantic crossing—an improbable turn of events for the son of a Presbyterian minister, a scholarship student with a passion for languages and literature. Thus before entering the Straits of Gibraltar Merwin treats his readers to an extended excursion through his formative years—from an impoverished childhood, to a Presbyterian boarding school, to Princeton, and then to the Stuyvesant family estate near Hackensack, New Jersey, each stop of which is rendered in luxurious prose. This journey through memory, which takes up more than half the book, makes his introduction to post-war Europe all the more amazing.

It is no small thing to enter the social orbit of the rich and titled after a childhood in Depression-era Scranton, Pennsylvania, circumscribed by an ever expanding list of the forbidden. There was little levity in the Merwin household. His stern, aloof, hard-working father meted out harsh punishment in a capricious manner; his mother made do with scant resources, financial and emotional; his discontent pervades the opening chapters. He remembers a glimpse of the Hudson River from his earliest years, when he went with his father to the church that soon would no longer require his services:

> One window of the study looked out over Hoboken and the harbor and the river, with the ferries coming and going, the freighters and liners catching the west light, and beyond them the jagged, gray, glittering skyline of New York, loom-

> ing in its silent distance, its own dimension. I had been allowed to accompany him on those occasions "if I thought I could keep quiet while he worked on the sermon. Did I think I could?" I thought I could, and I knelt on the blue velvet cushion on the window seat, gazing out through the leaded panes, or through the open casements—though usually his windows were tightly closed—watching the river, without a word, utterly rapt in the vast scene out in front of me, hearing my father muttering words of scripture ("Thou fool, this night shall thy soul be required of thee") somewhere far behind me. Whole trains were crossing the river on railroad ferries, all shades of orange in the sunlight. White puffs of steam climbed out of unseen whistles and horns, the distant sounds arriving, faint and faded, a long breath afterward. I was seeing something that I could not reach and that would never go away.

I have quoted this at some length to give a sense of Merwin's prose style and to suggest the quality of his attention, which is especially alert to the things of the earth. Indeed his work may be described as a continual grasping for that which lies just out of reach: points of departure and arrival described with what can only be called love for the transitory nature of our time here. He is always on the lookout for what can be retrieved and registered—clearly and accurately, with a fullness of expression not often on display in contemporary letters—and much of the pleasure of *Summer Doorways* lies in the sheer bounty of its descriptions. This is a gorgeous book.

It is also revelatory. At Princeton, where he studied with R. P. Blackmur and John Berryman, he befriended the son of a French writer killed in the Resistance, who in turn introduced him to Alan Stuyvesant—and the larger world. Stuyvesant, a demon-haunted man, hired Merwin to tutor his nephew for a summer on his estate, where the young poet spent his free time exploring the wilds, and then invited him to do the same at his villa in the south of France. The rich are different, as a certain American writer noted, and Merwin records the differences in uninflected tones. Alan gets drunk at an after-dinner show and makes a scene. A neighbor's wife attempts suicide. Things fall apart.

Much remains inexplicable, like the pair of ghost houses that Merwin saw once in his childhood and then could not find again—were they visions?—or the fact that his marriage seemed doomed from the outset. We learn tantalizingly little about Dorothy. The same holds for his friendship with Georges Belmont, a poet, novelist, and translator of Henry Miller, whom he visited nearly every day. Belmont, perhaps unbeknownst to Merwin, had been a high government official in the Vichy regime, an integral part of the Nazi machine; blacklisted after the war, he changed his name and reinvented himself—a story of compromise told in exemplary detail in

Vincent Giroud's essay, "Transition to Vichy: The Case of Georges Pelorson" (*Modernism/Modernity*, volume seven, number two, 2000). Merwin seems to intuit that something is amiss: the "chronic disappointment" of Belmont's wife is directed at her husband, who in Merwin's words is "somewhat at the mercy of his circumstances." Perhaps it is no coincidence that immediately after extolling Belmont's virtues Merwin introduces John Lodwick, an Irish writer and an authentic war hero tormented by his experiences in the Resistance. It is, to say the least, disconcerting to hear them discuss the Devil's bargain in Thoman Mann's *Doctor Faustus*.

In the last decade Merwin has published several volumes of poems, including *The Pupil* and *Present Company*; a book-length narrative poem, *The Folding Cliffs*; and a new and selected, *Migration*, which won the National Book Award. He has also brought out translations of Jaime Sabines, Dante's *Purgatorio*, and *Sir Gawain and the Green Knight*, as well as two works of prose, *The Mays of Ventadorn* and *The Ends of the Earth*—in short, another flowering by one of our most important, and innovative, literary artists. *Summer Doorways*, which is a kind of prequel to *The Mays of Ventadorn*, his meditation on the world of the Provençal poets, and to *The Vixen*, his acclaimed sequence of poems set near the farmhouse he restored in France, is essential reading.

At the end of the summer the Merwins joined the entourage of Comtessa Maria Antónia de Braganza, of the deposed Portuguese royal family, who orchestrated her return to her homeland in grand style. Once again Merwin found a magical place, which, alas, he had to leave all too soon. And it is this sense of the fleeting, integral to his poetry and prose, which finds its truest expression in the final paragraph of the book:

> But when we left the quinta I had seen something that I was to come to in various forms before I was old enough to be able to look back and recognize it. The move away from the valley of the Ceira would lead through years in which, again and again, I would have the luck to discover, to glimpse, to touch for a moment, some ancient, measureless way of living, of being in the world, some fabric long taken for granted, never finished yet complete, at once fixed as though it would never change, and evanescent as a work of art, an entire age just before it was gone, like a summer.

The luck is ours that Merwin has repeatedly found literary measures for these ways, of being in the world. And the secret of his work is that he takes nothing for granted. He has a knack for recognizing what is about to disappear—light and love—and transforming it into memorable speech: light into love.

STOMPING THE BLUES: KEVIN YOUNG AND THE NEW IDIOM OF AMERICAN POETRY

Jelly Roll: A Blues. Kevin Young. New York: Knopf, 2003. *Blues Poems*. Edited Kevin Young. New York: Knopf, 2003.

Ivy G. Wilson

In the foreword to a recent edited volume of poetry, Kevin Young notes that the blues are "feelings and states of mind that are hard to describe—some might say that don't properly exist—until we have a word for them." The genealogy of the blues as an aesthetic form, from the slave song and the work song through jazz, as well as both early rock-and-roll and rhythm-and-blues, is well-documented. But it is worth recalling that the blues were born at a moment in U.S. history when the residues of slavery were still yet too noticeable and the promise of equality still too far away, subjecting many African Americans to what W.E.B. Du Bois called a "peculiar sensation," or, as Young states it, to "feelings and states of mind that are hard to describe." How is it then, one might ask, that an aesthetic born out of the near impossibility of being black in these United States reverberated with such a wide range of poets from W.H. Auden to Sonia Sanchez, John Berryman to Gustavo Pérez Firmat? How is it that the blues became idiomatic?

Young's edited collection, *Blues Poems,* and his own volume, *Jelly Roll*, both published in 2003 by Knopf, are part and parcel of more recent work on the blues, as well as a continuation of the poet's own fascination with African-American cultural production, especially music. Some of these books include works by ethnomusicologists and others, such as Angela Davis's *Blues Legacies and Black Feminism* (1999) and Eric Sackheim's *The Blues Line* (2003) and, more specifically on Jelly Roll Morton, a new edition of Alan Lomax's *Mister Jelly Roll* (2001), Phil Pastras's *Dead Man Blues* (2001), and *Jelly's Blues* (2003) by Howard Reich and William Gaines. Young himself has been enthralled with music, as evidenced by an earlier edited collection, *Giant Steps* (2000), after John Coltrane's famous album, published in 2000, which includes a discography and the recent revamp of an earlier volume of poems to create *To Repel Ghosts: The Remix* in 2005. Given its presence in American culture, especially African-American poetry and letters, it is not surprising, then, that Young would pick up the blues.

Blues Poems and *Jelly Roll* reveal the grandeur of the blues; their contours, their vicissitudes, and their nuances not only illustrate their appeal to poetry but reveal the blues as poetry. Many of his selections for the Everyman's Library Pocket Poet series demand this kind of recognition, as with Ma Rainey's "See See Rider Blues" and Son House's "Death Letter Blues." The collection is sub-divided into discernible parts: "Standards," "Some Songs," "Form," "Facing Off," "Figures," "Freight," and "Finale." Young includes expected songs and poems such as Langston Hughes's "The Weary Blues," Richard Wright's "FB Eye Blues," Bessie Smith's "Backwater Blues," Robert Johnson's "Hellhound on My Trail," Big Mama Thornton's "Hound Dog," and Sherley Anne Williams's "Any Woman's Blues." The first section "Standards" is comprised of blues poems written before World War II and includes verses from Claude McKay, Nicolás Guillén, Muriel Rukeyser, and Gwendolyn Brooks. Poems on Muddy Waters, Leadbelly, Langston Hughes, and Big Mama Thorton can be found in the "Figures" section and, in the "Finale," there are poems for Bessie Smith, including the august "Homage to the Empress of the Blues" by Robert Hayden and Michael S. Harper's "Last Affair: Bessie's Blues Song." Young also selects John Berryman's "Dream Song [no. 40]" for the volume, itself a precursor to *John Berryman: Selected Poems* that Young edited for the American Poets Project of The Library of America in 2004.

Blues Poems is representative, if not comprehensive, and the extraordinary resonance of the blues is displayed in many of the poems that Young chooses for the sections "Facing Off" and "Freight." One of the most admired poems in contemporary American literature, Sonia Sanchez's "Blues Haikus," illuminates the haiku by animating it with the blues—"let me be yo wil / derness let me be yo wind / blowing you all day" (110). In the section "Freight," Young identifies poems that have transported—as much as transformed per se—the blues aesthetic into contemporary literature. Included in "Freight" is a resplendent slither from Albert Murray's *Conjugations and Reiterations* (2001)—a fitting selection from the author of *Train Whistle Guitar* (1974), whose writings, along with those of his contemporary Ralph Ellison, are imbued with the music and lyricism of black life in the U.S.

> old grandpa stole away
>   north by freedom train
> old grandpa snagged
>   that underground freedom train
> booked his passage through the grapevine
>   stashed his pack
> and prayed for rain, I mean heavy rain (208)

Murray's verse here riffs on the conventional chord progression of twelve bar blues. The image of the train is significant not only as an icon in the African-American imagination but also as a symbol of African American cultural and literary production that links Ma Rainey, Bessie Smith, and Robert Johnson (among others) to Yusef Komunyakaa, Toi Derricotte, and Bob Kaufman (among others), and, concomitantly, the blues to poetry, as boxcars of the train.

With poems by Sherman Alexie, Gustavo Pérez Firmat, Marilyn Chin, and Allen Ginsberg, "Facing Off" is the section that most overtly reveals how the blues have seeped into the broader precincts of American language, changing and heightening the measure of an American idiom altogether. Alexie's "Reservation Blues" demonstrates how the blues can be transplanted from one place to another, promising to expand the panorama of America itself.

> I ain't got nothing, I heard no good news
> I fill my pockets with those reservation blues
> Those old, those old rez blues, those old reservation
> blues
> And if you ain't got choices
> What else do you choose? (134)

If one of the most identifiable characteristics of the blues is its use of call-and-response, Alexie's poem approximates this interactive mode with its instructions for the reader to repeat the chorus twice more rather than simply have them (re)printed within the domain of the poem. In forcing the reader to remain momentarily in this stanza, to redouble back to it again (and again), Alexie fabricates a sensation of being immobilized, reproduces the feeling of being caught in an existential predicament, and intimates the brutal history of Native America that the phrase "rez blues" can only nominally conjur. Indeed, it is this stanza in particular where some of the qualities of the blues as a form (the extension of the classic three line structure, for example) and their philosophical themes (nihilistic, existential, humanistic) become perceptible—accentuated by Alexie's use of dialect, a particular grammar of language (and motives) so fundamental to the blues.

While only a few of Young's poems in *Jelly Roll* make use of dialect, all of them exude the aesthetics, philosophy, and, alas, feelings, of the blues. Young occasionally uses words like "yr" and "everythang," but the poem that conspicuously approximates dialect is "Errata." It does so by fabricating a feigned dialect, however, one that is the by-product of having been bruised by a love that prevents the tongue from speaking straight. One of the poems that most embodies the impulse of the blues is "Early Blues."

Once I ordered a pair of shoes
But they never came.

Young captures the anticipation of an arrival that will never come, of loneliness as an unyielding affect, of continually waiting in vain for love, as a veritable mood indigo. Fraught and unadorned, "Early Blues" and "Field Song," at two lines apiece, are the shortest poems in the volume. The lines are sparse not meager, a visual resonance of the yearning for more—more flesh, more desire, more freedom. As poems that underscore the two-line structure of the stanzas of many of the poems in *Jelly Roll*, "Early Blues" and "Field Song" are parallel analogues that correlate the origins of the blues with the long hangover of the peculiar institution.

Ineluctably perambulating about *Jelly Roll* is the motif of enslavement, appearing, as it does, to signal both the intoxicating splendor of the idea of freedom as well as the imprisonment of the body and soul after the love has gone. In one of the earliest poems in *Jelly Roll*, the narrator of "Cakewalk" equates a lover to the free space of the mythic North, only to fall into regretful lament for having failed to read "the moss on the tree" (8). "Cakewalk" approximates some of the themes of the lines quoted from Murray's "Aubades" and Young, himself, has a poem entitled "Aubades" in *Jelly Roll*. If the history of chattel slavery and its aftermath in the U.S. has to remain, for the most part, a prefiguration and a metaphor in *Jelly Roll*, its most visceral impression can only emerge as a trace in "Dixieland."

to see both our bodies

knocked out—dragged
quicksand down—

they'll put up posters—
have you seen—all over town—

Days later we'll be drug
naked from the swamp

that is us—re—
suscitated, rescued—

the cops without one clue. (9)

The narrator is speaking of a love that must persist, even if it must take refuge in the dregs of the swamp, but the image also recalls those escaped runaways in the nineteenth-century who, in fleeing slavery, were forced to live—and die—in the bowels of the bayou.

Love may set you free, but unrequited love yields nothing save its own jail-sentence—and Young's poems in *Jelly Roll* bear this sentiment out. Like the other dominant images of the collection—trains, trees, and the cross-roads—being condemned to a figurative jail is a recurrent theme.

> I weaved the road
> home. Pulled over
>
> the police offered me
> 2 choices—their bright
>
> lights making me
> mole—see
>
> the inside
> of jail, or forget
>
> all about you.
> How I have grown used
>
> to the dark! Once
> I did not dare
>
> whisper, utter your
> name—but here, in flashes
>
> of light I am unafraid. You
> you you I says
>
> & mean it! Confess
> nothing. Make me
>
> a deal, backroom, bail— (65-66)

Like the person who refuses to sign a false confession, the subject in "Jive," when faced with such a decision, admits, in fact, there really is no decision to be made at all. The narrator would rather hold on to the memory of the beloved and be confined with it alone—even if the presence of the beloved must now reappear as an auditory hallucination, as with the compulsory repetition of "you you you" that would make even John Lee Hooker envious.

Young extends this theme of a love long forgone but impossible to relinquish throughout *Jelly Roll.* In "Anthem" the poet compares the after effects of a love gone south to a chain gang that instinctively, "even without / a guard," unconsciously "breaks rocks out / of habit" (130). In "Fish Story," the adored is made the equivalent of a religion, or, more precisely, something more than a religion—indeed, a love supreme.

> For you I would give up
> God—repeal
>
> once & for all, unkneel—
> you are beautiful (116)

The presence of "I" in the blues is strong, but the presence of "you" is even more commanding. The first person subject in the blues aesthetic is frequently searching for something that is near but nonetheless distanced, sometimes in sight but not within reach—as in Young's "Drum Talk" ("I cannot bear to become / something far-off / from you" [89]). The first person subject is almost a false designation, a position that is incomplete without its complement, its other necessary half.

One of the astonishing maneuvers of *Jelly Roll* is that, in a volume that apparently derives its title from the famed pianist, Jelly Roll Morton himself does not make a noticeable appearance. Other figures appear, if only momentarily, such as Bessie Smith and John Henry, but, as a governing impulse, Young takes his cue from the blues to craft the poems of *Jelly Roll.* The poems here, like those of *Blues Poems*, signal the majesty of the blues, the resonances of the blues that allows us to speak through its idioms and tongues, and prompt us all to stomp to the blues.

EDITORS SELECT

The Poem That Changed America: "Howl" Fifty Years Later, edited by Jason Shinder, Farrar, Straus and Giroux, 2006. This is a curious anniversary. Now tamed by anthologies, classroom teaching, and Ginsberg's own later persona as a kind of allowed fool in the court of American culture,"Howl" was once seen as an outrage. I don't think it changed the nation, but it did change the national poetry. Most contributors to this book look with nostalgia back to the time when they first read Ginsberg's poem. They were young and the world was very different. Some of them—Mark Dotty, Frank Bidart—were clearly influenced by "Howl" in their own writing. Others—Andrei Codrescu in communist Romania—found it subversive in ways an American could hardly imagine. (And untranslatable in Romanian: "angelheaded hipsters" became something like "fashionable angels," and the "angry fix" that the best minds of Ginsberg's generation looked for through the "negro streets at dawn" turned out to be an "injection.") Robert Pinsky rightly sees "Howl" as "the world's least postmodern poem" and something that, if it were "published for the first time tomorrow," would unsettle "our postmodern cool." He also recalls how uncool his own teenage ear was at hearing Ginsberg's concluding litany properly—"Holy Peoria!", "Holy Istanbul!", etc. His reading made them sound like "Holy Cow" and "Holy Moly." Sven Birkerts remembers a cadence that "undid in a minute's time whatever prior cadences had been voice-tracking [his] life," a "voltage" that was almost too great. Such early responses are worth pondering, even if what one was living with in those years looked more like the palm at the end of the mind than Carl Solomon.

Some recent books by contributors. Michael Anania, *Heat Lines*, Asphodel Press, 2006. This is Anania's second book since his *Selected Poems* of 1990, and more substantial than the intervening *In Natural Light* (though without the accompanying CD). It may be Anania's best single volume of poems. Geographies range from a highway in Nebraska to a village in Calabria. As always with Anania, the images are indelible and the music is elegant. Richard Burns, *The Blue Butterfly*, Salt Publishing, 2006. Burns's book is an extended meditation upon the 1941 massacre at Kragujevac, Yugoslavia, and an elegy for the victims. Written in many forms ranging from "found" poetry to villanelles and sonnets, the volume also contains a prose history of the massacre and photographs of the atrocity. A single couplet, titled "War again: Yugoslavia 1992," reminds the reader in a new century how quickly one horror can be forgotten as the next arrives: "Watch where you walk. You think you tread on stones? / You're wrong, my friend. It is your brother's bones." Wayne Miller, *Only the Senses Sleep*, New Issues, 2006. This is an unusually strong first book. In a starred review, *Publishers Weekly* finds that the poems "dissolve the boundaries between things and across time, so that the strangeness of the world is apparent. The epigraph from Elizabeth Bishop is suggestive: "...since / our knowledge is historical, flowing, and flown." Neil Shepard, *This Far from the Source*, Mid-List Press, 2006. Shepard's book moves in space from Virginia to Vermont to Corfu and back to Vermont, in time from memories of adolescence in the 60s, through marriage, the loss of friends and neighbors, poetry in America from the Fugitives to the Beats, to the birth of a daughter and what seems to be the present, working as a guest in Hayden Carruth's writing shack. The poems sometimes resemble Carruth's Vermont poems, or those of John Engels, or the New Hampshire poems of Donald Hall and even Frost. But there are also a number of poems that turn on themselves to examine language in a way that makes Shepard's work sound more contemporary than that of the poets just named: "Yet another metamorphic / swimming hole, waterfall / where language fails. // *Gneiss, schist, slate.* / You can hear nouns metamorphose to verbs, *gnarl, shiver, split,* // then strip down, tumble / in granitic kettle-holes / and camouflage themselves..." Just as we go to press Nadine Sabra Meyer's *The Anatomy Theater*, Harper Perennial, 2006, has arrived. It takes much of its grim subject matter from anatomy texts of the 16th century and Mark Chagall's flying figures in the sky over Vitebsk transformed into victims of Stalinist terror. The book is framed by two poems about John Donne—on his deathbed, and wrapped in his shroud. It is brilliant and harrowing work. We hope to review most of these books properly in a future issue.

Two from Ahsahta Press. The Ernest Sandeen Prize-winning poet Janet Holmes is now directing Ahsahta, which has been a very interesting and enterprising poetry publisher for some time. New books for 2006 include Kate Greenstreet's *Case Sensitive* and Aaron McCollough's *Little Ease.* Greenstreet's book consists of five handmade chapbooks made by a character who has been driving across the country. This Emily Dickinson on the road travels with a number of books and is listening to a novel. In an author's note, Greenstreet writes that her character "has experienced a fracture in her life, a sudden opportunity. Her traveling companions are two books of Lorine Niedecker's letters, writings of Agnes Martin, the letters and journals of Paula Monersohn-Becker, a biography of Marie Curie, and a collection of interviews with Louise Bourgeois. When she stops to eat, she brings a book into the truck stop with her, also her journal. Writing down some of her thinking from the past 50 miles, she is reminded of a comment of Modersohn-Becker's to Rilke, which soon shares the page with observations about radium and a few scraps of conversation from the neighboring booth. Poems arise." McCollough's *Little Ease* takes its title from the name of a cell in the Tower of London in which the prisoner could neither lie down nor stand up. The book deals with prisons of all kinds and, as McCollough says, "dilates back and forth between my feeling of attraction and repulsion for bondage and my assignment of such feelings to personal and public habits of behavior and affect."

Four unclassifiable books. Notre Dame MFA graduate Jenny Boully has published a second book, *[one love affair]**, Tarpaulin Sky Press, 2006. Readers of Boully's *The Body* will like it. The title itself suggests the ludic character of Boully's writing, and the genre-defying discourse that combines prose poem with essay and memoir. *The Body* contained only footnotes at the bottom of otherwise empty pages. This book fills the pages, but also depends on the conventions of scholarly machinery. Caroline Bergvall, *Fig*, Salt Publishing, 2005. Poet and performance artist Bergvall presents a wide variety of work from performance pieces to quasi-concretist configurations to more reader-friendly texts such as the title piece and the autobiographical conclusion of "Gong". As the blurb has it, Bergvall "exploits multilingual speech, language games, sited texts and verbal noise in her exploration of poetic practice and its reception." Martin Corless-Smith, *Swallows*, Fence Books, 2006. Fence has the praiseworthy mission of "publishing challenging writing distinguished by idiosyncrasy and intelligence rather than by allegiance with camps, schools, or cliques." It aims to "support writers who might otherwise have difficulty being recognized because their work doesn't answer to either the mainstream or to recognizable modes of experimentation." *Swallows* certainly fits the bill. In some ways a continuation of Corless-Smith's *Nota*, listed in an earlier *Editors Select*, and still drawing on Burton and Thomas Browne, the new book treats swallows as alien in a house in the same way a nightingale is alien to the air and the soul is alien to the body (*Anatomy of Melancholy*). The central house in what is also a book of houses is the house of words, but also Horace's Sabine Villa, which Corleless-Smith explores like a verbal archaeologist—but also like a swallow. The book is hard to describe, but it is original and moving. *NDR* contributor Ray Di Palma has published a bilingual edition English/Italian edition of *Caper*, with translations by Gian Maria Annovi and drawings by Roy Dowell. Available from NLF Editions, 29010 Castelvetro Piacentino, Piacenza, Italy.

Two from Wake Forest. Thomas Kinsella, *Collected Poems*, 1956-2001, Wake Forest University Press, 2006. This closely printed volume of 380 pages is the life's work of a major Irish poet whose poetry should be read beside Heaney's, Mahon's, Boland's, Montague's and Muldoon's. Although not as well known in this country as the other five, Kinsella is a master. Vona Groarke's *Juniper Street*, Wake Forest, 2006, is more of an interim report since the publication of *Flight and Earlier Poems*, a new and selected volume reviewed by James Wilson in an earlier issue of *NDR*. The new book begins to show the influence of living in the US, where Groarke now teaches at Wake Forest itself—which is "dedicated to Irish poetry," as the WF logo proudly declares.

Four prizewinners. David Roderick, *Blue Colonial*, APR, 2006. *Blue Colonial* is the winner of this year's APR/Honickman first book prize, chosen by Robert Pinsky. The poet is a native of Plymouth, Massachusetts, and writes poems about Plymouth colony and early colonial figures such as William Bradford, John Alden and John Billington that occupy a space somewhere between Robert Lowell's poems on early America and those in the long sequence by Daniel Hoffman about William Penn called *Brotherly Love*. He also writes personal poems about his family and childhood in the blue colonial house where he grew up. Mary Rose O'Reilley, *Half Wild*, Louisiana University Press, 2006. This book is the new Walt Whitman Award Winner of the Academy of American Poets. It was chosen by Mary Oliver for "a style that celebrates...that mystery we call the soul." The poems are never longer than a page, written in short lines, austere to the point of risking meagerness. The best of them, however, have a concentrated power, such as in "The Lost Child": "Do not pity the lost child / She has been lost so long, / she has become half wild." The previous year's Whitman award went to Geri Doran for *Resin*, Louisiana University Press, 2005, and was selected by Henri Cole. Doran's style is also austere, but not so stark in its engagement with ethical, moral, political and spiritual issues as O'Reilley's. Among last year's National Poetry Series winners, Corine Lee's *PYX*, Penguin, 2005, is perhaps the most interesting. Chosen by Pattiann Rogers, *PYX* is as edgy in its music and zany in its diction as the O'Reilley and Doran books are restrained. The title alludes to the box containing communion wafers, which is here implicitly compared to the book with its poems ready for consumption. The work in this volume sparks, amuses, saddens and transfigures both the sacred and profane.

Four from ND Press. Sonia Gernes, *What You Hear in the Dark*, 2006. Emerita Notre Dame professor and Creative Writing Program veteran's new collection, which contains poems selected from three earlier volumes, (*Brief Lives*, *Women at Forty*, and *A Breeze Called the Fremantle Doctor*) plus a number of new poems, has received praise from John Engels ("an outer eye for the personal and immediate and an inner for the most closely-held truths of the community") and Gary Gildner ("one of those rare, loving, heartbreaking books that has come together as all the necessary parts of a life come together"). Janet Holmes, *F2F*, 2006. The former Sandeen Prize Winner (*The Green Tuxedo*, 1999) shapes her new volume from a dialogue between face-to-face instant messaging lovers who morph into Echo and Narcissus, Eurydice and Orpheus, and other mythic couples. Jude Nutter, *The Curator of Silence*, 2006. Nutter's volume is winner of the 2007 Sandeen Prize. Judith Minty says "these astonishing poems take my breath away with their beauty and deeply held knowledge." The volume will be reviewed by Jeremy Hooker in our next issue. And, one volume of fiction: Bill Meissner, *The Road to Cosmos*, 2006. Poet Meissner's second collection of short stoires—stories praised by Richard Ford ("They say what we all should say but usually can't") and Tim O'Brien ("He knows his small towns, but beyond that, he knows the workings of the human heart")—surveys a corner of the country so completely it can be called Meissner Land, a world both vanished and yet contemporary and continous, carefully captured and preserved.

Jason Berry, *Last of the Red Hot Poppas*, Chin Music Press, 2006. New Orleans and Louisiana pre-Katrina, but a novel, Berry's first, that makes Katrina's aftermath predictable. Political corruption galore, mixed with human frailties, exposed by a writer who knows his way around the territory, full of humor and rue. Berry is also the author *Lead Us Not into Temptation*, one of the earliest (1992) and most perceptive books on the Church's molestation crisis of the last two decades.

Tom Coyne, *Paper Tiger*, Gotham Books, 2006. Coyne, a ND creative writing program alum, after his successful first novel, *A Gentleman's Game*, turns to nonfiction, but doesn't abandon the subject: subtitled "An Obsessed Golfer's Quest to Play with the Pros," Coyne details a year preparing to conquer the PGA's Qualifying School and thereby be turned into a "pro," a state devoutly to be wished for. Coyne's account is full of earned wisdom, wry observation and love of the game, as well as for all the characters that populate the all-too-full world of amateur and professional golf.

Kelly Kerney, *Born Again*, Harcourt, 2006. Kerney, another ND alum, is the first former Nicholas Sparks postgraduate fellowship winner to publish a novel—and it's a humdinger, an amazing investigation of evangelical America's family values, full of exacting truths and provocative characters. This blue-collar tale of life's many travails by a golden-voiced young author leaves an indelible impression on both the heart and the mind.

Michael Collins, *Death of a Writer*, Bloomsbury USA, 2006. One of the first graduates of ND's creative writing program, Collins' eighth book, the fourth novel with an American locale, the battered Midwest embracing Lake Michigan, the first of which, *The Keepers of Truth*, was short-listed for England's Booker Prize. This time the setting is a backwater college campus that Collins' characters inhabit—including the main character, a writer/professor who has decided to stop writing, depriving the lovers of literature of "more not to read," and who spends most of the novel in a self-induced coma. More than one crime is committed here and Collins describes both the central murder and various assaults on American letters with equal gusto. Another captivating way station in an unique literary journey.

Leslie Epstein, *The Eighth Wonder of the World*, Handsel Books, 2006. Epstein's tenth fiction, a novel compared to the work of Thomas Pynchon, William T. Vollman, and Joseph Heller. But, it mostly resembles the work of Epstein himself, beginning with his 1979 novel, *King of the Jews*: history and imagination, wonders and absurdity, horror and hilarity—a major work by a tireless and brave writer.

CONTRIBUTORS

Michael Anania's most recent collection of poems, *Heat Lines*, was published last year. Recent books include *Selected Poems* and *In Natural Light*. Anania lives in Austin, Texas and on Lake Michigan. **Robert Archambeau** is associate professor of English at Lake Forest College. He is the author of *Home and Variations* and editor of *Word Play Place*. **Ciaran Berry** received his MFA from New York University where he currently teaches on the Expository Writing Program. His work has appeared in *Poetry Ireland Review*, *Gettysburg Review*, *Prairie Schooner*, *AGNI*, *The Threepenny Review*, *Green Mountains Review*, *The Southern Review*, *Ontario Review*, and *The Missouri Reiew*. He is originally from the northwest of Ireland. **Drew Blanchard** is a doctoral candidate at the University of Wisconsin-Milwaukee. He received his MFA from the Ohio State University. He is the author of the chapbook *Raincoat Variations* and his poems have appeared or are forthcoming in, among others, *Mudfish*, *Maize*, and the anthology *Best New Poets 2006* from the University of Virginia. **Matt Bondurant**'s first novel *The Third Translation* was published in 2005 and has been translated into fourteen languages worldwide. His work has recently appeared in *Glimmer Train*, *The New England Review*, and *The Hawaii Review*, among others. Matt currently lives in Alexandria, Virginia, where he teaches at George Mason University and is working on a second novel. **Sarah Bowman** is a 1999 graduate of the Notre Dame Creative Writing Program. She is a tenure-track instructor in the Department of English at Wright College, one of the City Colleges of Chicago. **Peg Boyers** is executive rditor of *Salmagundi* magazine and author of a book of poems, *Hard Bread*. Her second book, *Honey with Tobacco*, comes out this year. **Trent Busch** is from Georgia where he writes and makes furniture. His poems have appeared in *The Best American Poetry*, *Poetry*, *Hudson Review*, *Southern Review*, *Georgia Review*, *The Kenyon Review*, *American Scholar*, *The Nation*, *The Threepenny Review*, and elsewhere. **Laton Carter**'s first collection of poems *Leaving* won the 2005 Stafford-Hall Oregon Book Award. He lives in Eugene. **Kim Chinquee**'s recent work has appeared in *Noon*, *Conjunctions*, *Denver Quarterly*, *Fiction International*, *The Pushcart Prize XXXI: Best of the Small Presses*, and other journals. She teaches creative writing at Central Michigan University. **Jenny Cookson** has just completed her MA in Creative Writing at the University of Colorado, Boulder, where she was the poetry editor for *Square One*. She was previously an assistant editor at Doubleday Broadway Publishing Group. Her work has appeared or is forthcoming in *Five Fingers Review*,

Red Chair, *Shove*, *Peloria*, and *Alice Blue*. **Patricia Corbus**' poems have appeared in various reviews, including *The paris Review*, *The Georgia Review*, and *The Madison Review*. Her first collection of poetry is entitled *Ashes, Jace, Mirrors*. **Trevor Dodge** is the author of *Everyone I Know Lives On Roads* and *Yellow #10*. His work has appeared in *Plazm*, *Gargoyle*, *Black Ice*, *Two Girls Review*, *Fiction International*, *Natural Bridge*, *Rain Taxi*, and *Review of Contemporary Fiction*. He can be found online at www.trevordodge.net. **James Doyle**'s new book, *Bending Under The Yellow Police Tapes,* will be published this year. He is married to poet Sharon Doyle. He has poems coming out in *Mid-American Review, Xavier Review, River Styx, Appalachia,* and *West Branch.* **Kevin Ducey** has published the Honickman prize-winning volume of poems, *Rhinoceros*. He lives in Madison, Wisconsin. **K.E. Duffin**'s book of poems, *King Vulture*, was published in 2005. Her work has appeared in *Agni*, *Chelsea*, *Denver Quarterly*, *Harvard Review*, *Hunger Mountain*, *The New Orleans Review*, *Ploughshares*, *Poetry*, *Poetry East, Prairie Schooner*, *Rattapallax*, *The Sewanee Review*, *Southwest Review*, *Verse,* and many other journals. Her poems have also been featured on *Poetry Daily* and *Verse Daily*. A painter and printmaker, Duffin lives in Somerville, Massachusetts. **Diane Furtney**'s poems and translations (French, Japanese) have appeared in numerous magazines. Under the pseudonym D.J.H. Jones, she is the author of *Murder at the MLA*, a comic mystery novel. She works in the plant biology department at the Ohio State University. **Robert Estep** is a musician and writer who lives and works in Houston, Texas. He is currently working on short prose pieces intended for a larger sequence, loosely borrowing themes and rhythms from the work of the Scottish composer Ronald Stevenson, and especially his extended piano composition "Passacaglia on DSCH". **Kass Fleisher** is the author of *The Bear River Massacre and the Making of History*; *Accidental Species: A Reproduction*; *The Adventurous*; and *Talking Out of School: Memoir of an Educated Woman*. She is assistant professor of English at Illinois State University in Normal. **Catherine Gass** received her MFA in photography from the School of the Art Institute of Chicago where she is currently a professor in the photography department. She is also the photographer for The Newberry Library in Chicago. Her work has been previously shown at the Organization for Independent Artists (New York), Kaufman Arcade (Minneapolis), the Noyes Cultural Center, Artemsia, the Randolph Street Gallery (Chicago), and elsewhere. **Eckhard Gerdes** has published several novels. He has four novels coming out in the next few months: *Przewalski's Horse*, *The Million-Year Centipede*, *The Unwelcome Guest,* and *Nin and Nan*. He also edits the *Journal of Experimental Fiction* series of books. **Robert Gibb**'s books include

The Burning World, and *The Origins of Evening*, which was a National Poetry Series winner. A new book, *World over Water*, is due out this year. **Stephen Gibson** is author of two poetry collections, *Masaccio's Expulsion* and *Rorschach Art*, and a fiction collection *The Persistence of Memory*. **Lorrie Goldensohn**'s *American War Poetry* was published last year. **Ian Harris** is an MFA candidate at Columbia College in Chicago. His recent work has appeared or is forthcoming in *Wisconsin Review*, *Kenyon Review*, *Mid-American Review*, and *Agni* Online. **Henry Hart**'s most recent book is *James Dickey: The World as a Lie*. He is currently finishing a novel entitled, *In the Shadow of the Great Wall*, and teaches English at the College of William and Mary. **John Hennessy**'s poems have recently appeared in *Fulcrum*, *The New Repbulic*, and the *Yale Review*. His collection, *Bridge and Tunnel*, was published last year. **Dennis Hinrichsen**'s most recent work is *Cage of Water*. With Gerry LaFemina, he co-edits *Review Revue*, a journal devoted to the review of contemporary poetry. **Johnny Horton** lives in Seattle. He's published work in *Willow Springs*, *RE:AL*, *The Laurel Review*, and other magazines. **Leo Jilk** lives in Bronx, New York. **Tim Kahl**'s work has been published or is forthcoming in *Prairie Schooner*, *American Letters & Commentary*, *Berkeley Poetry Review*, *Fourteen Hills*, *George Washington Review*, *Illuminations*, *Indiana Review*, *Limestone*, *Nimrod*, *Ninth Letter*, *South Dakota Quarterly*, and dozens of other journals. He has translated Austrian avant-gardist, Friederike Mayröcker; Brazilian poet, Lêdo Ivo; and the poems of the Portuguese language's only Noble Laureaate, José Saramago. **John Kinsella** is an Australian poet, novelist, critic, essayist and editor. **Susanne Kort** is a psychotherapist practicing in Jalisco, Mexico. Her poems have appeared in the *Seneca Review*, *Indiana Review*, *Grand Street*, the *Iowa Review*, *Seattle Review* and others in the U.S., and in journals in Ireland, Canada and England. **Sarah Lindsay** is the author of two books in the Grove Press Poetry Series: *Primate Behavior* and *Clutter*. She lives in Greensboro, North Carolina, where she works as a copy editor. **Moira Linehan**'s manuscript, *If No Moon*, was selected by Dorianne Laux as the 2006 first prize winner of the Crab Orchard Series in Poetry Open Competition. It will be published this year. **William Logan**'s most recent book of poetry is *The Whispering Gallery*, and his most recent book of essays and reviews is *The Undiscovered Country*. The latter received the National Book Critics Award in Criticism. **Paul Maliszewski**'s writing has appeared in *Granta*, *Paris Review*, and *Harper's*. **Christopher Merrill**'s most recent book is *Things of the Hidden God: Journey to the Holy Mountain*. He directs the International Writing Program at the University of Iowa. **W.S. Merwin** is a Pulitzer Prize-winning poet and essayist. **Peter Michelson** publishes essays, poetry and literary criticism in a variety of journals. He has taught at Notre Dame and Northwestern universities and at the University of Colorado, where he served several stints as director of its Creative Writing Program. His books include *The Eater, When the Revolution Really,* and *Speaking the Unspeakable.* **Jenny Morse** is currently finishing her Master's degree in Creative Writing at the University of Colorado, Boulder. **Jay Neugeborn** is the author of 14 books, including prize-winning novels *The Stolen Jew* and *Before My Life Began.* **Carol Novack** is the author of a book of poems published in Australia, where she received a writer's grant equivalent to an NEA. Her writings can and will be found in many publications, including *The Penguin Book of Australian Women Poets, Action, Yes, American Letters & Commentary, Anemone Sidecar, Big Bridge, BlazeVOX, Del Sol Review, Diagram, First Intensity, 5_Trope, La Petite Zine, LIT, Milk, Orphan Leaf Review, Salt Flats Annual, Salt River Review,* and *Segue.* She publishes and edits the e-journal *Mad Hatters' Review.* **Jude Nutter** was born in North Yorkshire, England, and grew up in northern Germany. Her poems have been been widely published and received numerous national and international awards. She is the author of two full-length collections: *Pictures of the Afterlife* and *The Curator of Silence*, which was awarded the 2007 Ernest Sandeen Prize and published by the University of Notre Dame Press. **Kristy Odelius** is a poet and Assistant Professor of English at North Park University. Her work has appeared in *Chicago Review, ACM, Foreword, Diagram,* and others. **Andrew Osborn** teaches literature and writing at Whitman College in Wall Walla, Washington. His poetry and articles about poetry have appeared in such publications as *American Letters & Commentary, Bat City Review, Contemporary Literature, Denver Quarterly,* and *The Wallace Stevens Journal.* **Gwendolyn Oxenham** received her MFA in creative writing at Notre Dame in 2005. She played soccer at Duke University and she is currently the recipient of the Nicholas Sparks Prize, a post-fellowship MFA year. **John Peck**'s recent books are *Collected Shorter Poems 1966-1996,* and *Red Strawberry Leaf: Selected Poems 1994-2001.* **Raymond Perreault** (1933-1991) lived in Provincetown for 30 years, was a bartender at several popular nightspots, spent 20 winters in Haiti. **Donald Platt**'s second book, *Cloud Atlas,* won the Verna Emery Poetry Prize. His poems have recently appeared or are forthcoming in *The Georgia Review, Kenyon Review, AGNI, Field, Chelsea, Antioch Review, Cream City Review, Black Warrior Review, Michigan Quarterly Review, The Iowa Review, Southwest Review,* and *The Southern Review.* His third book, *My Father Says Grace,* will be published this spring. He is associate professor of English at Purdue University. **Göran Printz-Påhlson** (1931-2006) was a world-renowned poet, critic, translator, and scholar. **James S. Profitt** is a freelance journalist in Cincinnati. His poems and fiction have appeared in *Rattapallax, Tampa Review, Rattle, West Wind Review* and elsewhere. **Rachel Richardson** recently completed a Wallace Stegner Fellowship in poetry, and currently teaches in North Carolina. Her poems have appeared in *Shenandoah, Crab Orchard Review, Ninth Letter*, and other journals. **Shane Seely**'s poems have recently appeared or are forthcoming in *Prairie Schooner, River Styx, Poems & Plays*, and other journals. He is a Senior Lecturer in the English Department at Washington University in St. Louis. **R.D. Skillings** is chairman of the writing committee of the Fine Arts Work Center in Provincetown. **R.T. Smith** edits *Shenandoah* for Washington & Lee University. His most recent book is *Uke Rivers Delivers*, and his new book of poems, *Outsider Art*, is forthcoming. **Jesper Svenbro** is a Swedish poet and classical philologist. He is director of research at Centre Louis Gernet in Paris, and was recently elected to the Swedish Academy. **Lars-Håkan Svensson** is a professor at the University of Linköping, Sweden. He has published three volumes of poetry and has translated John Matthias, Paul Muldoon, Les Murray, Pindar, Sophocles and others into Swedish. **Emily Tipps** lives in Boulder, Colorado. **Jennifer Tonge**'s poems have appeared most recently in *Poetry* and *The Hayden's Ferry Review*. She lives in Salt Lake City. **Deb Olin Unferth**'s fiction has appeared in *Harper's, Conjunctions, Fence, NOON*, the Pushcart Prize anthologies, and elsewhere. Her first book is forthcoming from McSweeney's. **Ryan G. Van Cleave**'s most recent books include a poetry collection, *The Magical Breasts of Britney Spears*, and a creative writing textbook, *Behind the Short Story: From First to Final Draft*. He teaches creative writing and literature at Clemson University. **James Walton**, Professor Emeritus of English at the University of Notre Dame, has published a novel, *Margaret's Book*, a collection of Anglo-Irish political correspondence, *The King's Business*, and essays on British literature from Defoe to Joyce. He has recently completed a critical study of the fictions of Joseph Sheridan Le Fanu. **Igor Webb** is Professor of English at Adelphi University. His "Reading Mary Barton" appeared in the Winter 2005 issue of *Literary Imagination*. **Mike White** has recent or forthcoming poems in magazines including *Poetry, Verse, The Iowa Review, The Antioch Review, Colorado Review, Pleiades*, and *River Styx*. He serves as co-editor of *Quarterly West*. **Wallis Wilde-Menozzi** has recently published a series of poems, *The Heron Songs*. A dozen of her essays are being translated into Italian by Moretti and Vitali. Her memoir *Mother Tongue: An American Life in Italy* is also being translated. She has finished a novel set in Florence. **Ivy Wilson** teaches courses on African American literature and the literatures of the black diaspora more broadly. His book, *Specters of Democracy: Blackness and the Aesthetics of Democracy*, is forthcoming from Oxford University Press. **James Matthew Wilson** is a Sorin Research Fellow at Notre Dame. His essays appear regularly in *Contemporary Poetry Review*; his poems can be found in *Measure* and *The Dark Horse*. **Jiri Wyatt** is author of *Against Capitulation*. His work has appeared in *The New Yorker*, *Partisan Review*, *The American Scholar*, and others. **Lon Young** grew up in Michigan's Upper Peninsula. Now living in Utah, Lon teaches music to middle schoolers.

SUSTAINERS

Anonymous

Nancy & Warren Bryant

Kevin DiCamillo

Gary & Elizabeth Gutchess

John F. Hayward

Samuel Hazo

Tim Kilroy

Richard Landry

Steve Lazar

Carol A. Losi

Jessica Maich

Vincent J. O'Brien

Kevin T. O'Connor

Daniel O'Donnell

Beth Haverkamp Powers

Mark W. Roche

In Honor of Ernest Sandeen

John Sitter

In Honor of James Whitehead

Kenneth L. Woodword

Sustainers are lifetime subscribers to the *Notre Dame Review.* You can become a sustainer by making a one-time donation of $250 or more. (See subscription information enclosed.)

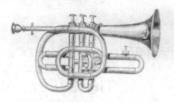

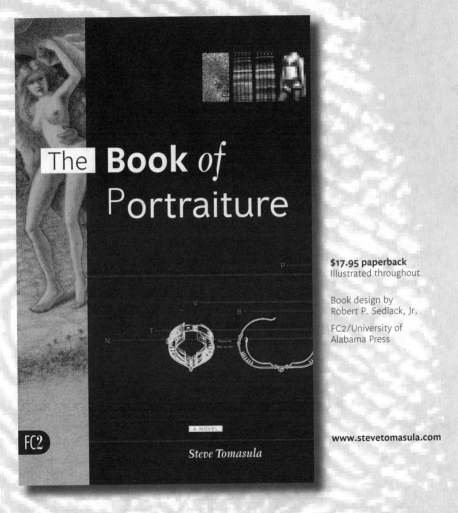

SYCAMORE REVIEW

LITERATURE, OPINION, AND THE ARTS

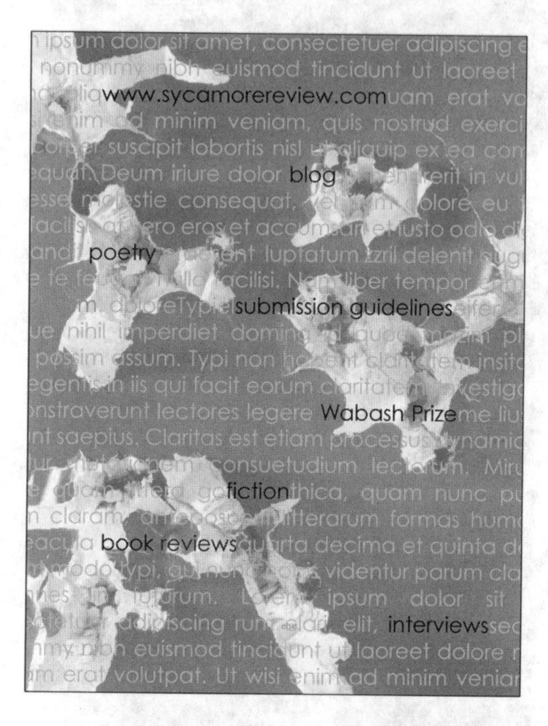

WINTER/SPRING 2007 VOLUME 19, ISSUE 1

INTERVIEWS WITH MICHAEL MARTONE, DAVID YOUNG AND NATALIE AND DREW OF MARRIED TO THE SEA